CORRUPTION & DEMOCRACY IN LATIN AMERICA

CORRUPTION & DEMOCRACY IN LATIN AMERICA

EDITED BY **CHARLES H. BLAKE** &
STEPHEN D. MORRIS

UNIVERSITY OF PITTSBURGH PRESS

Published by the University of Pittsburgh Press, Pittsburgh, Pa., 15260

Copyright © 2009, University of Pittsburgh Press

Manufactured in the United States of America

Printed on acid-free paper

10   9   8   7   6   5   4   3   2   1

Library of Congress Cataloging-in-Publication Data

Corruption and democracy in Latin America / edited by Charles H.
Blake and Stephen D. Morris.

p. cm. — (Pitt Latin American series)

Includes bibliographical references and index.

ISBN-13: 978-0-8229-6023-2 (pbk. : alk. paper)

ISBN-10: 0-8229-6023-0 (pbk. : alk. paper)

1. Political corruption—Latin America.   2. Democracy—Latin
America.   3. Latin America—Politics and government—1980–
I. Blake, Charles H., 1962–   II. Morris, Stephen D., 1957–

JL959.5.C6C67 2009

320.98—dc22   2009000807

CONTENTS

CORRUPTION &
DEMOCRACY IN
LATIN AMERICA

STEPHEN D. MORRIS AND CHARLES H. BLAKE

Introduction **Political and Analytical Challenges of Corruption in Latin America**

In countries such as mine, gaining office . . . is akin to political plunder: the position offers a blank cheque and the guarantee of great personal enrichment.
                                        Rigoberta Menchú

Corruption—usually defined as a violation of the norms of public office for personal gain (Nye 1967)—captures news headlines and the imagination, especially in a democracy. Since the celebrated return of democratic rule to most of Latin America beginning in the 1980s, scandals involving sitting or former presidents, governors, ministers, and other top government officials have rocked virtually every country in the region. The more spectacular cases have featured illegal campaign funds and expenditures; presidents bribing members of congress for their votes; the illegal sale of arms by top government and military officials; multimillion-dollar graft, fraud, kickbacks, and bribes involving government contracts, state concessions, and the privatization of state-owned enterprises; judges selling verdicts; law enforcement officials working for or protecting drug traffickers or engaged directly in kidnapping and theft; drug traffickers running their operations from prison or even walking free at will.

1

Beyond the more high-profile cases—the tips of real and imagined icebergs—substantial evidence suggests that in much of Latin America corruption permeates daily life. From acquiring varied licenses and permits to dealing with a routine traffic violation, corruption is often the rule rather than the exception. Transparency International's Global Corruption Barometer 2005 survey, for instance, found 43 percent of respondents in Paraguay and 31 percent in Mexico admitting to having paid a bribe just within the past twelve months. In *Latinobarómetro's* regional survey in 2004, an average of 42 percent of respondents ranked the probability of paying a bribe to the police as high, while 35 percent expressed the same ease of bribing a judge. One poll in 2003 even calculated the average bribe in Peru at sixty-four *soles* (about eighteen dollars): six dollars to slip merchandise past customs agents or speed up the installation of water services; fifteen dollars to obtain a building permit, a driver's license, or to work as a street vendor; and fifty cents to visit a hospital patient outside regular visiting hours (cited in Fraser 2003).

The perception that Latin American politicians and government institutions are corrupt runs even deeper than actual involvement or victimization rates (see Seligson 2006). When the European Values Study Group and World Values Survey Association (EVSG & WVSA 1995–1997) asked people in seven countries about the extent of corruption, substantial majorities in Argentina, Brazil, Colombia, Mexico, and Venezuela considered "almost all" or "most" public officials to be corrupt. Argentina led with 89 percent of respondents holding this view (EVSG & WVSA 2005). Only in Chile and Uruguay did a slim majority claim that only "a few" were corrupt. Similarly, when asked to calculate the percentage of civil servants who are corrupt, the average for seventeen Latin American countries surpassed 70 percent (Lagos 2003). Congress, the police, and political parties are held in similarly low (if not lower) esteem as are the bureaucrats. And the public is not alone in holding such views. Surveys of legislators, outside experts, and business executives all say basically the same thing (see Brinegar 2003; Canache and Allison 2005). Using polls measuring the perceptions of business executives and development experts, Transparency International has classified the countries of Latin America among the most corrupt in the world since they began elaborating their Corruption Perception Index (CPI) in 1995. In the 2007 CPI, the twenty countries of the region registered an average score of just 3.4 on a scale of 10 (low corruption) to 0 (high) scale.

Whether referring to the fantastic, the quotidian, the real, or the imagined, most would agree that corruption has haunted the countries of Latin America from the beginning. It is neither new nor unique to the current democratic governments. Historical analyses—by Burkholder and Johnson (1994), Ewell (1977), Gibson (1966), Hopkins (1969, 1974), McFarlane (1996), Nef (2001), Posada-Carbó (2000), Phelan (1960), Whitehead (2000a, 2000b), and others—all point to elaborate networks of corruption, rampant paternalism, extensive use of government revenues for personal use, and weak rule of law permeating both colonial and postcolonial Latin America under civilian- and military-led governments. Thus, while some military officers during the twentieth century blamed democracy for the existence of corruption in various Latin American countries, it is abundantly clear that corruption predates the emergence of democracy.

But democracy has a complex and multifaceted relationship to corruption (Doig and Theobald 2000; Johnston 1999, 2005a; Rose-Ackerman 1999; Warren 2004). Democracy creates new means of acquiring and exercising power and wealth, conditions often giving rise to new opportunities for corruption. For example, schemes to buy legislative votes or to influence illegally the votes of citizens in general elections are more tempting in a democracy. At the same time, democracy nourishes popular demands and pressures for good government and accountability—forces driving societal and government pressures to detect and punish corruption. As a result, democracy lofts corruption high onto the political and the analytical agendas. The spread of democracy—together with economic liberalization and the end of the Cold War, as we will see—played a major role in sparking unprecedented global and scholarly attention to corruption beginning in the mid-1990s, and it continues to inform research on corruption. Democracy brings government affairs more out into the open, often exposing once hidden practices of wrongdoing via greater freedom of the press and, over time, via greater checks and balances within government itself.

Fundamentally, democracy heightens the importance of corruption because corruption strikes at the very heart of democracy itself. By converting collective goods into personal favors, corruption represents a basic denial of justice (Johnston 2005a). By denying citizens access and a role in determining collective decisions and actions, corruption disempowers. Corruption, in short, undermines the essence of citizenship, distorting and crippling democracy. Even the perception of corrupt politicians and institutions erodes the basic foundations of trust upon which democracy must rest (Warren 2004). In a sense, then, corruption and democracy represent antithetical forces, one embodying the ideal of curbing corruption; the other threatening to undermine the very meaning and existence of democracy itself.

For the countries of Latin America, the issues linking corruption and democracy today pose important political and analytical challenges. The political challenge centers on the continuing struggles of the region's democracies to reduce the real and perceived levels of corruption in countries where the dynamics of corruption combine historical roots with an ability to adapt to new events in an effort to avoid detection and prosecution. For the reasons noted earlier, corruption represents an obstacle to the further deepening and consolidation of democracy. The major analytical challenge, in turn, stems from the nature of the subject matter: how can one gather sufficient information to understand fully an illegal activity? Though certainly much has been learned about this once-obscure political phenomenon, our understanding remains partial at best. A host of theoretical and methodological problems continue to plague the study of corruption. Ultimately, these political and analytical challenges fold together: a greater understanding of corruption can help governments to combat corruption, while public efforts to limit corruption provide a more open landscape in which to study the dynamics of corruption. The current collection responds to these dual challenges, addressing various aspects of the corruption-democracy nexus.

RESEARCH IN THE MID-TWENTIETH CENTURY

For years, an assortment of analytical and political obstacles limited scholarly and political interest in corruption. Analytically, the study of corruption suffered initially from lack of a clear and concise definition, particularly one that could travel well across national boundaries or through time (see Heidenheimer 1970; Johnston 1996; Nye 1967; Philip 1997, 2002; Scott, 1972a; see the discussion here by Bailey). This search for a consensual definition was made more difficult by the lack of a firm institutional grounding in an academic discipline. Corruption occasionally emerged as a topic in anthropology, business administration, economics, history, political science, public administration, and sociology, but it rarely captured sufficient attention to spark the development of a consistent methodological approach within or across these disciplines. This lack of agreement over how to conceptualize corruption was, in turn, exceeded by a more tangible obstacle—the shortage of solid, nonanecdotal evidence needed to gauge the extent of corruption within a country. Without comparable information in place to describe conditions across countries, it was difficult (to say the least) to test hypotheses cross-nationally.

The scarce efforts to overcome these conceptual and measurement difficulties had to overcome a fourth obstacle. Many observers in and out of academia claimed that corruption was of limited importance in the broader scheme of things. In developed countries, many saw corruption as an aberration, hardly warranting much attention. Some considered it ephemeral and transitory. Others argued that it was overly moralistic, even paternalistic, to study the dynamics of corruption in developing countries. Moreover, in such settings the issue of corruption often seemed to pale in comparison to more important matters like wrenching poverty, brutal repression, and the need for democracy. Still others saw corruption as functional in the process of development (for a review of the literature on this debate, see Heidenheimer and Johnston [2002] or the four-part series edited by Williams [2001]).

Political realities during the first few decades following World War II further constrained the study of corruption. A veneer of silence at the international level enveloped the issue. The major global political and economic powers showed virtually no inclination to expose the corruption of their political allies or business partners or to fund those who might. Corruption took place in the shadows, often within dark authoritarian settings. And it often seemed that global political and financial interests wanted it to stay in those shadows. Despite the restrictions on U.S. companies to engage in corruption through the Foreign Corrupt Practices Act of 1977, for strategic reasons U.S. foreign policy largely ignored the corruption of others. The IMF and World Bank did so as well, pointing to their mandates as prohibiting them from touching such "political" matters. In turn, while many scholars and citizens in developing countries acknowledged widespread corruption, the presence of authoritarian regimes during much of this period greatly limited the scope of debate and discussion on the topic.

Together with the analytical problems, this political situation relegated the study of corruption to the sidelines. A relatively small group of scholars engaged in extensive debate over how to define corruption. Several scholars conducted historical case studies of corruption in developed and developing countries. Some engaged in an intense debate over whether corruption was perhaps functional in the process of economic and political development. In turn, this small, dispersed scholarly community elaborated theoretical propositions and hypotheses regarding the cross-national dynamics of corruption that remained largely untested (see Heidenheimer 1970; Heidenheimer, Johnston, and LeVine 1989).

Things have changed rather dramatically from the 1980s forward as democracy, economic liberalization, and the end of the cold war have altered fundamental perceptions about the nature and the importance of corruption. Neglect transformed into (often) intense global interest. The spread of democracy played a major role in this process, as noted earlier. It fed popular demands for accountability and transparency, spotlighted previously hidden areas of corrupt activities, and pushed government and nongovernment actors to take the issue seriously. In like manner, economic liberalization and economic globalization opened up once-closed businesses to international competition and fomented trade and foreign investment. By converting corruption into an unfair competitive advantage, economic globalization pushed it into the limelight. At almost the same time, the conclusion of the cold war removed the strategic veil enveloping the issue, prompting the major political and economic powers to recast corruption as not only an addressable issue but also a prime obstacle to the emergent post–Cold War, liberal world order.

As a result, by the mid-1990s the IMF, the World Bank, and the U.S. government had dramatically shifted their attention and their funding priorities to this once neglected issue. The international financial institutions overcame their mandates simply by redefining corruption a matter of "governance," hence no longer a "political issue" (Elliott 1997; Hall 1999). Symbolizing and spearheading this newfound attention to the issue of corruption at the international level was the creation of the Berlin-based organization Transparency International (TI) in 1993 by a former official of the World Bank. Patterned on Amnesty International, TI stimulated global awareness and mobilized national and international efforts, first to understand and then to combat corruption. Together these political trends created a growing awareness of the scope of corruption in Latin America and elsewhere. They sparked the development of policy strategies and international conventions designed to fight corruption in the Organization of American States (OAS), the Organization for Economic Cooperation and Development (OECD), and the United Nations (UN). The newfound attention also fashioned strong international pressures on domestic governments to institute reforms. Latin America, as we will see, became caught up in this global shift, authoring the first regional treaty to battle corruption and hosting extensive IMF, World Bank, and U.S. government programs designed to assess and fight corruption.

Academic trends, of course, often mimic political tides. As the political context shifted, so, too, did the academic treatment of corruption. Greatly reinvigorated, studying corruption now became central to understanding the challenges and the course of democratic and economic development. The study now moved from the sidelines to the mainstream: understanding corruption became a critical piece in questions regarding economic liberalization and democratization. Internationally, fighting corruption became a guiding task of aid programs and the topic of international agreements: mandates that required extensive research and analysis.

But beyond the growing rhetorical and funding emphasis on corruption, perhaps the greatest impetus to its study during this time came from the development and diffusion of comparative data gauging corruption across countries by high-profile organizations such as TI and the World Bank (Kaufmann, Kraay, and Zoido-Lobaton 1999; Kaufmann, Kraay, and Mastruzzi 2002). Using opinion surveys of experts, business and financial executives, development officials, and the general public, scholars elaborated measures of the perceived level of corruption using common techniques that made the data more comparable than ever before. These measurement efforts facilitated the cross-national testing of hypotheses about the determinants and the effects of corruption. The data unleashed a tidal wave of research.

The new, cross-national empirical research on corruption took the study to new heights, generating a wealth of more robust findings. The most abundant stream of research deciphers the economic, cultural, and political determinants of corruption. Cross-sectional studies that examine economic factors consistently find that corruption is inversely related to economic and human development (Ades and Di Tella 1999; Goldsmith 1999; Mauro 1995, 1997; Johnston 1999; Montinola and Jackman 2002; Xin and Rudel 2004). In addition, cross-sectional studies reveal that an additional series of socioeconomic conditions and policies may be influential, such as open economies (Paldam 2002; Sandholtz and Koetzle 2000), economic competitiveness and freedoms (Ades and Di Tella 1994, 1997a, 1997b, 1999; Goldsmith 1999; Graeff and Mehlkop 2003; Sachs and Warner 1995), neoliberal economic policies (Gerring and Thacker 2005), income equality (Paldam 2002), and the absence of large resource endowments (Ades and Di Tella 1999; Leite and Weidmann 1999; Montinola and Jackman 2002). Many of these findings bolster the claims of neoliberal and international reformers who consistently prescribe free market reforms to counter corruption. They asserted that economic liberalization limits corruption by reducing government regulation, cutting taxes, enhancing competition, and eliminating rent-seeking opportunities. In turn, although many theoretical writings also allude to the size of government as a determinant of corruption (Rose-Ackerman 1999; Shleifer and Vishny 1993), empirical studies show no firm correlation between government spending and corruption. Analysts are quick to point out that many of the least corrupt governments in the world, like Finland and Sweden, indeed support large budgets and extensive social welfare programs. At a more refined level, however, studies link regulatory burden, red tape, high entry regulations, low salaries, high discretion levels, opaque bureaucracies, and a limited rule of law to corruption (Bardhan 2006; Brunetti and Weder 2003; Djankov et al. 2002; Kaufman 1997, 1999; Kraay and Van Rijckeghem 1995; Rauch and Evans 2000; Van Rijckeghem and Weder 2001).

Cross-national empirical studies also highlight a range of cultural factors that can influence corruption. These include low levels of interpersonal trust (La Porta and Vannucci 1997; Seligson 1999, 2002), the absence of British legal and colonial traditions (Blake and Martin 2006; La Porta et al. 1999; Lederman, Loayza, and Sores 2005; Sandholtz and Koetzle 2000; Swamy et al. 2001; Treisman 2000), low proportions of Protestants (Blake and Martin 2006; Sandholtz and Koetzle 2000; Treisman 2000), less female empowerment (Dollar, Fishman, and Gatti 1999; Swamy and Knack 2001), higher crime rates (Soares 2004), limited press freedoms, ethnolinguistic factionalism (Mauro 1995), and a generalized tolerance toward corruption. In turn, microlevel studies of individual attitudes and opinions add further to our understanding of the cultural determinants of corruption and particularly popular perceptions of corruption. Such studies point to the impact of interpersonal trust, tolerance, and permissiveness on perceptions of corruption. In addition, studies by Gatti (2003), Miller (2006), and Mocan (2004) and formal models by Andvig (1996), Andvig and Moene (1990), Mishra (2006), and Tirole (1996) highlight the role of societal factors in influencing citizens' perceptions of corruption and their participation in corrupt acts. Many of these, as we will see, come from studies of corruption in Latin America.

The multiple cross-national studies fail to offer consistently conclusive results regarding the political determinants of corruption. Despite extensive theoretical arguments linking democracy to the absence of corruption, research shows a rather ambiguous relationship linking the two (see Rose-Ackerman 1999). Cross-nationally, at least, contemporary democracy and current levels of political freedoms seem very weakly related to the level of corruption (Goldsmith 1999; Sandholtz and Koetzle 2000). However, it does appear that a longer exposure to democracy tends to lower the level of corruption over time (see Blake and Martin 2006; Gerring and Thacker 2004; Lambsdorff 1999; Thacker, this volume; Treisman 2000). The implication of this finding is particularly relevant for Latin America in that it affirms the notion that the emergence of democracy by itself does not ensure a reduction in corruption. Instead, as we will explore, the role of democracy as a check on corruption centers on its ability to foster a network of governmental and nongovernmental accountability mechanisms that take time to develop. In many countries in and beyond Latin America, the emergence of these mechanisms—including an independent judiciary, a well-paid civil service, a media sector able and willing to conduct investigative journalism on corruption, and a set of interest groups dedicated to the reduction of corruption—remains a work in process.

A smaller set of new empirical research explores the economic and political consequences of corruption. These studies find strong support for the notion that the effects of corruption are negative, putting to rest many of the functionalist contentions of the 1960s and 1970s (Huntington 1968; Nye 1967). As regards the economic consequences, such studies show rather conclusively that corruption discourages productive investment, distorts trade and government spending priorities, worsens poverty and inequality, and, most important, reduces overall levels of economic growth (Ali and Isse 1999; Kaufmann and Wei 1999; Lambsdorff 1999; Mauro 1995, 1997, 2002). Politically, the effects are equally pernicious. Studies show corruption erodes popular trust in political institutions, undermines generalized trust in others, distorts political participation, and reduces overall regime legitimacy (Anderson and Tverdova 2003; Della Porta 2000; Seligson 2001a, 2001b, 2002, 2004, 2006). Together, these robust findings support the view that corruption threatens or distorts both economic development and democracy.

These new studies breed policy change by informing current anticorruption approaches. Coordinated through governmental and nongovernmental international organizations, particularly the high-profile TI, the prevailing approach stresses the need for economic reform—the strengthening of the protection of private property and the rule of law; the reduction of state regulations—the elimination of red tape and the downsizing and professionalizing of the bureaucracy; the broadening of press freedoms and electoral competition; and greater citizen involvement to apply the needed pressures for reform and to alter public tolerance of corruption. Such approaches are enshrined in international conventions, aid agreements, NGO mission statements, anticorruption tool kits, and governmental anticorruption programs.

THE STUDY OF CORRUPTION IN LATIN AMERICA

For decades, the study of corruption in Latin America followed the broader pattern of neglect discussed earlier. Although most people acknowledged deep-seated corruption throughout the region, until recently few wrote, spoke, or really did much about it. Anecdotes, allegations, and even jokes frequently filled the gaps left by the lack of data on corruption, the limited access to governmental information, and a general unwillingness by scholars, journalists, and political activists to tamper with what seemed to be Pandora's box. A simple search of the flagship *Latin American Research Review*, for example, shows that while about one hundred articles mention corruption, only three titles contain the term. Two articles are historical treatments of corruption in Venezuela and Brazil, and the other, a book review essay (Horowitz 2005; Smallman 1997; Yarrington 2003). This generalized inattention can be seen from an opposing angle as well. Of the 130 reprinted articles and original chapters appearing in the three editions of the classic reader on political corruption by Arnold J. Heidenheimer and associates (1970, 1989, 2002), only two focus on Latin America (both by Laurence Whitehead 1989, 2002) compared to fourteen on Asia and twelve on Africa.

Today, the situation is quite different. Fed by global and regional developments and sparked by the high-level scandals mentioned at the start of this chapter (particularly the impeachments of Venezuelan President Carlos Andrés Pérez and Brazilian President Fernando Collor in the early 1990s), corruption emerged as the leitmotif of the 1990s and 2000s. It is now part and parcel of major research agendas inside and outside the region, the target of "reformist" governments, national and international NGOs, international organizations, and an assortment of journalists and scholars working in the region, and, it seems, the "silver bullet" explaining everything from the failures of economic and political reforms to the region's persistent inequality. Three themes—institutional determinants, culture and public opinion, and anticorruption reforms—facilitate a brief review of this emerging literature.

INSTITUTIONAL INFLUENCES ON CORRUPTION

Because of the link between corruption, economic structures, and democracy, the dominant theme in the more qualitative research on corruption in Latin America centers on understanding the relationship between corruption and the recent processes of economic liberalization and democratization. This literature focuses on one overarching research question: why, despite the theoretical expectation that economic liberalization and democratization would reduce the levels of corruption (Whitehead 2000a, 2000b, 2002), does the evidence suggests otherwise? Indeed, in the years following the return to democracy of the 1980s, corruption in Latin America has increased or has failed to fall appreciably (Weyland 1998; Geddes and Neto 1992, 1999; Brown and Cloke 2004, 2005).

Responses to this central query vary. Some attribute the resilience of corruption to the pursuit of market-oriented reform amid economic crisis. Manzetti (1994) and Manzetti and Blake (1996), for instance, hold that economic crisis and the reform imperative led to an increase in presidential discretionary power, thereby opening up new and unique opportunities for corrupt gain. This view helps to explain the corruption of the Pérez, Menem, and Collor governments, for example. Others point to the impact of economic liberalization on the growth of money laundering operations and drug trafficking (Whitehead 2002) or the impact of economic reforms on reducing the scope and role of the state's regulatory controls or even the pay of bureaucrats (Brown and Cloke 2005, 604; Van Rijckeghem and Weder 2001; and Di Tella and Schargrodsky 2003).

In turn, many authors attribute the resilience of corruption to the presence or absence of key political institutions. These studies point, for instance, to the increased role of elections (Skidmore 1999; Zovatto 2000), the design of party and electoral systems (Geddes and Neto 1992, 1999; Skidmore 1999; Rehren 1997), the institutional framework of presidential systems and federalism, and the rise of neopopulism as critical factors generating corruption. In Brazil, for example, Geddes and Neto (1992, 1999) attribute the rise of corruption in the early 1990s to the 1988 constitution and electoral laws, which hampered "the ability of the executive to a) build coalitions, and b) assure the loyalty of his or her supporters in Congress" (643). Weyland (1998) and Whitehead (2000a, 2000b, 2002), on the other hand, point to the rise of neopopulist leaders (see the discussion by Rehren in this volume).

In addition, new research also highlights the relative absence or weakness of prophylactic political institutions designed to inhibit corruption (Fabbri 2002; Fleischer 2002; Mainwaring and Welna 2003; Santoro 2004; Rodrigues 2004; Subero 2004). Analyses in this vein document a vast array of weak or nonexistent institutions in the region designed to provide horizontal accountability across governmental institutions (e.g., few checks and balances in executive-legislative relations, a politicized and/or overwhelmed civil service, underfunded or nonexistent oversight institutions, insufficient legal frameworks, and a weak judiciary). In turn, mechanisms of vertical accountability between citizens and their governments are also weaker than one would hope (e.g., limited press freedoms, weak civil society, unrepresentative parties, and limited governmental transparency in which access to government activities is restricted or even kept secret). Colazingari and Rose-Ackerman (1998), for instance, stress the lack of constraints on government power, an economic system dominated by a small number of families and firms, the lack of independent prosecutors, the use of public ethics laws to help silence the press, and the lack of administrative oversight. A major component is the lack of prosecution. Indeed, impunity—corruption's brother—remains remarkably high throughout the region. Despite the many cases of corruption that are made public, officials are rarely prosecuted. A report on compliance with the OAS treaty in February 2003 on Argentina, for instance, pointed to the lack of judicial sentences for dozens of civil servants convicted of corruption (cited in Santoro 2004, 10).

THE ROLE OF CULTURE AND PUBLIC OPINION

A second group of studies looks at corruption from the ground up, focusing on culture and public opinion. These studies explore the underlying values and views that support or sustain corruption, examine the nature of popular perceptions of corruption, and also use public opinion data to gauge the impact of corruption. Qualitative cultural studies link corruption to a generalized lack of respect for the rule of law in Latin America, to popular tolerance toward corruption and wrongdoing (Moreno 2002; Santoro 2004, 6), to the prevailing notion among the public that corruption actually works, to the primacy of personal relationships and family over universal norms (Correa 1985; Nef 2001), or to the gap separating popular expectations and economic capabilities (Nef 2001; Lipset and Lenz 2000). Writing in TI's *Global Corruption Report* (2001), for instance, Telma Luzzani points to the lack of respect for the law and public institutions, the sense that anything goes, and the view that bribery actually makes public administration work smoothly to explain widespread corruption in the region. Expressing a similar position, Argentine psychologist Roberto Lerner locates the problem in the prevailing social patterns in which people feel responsible for themselves and those close to them, but not for the community at large. "There's no concept of a common good—our country is made up of 'me' and 'you.' Until there's an 'us,' a true sense of common welfare, the *coima* [bribe] will continue to be accepted" (Fraser 2003).

Beyond narrative cultural studies, numerous scholarly works focus attention on public attitudes toward corruption. This approach stems in part from the use of surveys to measure corruption, but also reflects the notion that citizen views are central to sustaining corruption, to shaping public involvement in and support for mechanisms of vertical accountability (O'Donnell 1998), and to determining the impact of corruption on democracy (see the discussion by Bailey in this volume). Indeed, as we will see, many analysts consider citizen involvement the key ingredient in fighting corruption. Studies exploring public opinion confirm, first, that perceptions of corruption outpace the level of popular participation in actual corrupt exchanges (Seligson 2006; see also Morris, this volume). Democratization increased the perception of corruption, as Weyland (1998) contends. Furthermore, as Bailey notes later in this volume, corruption is often blamed for all types of national ills, particularly during times of crisis. Separate from its link to the actual occurrence of corruption, the perception of corrupt institutions and politicians plays an independent role in hindering political and democratic development. Studies of public opinion also provide insight into the determinants of individual perceptions of corruption and participation rates. Studies by Davis et al. (2004) and Canache and Allison (2005), for instance, link individual perceptions of corruption to generalized distrust in others and political institutions, a poor evaluation of the economy, and support for opposition parties. They also find that women, older respondents, and people with greater levels of political interest tend to perceive higher levels of corruption than do others. In contrast, males and individuals from the higher income and education brackets are more likely to be involved in corrupt activities or to be victims of corruption (Seligson 2006). Finally, research based on public opinion data also helps gauge the impact of corruption on popular support for the government or governmental institutions, feelings of legitimacy, patterns of political participation, and satisfaction and support for democracy. In this area, studies reveal that the perception of corrupt institutions influences people's expectations of paying or being asked to pay a bribe (Guerrero and del Castillo 2003); and that both perception and participation in corruption reduces regime legitimacy (Seligson 2001b, 2002, 2006) and satisfaction with democracy. One study looking at eleven countries in 2004 concludes that "corruption, along with citizen security concerns, has the most detrimental impact on citizens' confidence in democracy and democratic institutions" (Kite and Sarles 2006, 350). Despite this dangerous tendency, findings nonetheless vary over the impact of the perception of corruption on voting. According to McCann and Dominquez (1998), the perception of corruption in Mexico does not seem to lead to antisystem behavior or even voting for the opposition, but instead to lower voter turnout rates. Yet, in their analysis of Venezuela, Little and Herrera (1996) and Subero (2004, 371) blame corruption for voters' rejection of the traditional parties and the concomitant support for the outsider candidate, Hugo Chávez.

ANTICORRUPTION REFORM EFFORTS

Another dominant theme in the new literature on corruption in Latin America focuses on reforms. These include both normative and empirical perspectives. Some studies review the forces involved in exposing and pressing recent cases of corruption and anticorruption initiatives in the region (Boswell 1996; Maingot 1994; Tulchin and Espach 2000), U.S. government programs (see USAID 2005a), or particular countries such as Brazil (Fleischer 1995, 1997, 2002), Mexico (López Presa 1998), Peru (Lawyers Committee for Human Rights 2000), and Venezuela (Coronel 1996). Some emphasize the role of citizens, while others offer general policy recommendations and reform formulas focusing on institutions. The literature on reform, of course, grows out of the analysis of the determinants of corruption. Consequently, many offer a laundry list of the institutional and attitudinal reforms needed to address corruption. Schor (n.d.), for instance, notes the need to replace the prevailing system of authoritarian legality, which breeds mistrust, with a system of democratic legality, which fosters cooperation. Such a move, he contends, will enhance faith in rule of law. Whitehead provides a broader view of the changes needed, pointing to both preventive and corrective devices: "Underlying incentive structures would have to be refashioned, and anti-corruption monitoring reinforced. An ethos of public responsibility would have to be nurtured. Any progress on these fronts would take a considerable time, would vary with complex local conditions, and would require seriousness of purpose from a wide array of actors and institutions, both locally based and internationally. Such anti-corruption networks will only be durable, credible, and eventually successful, if they are willing to challenge entrenched interests and practices opposed to their agenda wherever they lurk" (2002, 816).

Discussion of reform provides a link between the explanatory studies focusing on institutions and those focusing on culture and public opinion. Though many seem to play down the role of culture as an underlying cause of corruption, the reform literature does stress the need to alter underlying popular attitudes and values in order to reduce corruption. Whether this means treating a symptom or a cause remains an open question in some minds. Nevertheless, many observers praise the role citizens have played in focusing attention on corruption, pressuring for change, and pushing for investigations of official wrongdoing (see Coronel 1996; Goodman 1994). According to Smulovitz and Peruzzotti (2000, 147), "Citizen action aimed at overseeing political authorities is becoming a fact of life and is redefining the traditional concept of the relationship between citizens and their elected representatives." Noting how the belief that corruption is uncontrollable or inevitable foments tolerance, Nieto (2004) stresses the need to convince people that corruption can be fought effectively. Such views build on the notion that without pressures from below—the essence of vertical accountability—there is no incentive for politicians to pursue reforms. As Schor (n.d.) and Husted (1999, 2002) assert, good laws are not the core solution to the problem of rule of law, but rather social movements that pressure government to respect rights.

Attention to reform also addresses key questions about the underlying conditions that facilitate or prevent effective reform, providing insights into the failure of recent initiatives. One major reason centers on the lack of political will: reforms fail if they do not take into account the realities of political survival (Geddes 1994; Groves 1967). Some studies note that many reform initiatives have seen little activity beyond the rhetorical. In the case of Brazil, for instance, Fleischer (2002, 7) points to the failure to implement the provisions of the OAS treaty and the lack of civil service and judicial reform. Others locate the lack of progress in the reformist approaches themselves. In the case of Mexico, Alejandro Poiré, for instance, criticizes President Fox's moderate, nonconfrontational approach that grew out of the president's need to work with the large bloc of Institutional Revolutionary Party (PRI) members of congress to enact crucial reforms. Others emphasize the lack of consistency of recent reforms with the region's values and culture. Husted, for example, contends that the demands of the OAS anticorruption treaty are largely incompatible with the culture: "In Latin America, since there already exist many anti-corruption laws on the books, there is considerable skepticism that reform will have an impact" (2002, 418). Reyes offers a similar diagnosis in assessing the failure of reform in Mexico: "no national reflection, no revising of moral values and ethics to build a new Mexico" (2004, 178).

As occurred elsewhere in the world, the rise of democracy in Latin America not only helped generate interest in the study of corruption, but it also helped bring the study more into the mainstream. Corruption is clearly not the only problem associated with such dominant issues today as the weak rule of law, the security crisis, the lack of democratic deepening, the crisis of political representation, the issue of accountability, or democratic consolidation. That said, exploring and understanding corruption does provide crucial insights into these areas (Diamond 1999; Foweraker and Krznaric 2002; Linz and Valenzuela 1994; Mainwaring and Shugart 1997; Mainwaring and Welna 2003; Mendez et al. 1999; O'Donnell 1994, 1998, 2003; Smith 2005).

ANALYTICAL AND POLITICAL CHALLENGES FOR
THE TWENTY-FIRST CENTURY

Today, two challenges dominate the discussion of corruption in Latin America. One set of challenges is analytical. Despite increasing scholarly attention and significant advances in our understanding of corruption in recent years, the study of corruption continues to face some methodological and theoretical shortcomings. From a methodological angle, many question the widespread use of single-dimension indexes measuring perceived levels of corruption. Such measures fail to differentiate among distinct types of corruption. In addition, the recent emphasis on cross-national measurement of perceived corruption provides useful information, but one should not confuse perception with participation in corruption itself. We have attained a much better understanding of why some countries and some individual citizens perceive more corruption, but the study of corrupt activity per se remains a frontier worthy of study. Moreover, significant questions remain regarding the validity and the precision of the survey-based measures of corruption that dominate the study of perceived corruption. Problems range from a bias toward business opinion and bribery forms of corruption, a lack of precision and comparability across studies (some polls look at the "problem," some at "pervasiveness," and others at "number of cases"), and the differing scales, sample sizes, and number of surveys per country (on methodological challenges, see Del Castillo 2003; Lancaster and Montinola 2001). Despite the use of annual polls, it is also difficult to look at change over time, because one "cannot tell us whether year-on-year differences reflect changes in 'real' levels of corruption, the addition of new data that improve the scale or other methodological difficulties that weaken it" (Johnston 2000, 13). This concern is particularly problematic given the genuine, policy-centered interest in anticorruption reform in which changes in the level of corruption over time are central.

In addition to these methodological shortcomings, thematic deficits also need to be addressed. Despite the aforementioned boom in interest, many substantive issues in the study of corruption have continued to receive minimal examination. We have cross-sectional studies that account for corruption on various single-dimension corruption indexes and rich case studies that focus on history, culture, and social context, as Johnston (2005a, 4) notes, but very little in between. Midlevel theory and research is still missing. There also remains a lack of cross-disciplinary research owing to problems of "definition, scope, comparability, meaning and importance across disciplines" (Duncan and Dutta 2006, 324). Economists tend to focus on bureaucratic corruption where there is an underlying assumption of a sharp distinction between public and private, while anthropological case studies point to the difficulty of drawing such divisions (see Gupta 1995). Political scientists tend to focus on explaining grand corruption, but often without incorporating cultural factors to the same extent as they examine political and economic factors. Economists even more frequently ignore value systems, reducing corruption to incentives and organizations, an approach that Bardhan (2006) calls somewhat naive.

Some also criticize what they see as an underlying theoretical bias in many current studies that reflects an economist's perspective, stresses rent-seeking opportunities, and thus echoes a neoliberal and antistatist bias. Brown and Cloke (2004, 2005), for instance, attack the tendency to treat corruption outside of its political and cultural context, to see it as merely a technical issue demanding a reduction in the size of the state and as a uniquely Southern phenomenon. Hall (1999) also criticizes the tendency to focus on corruption in the developing countries but ignore the corruption of developed countries' businesses that contribute to that corruption. In summarizing the state of the contemporary literature, Johnston argues that though the interest is good, "the vision that has emerged over the past decade is a partial one at best . . . the new emphasis on corruption has been limited in a variety of ways by the interests and worldviews of the organizations and interest spearheading debate and policy change" (2005a, 6).

The second major challenge is political. Despite the resurgence of democracy and the pursuit of market-oriented economic reforms, despite the booming political and scholarly interest in corruption, and despite the concerted efforts by national and international reformists to tackle it, corruption stubbornly thrives in Latin America. This view is supported by assessments of recent reforms by analysts and by mass publics alike. The annual CPI figures produced by TI, for instance, reveal little change over the past decade. A recent assessment by the organization of its Global Corruption Barometer, moreover, observes that respondents in Latin American countries were the most negative regarding change in recent years. Citizens in nearly all the countries examined perceived corruption to be on the rise; only in Argentina and Colombia did respondents *not* see an increase in corruption and only in the latter case some reduction (Transparency International 2005a). In *Latinobarómetro* surveys majorities in virtually every country express the view that corruption has indeed gotten worse or remained the same; very few people think it has declined. Once again, expert assessments seem to agree with public opinion. According to Herrera and Urueña, writing in TI's *Global Corruption Report*, "More than a decade after the transition to democracy planted hopes of reform, the region continues to be preyed upon by networks of elites who abuse their positions for illicit gain" (2003, 103). Rodas-Martinini also writing in the same report notes that the emergence of anticorruption initiatives in Mexico and Central American countries "has not generally been accompanied by appreciable improvements in government transparency" (2003, 90). Peter Eigen, the chairman of TI, described Latin America in 2002 in similarly discouraging terms: "Political elites and their cronies continue to take kickbacks at every opportunity. Hand in glove with corrupt business people, they are trapping whole nations in poverty and hampering sustainable development (cited in NotiSur 2002).

In short, neither international nor domestic reforms seem to have made much progress at the start of the twenty-first century. Although more than a decade has passed since the signing of the OAS treaty and nearly that since the OECD treaty, neither have had much of an impact (Husted 2002). Amid an upsurge in investigations and in high-profile public scandals, few corrupt officials ever spend time in prison. Even in the intensely investigated Collor case in Brazil, only two of his men were convicted, and one, his private pilot, for tax evasion (Fleischer 2002, 7). Despite institutional reforms, much remains to be done. Newly created anticorruption agencies and commissions have been attacked for lacking true autonomy. Perhaps even more disturbingly, there is a tendency for those promising to fight corruption during electoral campaigns to subsequently get caught up in accusations and scandals themselves. Fernando Collor, Alberto Fujimori, Fernando de la Rúa, and Luis Inácio (Lula) da Silva came to power cultivating an image of honesty and emphasizing anticorruption only to get immersed in major corruption scandals. These disappointments further undermine the image of anticorruption efforts and breed cynicism regarding politicians more generally. It may also set the stage for more radical promises and solutions. Though corruption is not consistently deemed the most serious national issue in public opinion polls across Latin America, it tends to be mentioned as a major problem. There is a growing concern that corruption, magnified by the failure of recent efforts to curb it, is slowly eating away at the foundations of democracy, hindering efforts to forge a more just society.

In a variety of ways, the studies presented here respond to these analytical and political challenges. Part 1 addresses the causes and the impact of corruption in the region from a cross-regional, global perspective. Strom Thacker builds on recent cross-national studies to explore the impact of democracy and economic policies on corruption. In addition, Thacker examines whether there is something unique about Latin America—a question that combines a nuanced study of political and economic institutions with a concern for the role of culture. Among the findings, Thacker shows that while democracy tends to lower the levels of corruption, this occurs only in the long term and that in the short term democracy has virtually no impact. Alfredo Rehren then builds on this finding, exploring how corruption continues to characterize the countries of the region despite recent transitions to democracy and how one might understand the resilience of corruption. Rehren explains how old forms of clientelistic-based corruption have given rise to two new forms of corruption: neo-populist-based corruption (which centers on the personalization of power, presidential autonomy, and the absence of institutional controls) and the financing of parties and campaigns. In the latter arena, corruption facilitates the flow of state resources to political campaigns and parties. Indeed, perhaps the greatest change in recent years, Rehren contends, has been the conversion of parties into virtual businesses. This middle-range study examines a substantive issue that had been neglected in many recent studies.

John Bailey shifts attention away from the underlying causes of corruption to discuss the consequences of corruption for democratic governability. Here, Bailey goes beyond gross generalizations about the impact of corruption to consider more precisely how different types of corruption—and differing perceptions of corruption—affect specific aspects of democratic governability. In disaggregating the impact of corruption, Bailey highlights the types of institutional scenarios considered the most prone to corruption in the region. He also challenges us to come to terms with various potential popular usages of the term "corruption."

Subsequent empirical-based studies in this section further develop ideas raised by both Rehren and Bailey. Perceptions of corruption and permissiveness toward corruption, as noted earlier, not only figure prominently in our data on corruption but are considered key components in facilitating corruption and shaping the impact of corruption in society. Manzetti and Wilson explore the issues of tolerance and the lack of confidence in government institutions. Rooted in theories of clientelism, the authors show how and why citizens in countries with weak institutions are more likely to support corrupt governments. Moreover, by showing how corrupt leaders perpetuate their hold on power by maintaining clientelistic relations, their study harbors important implications for those promoting accountability and anticorruption reforms. Using a similarly cross-national approach to examine the public's permissiveness toward corruption, Charles Blake also contributes to our understanding of perceptions and tolerance. He focuses on the role of popular attitudes toward the police in shaping tolerance toward bribe-taking. Like Thacker, Blake provides a cross-regional analysis and compares Latin America to the global pattern linking confidence in the police to the public's tolerance for corruption. The extremely low levels of confidence in the police found across the region are particularly noteworthy features of the cultural terrain in Latin America.

Part 2 presents innovative, middle-range research on corruption in Peru, Chile, Brazil, and Mexico. José R. López-Cálix, Lorena Alcázar, and

Mitchell A. Seligson focus on one specific government program in Peru—the Vaso de Leche program—to determine the pattern of budgetary leakage. Using a new methodological tool known as PETS (Public Expenditure Tracking Survey), the authors provide important insights into the question of whether decentralization enhances or diminishes accountability. Adam Brinegar then examines public views toward corruption during the 2002–2003 scandals in Chile. Adding further to the literature on public opinion and the findings of Davis et al. (2004) and Canache and Allison (2005), he explores the role of partisanship in shaping attitudes toward corruption and vote choice. He also explores the distinct discourses on corruption of the major political parties. Turning our attention to Brazil and to the third theme in the literature, reform, Matthew Taylor analyzes the structure and nature of accountability in Brazil's new democracy. His study centers on the salience of the process by which responsibility for allegedly corrupt acts is allocated and how accountability is enforced by public institutions, the private sector, and society as a whole. Above all, the Brazilian experience highlights the disconnection between perceptions of corruption and perceptions of accountability; it shows how perceptions of the widespread absence of accountability feed frustrations with the broader political system. Stephen Morris concludes this section by focusing on the relationship between corruption and democracy in Mexico at the state level. He examines the impact of increasing democratic competitiveness on changes in both corrupt activity and the perception of corruption—thus unifying two streams of research that have been kept separate in most research. He also explores the impact of corruption on support for incumbents.

These studies respond to the analytical and political challenges by addressing new questions and by employing innovative methodological and theoretical approaches. In contrast to the broad generalizations drawn from cross-national research on corruption, for instance, Thacker and Blake tackle the question of how the region itself differs from the broader trends, contributing thus to the elaboration of middle-range theory that is more sensitive to the possibility that culture matters. The work by Bailey and Rehren similarly goes beyond the broad discussion in the literature on corruption and democracy to focus on the more detailed aspects and nuances of how specific aspects of democracy in Latin America have recrafted the patterns of corruption and how they affect governability. Blake and Brinegar's analyses similarly take the current work on public opinion about corruption to a new level by focusing more precisely on the determinants of those views. Their approach helps us better understand the nature of public opinion and its potential role in the fight against corruption. Wilson and Manzetti, in turn, focus on an important and heretofore unexamined question: why citizens sometimes support corrupt governments. Meanwhile, the analysis by Morris on Mexico looks beyond the traditional cross-sectional assessments of cause and consequence to focus on the critical issue of change and the factors shaping the ability of government to decrease corruption itself (and not just its perception). Like Morris, Taylor also goes beyond current studies fastened to a cross-national approach to look at corruption at the subnational level. Finally, López-Cálix, Alcázar, and Seligson develop and show the utility of PETS: a critical diagnostic tool in the struggle against corruption that will help orient future studies (see Reinikka and Svensson 2006). They also focus on the critical issue of decentralization and its contributions to facilitating or inhibiting corruption. Like Morris's research, their study also shifts the focus away from the perception of corruption toward its occurrence.

Taken together, the studies in this volume offer what we hope will be stimulating new research on an old problem. In addition to improving our understanding of corruption's causal dynamics and its influence on democracy, we hope that this heightened understanding can help to identify some paths toward reducing the prevailing skepticism regarding the resilience of corruption during the third wave of democratization in Latin America. We will return to these concerns at the end of this volume.

PART I   **CAUSES AND IMPACTS OF CORRUPTION IN LATIN AMERICA**

STROM C. THACKER

1 Democracy, Economic Policy, and Political Corruption in Comparative Perspective

A vibrant literature on political corruption has emerged in recent years. As reviewed in the prior chapter, much of this work has consisted of cross-national, statistical analysis, while other studies have adopted a qualitative case study and comparative approach. Fewer have employed region-specific quantitative approaches.[1] Among the myriad factors that influence levels of political corruption around the world, recent studies have examined in greater depth the impact of political institutions and public policies on political corruption. This chapter employs a quantitative methodology and a cross-national data set to examine both global patterns and the manner in which Latin America fits into those broader trends. Specifically, it examines relationships between democracy and political corruption, and between economic policies and political corruption. Does the relationship between democracy and corruption in Latin America follow a pattern similar to that obtained elsewhere? Do economic policies exhibit the same kind of effects on corruption in Latin America as they do globally? If any differences appear, how might we account for them?

Latin America as a region is widely viewed as suffering from high levels of political corruption (see Weyland 1998), defined here as an act by a public official (or with the acquiescence of a public official) that violates legal or social norms for private or particularistic gain.[2] From the 1980s forward, Latin America has undergone a dramatic process of both political and economic opening. Country after country has democratized and most also adopted neoliberal economic reforms. Many studies have examined the political and economic effects of corruption in Latin America (and elsewhere) (e.g., Morris 1999; Seligson 2002).

Fewer have examined the impact of democracy and economic reforms on corruption in Latin America (Weyland 1998). But recent cross-regional studies suggest that democracy and neoliberal economic reforms can affect corruption. Democracy may reduce political corruption, especially over the long term (Blake and Martin 2006; Bohara, Mitchell, and Mittendorf 2004; Chowdhury 2004; Emerson 2006; Gerring and Thacker 2004; Lederman, Loayza, and Soares 2005; Montinola and Jackman 2002; Sandholtz and Koetzle 2000; Serra 2006; Treisman 2000). There is some evidence that more market-friendly economic policies inhibit corruption, as well (Akhter 2004; Gerring and Thacker 2005; Ganuza and Hauk 2004; Goldsmith 1999; Sandholtz and Gray 2003; Treisman 2007). Given its recent history of political and economic reform, why does corruption persist in Latin America? Is there something peculiar, perhaps immeasurable by conventional means, that makes Latin America an "outlier," or do patterns in Latin America fit existing explanations well and reflect broader trends seen elsewhere around the world?

DEMOCRACY AND POLITICAL CORRUPTION

Causal explanations of political corruption abound, as do studies on the effects of different political institutional arrangements on important outcomes like economic growth, human development, and political stability, among others. Yet only recently has significant attention been paid to the theoretical and empirical links between corruption and political institutions. One of the more important institutions in this literature is democracy.[3] What effect does democracy have on political corruption? Are democratic regimes less corrupt than their authoritarian counterparts?

Early studies found somewhat ambiguous results when testing the relationship between democracy and corruption. Others have suggested that these prior null findings are an artifact of the manner in which democracy is conceptualized and measured (Blake and Martin 2006; Gerring and Thacker 2004). In particular, attempts to link annual measures of democracy with contemporaneous measures of political corruption reveal inconsistent patterns. Many of the individual benefits of corruption accrue in the short term, while its societal costs are both more widespread and more likely to accumulate over time (via their potentially dampening, additive effect on investment and growth, for example). A historic measure of democracy that captures both its duration and strength over a long period of time may, therefore, yield more satisfying results.

Before examining the empirical relationship between democracy and corruption, let us explore its conceptual underpinnings. Why should democracy be expected to lead to lower levels of political corruption? Additionally, should we expect democracy to yield immediate, short-term benefits, or are its potential salubrious effects more likely to emerge only over a long period of time? Historical work suggests that democracy and authoritarianism construct deep legacies, extending back several decades, perhaps even centuries (Collier and Collier 1991; Hite and Cesarini 2004; Linz and Stepan 1996; Mahoney 2002). It follows that we should concern ourselves with the accumulated effect of these historical legacies, not merely their contemporary status. This chapter contends that the effects of political institutions are likely to unfold over time—sometimes a great deal of time—and that these temporal effects are cumulative.

This section identifies three (among many) potential causal pathways linking democracy with political corruption that take into consideration the possible temporal characteristics of this relationship. This chapter does not argue that democracies are pristinely or uniformly clean, for long-standing democracies such as the United States still suffer from corruption scandals. Rather, the purpose here is to understand better the long-term impact of democracy compared to other systems of government, holding other things equal.

First, competition among elites for voters' favor should produce a situation in which elites are accountable to the citizenry—at the very least, to a plurality of the voting electorate.[4] Since political corruption is typically unpopular among those who do not receive its direct benefits, democratically elected leaders may be more likely to run a clean government than leaders who maintain their positions through other means.[5] The latter sort of leaders may be better able to weather discontent from the masses than their democratic counterparts because they typically face a much smaller "selectorate" (Bueno de Mesquita et al. 2003). As long as the authoritarian regime's core constituency (e.g., the military, ruling party, and economic elites) remains well compensated, possibly through corruption itself, it is unlikely that social discontent will threaten rulers' control over the state. Democratic politicians, on the other hand, may face similar material incentives for engaging in corruption and may even benefit politically from it in the short run. But we can expect the logic of democratic competition to create relatively fewer incentives and more disincentives to corruption than an authoritarian regime.

In the short run, however, there is no obvious reason why democratically elected rulers would benefit from incurring present costs for the sake of future gains unless their time horizons have shifted to a longer-term perspective. This shift, in turn, is unlikely to occur in the early years of a recently democratized polity, where institutions are in flux, parties and party systems nascent and unstable, and voter affiliations ephemeral. Faced with political uncertainty and instability, politicians in this context may face incentives to pursue short-run goals at the expense of long-term ones (Haggard 1991). In a long-standing democracy, by contrast, it seems plausible that leaders are more likely to have longer time horizons. To the extent that longer time horizons increase incentives to combat corruption, established democracies should demonstrate lower levels of corruption.

Second, the institutions of democracy tend to foster a well-developed civil society, including watchdog groups and independent media. Political rights and civil rights are highly correlated,[6] and the existence of civil rights typically leads, over time, to a dense network of voluntary associations (Boone and Batsell 2001; Parker 1994; Webb 2004). Democracy is also associated with a vibrant, independent media that can investigate, scrutinize, and publicize allegations of political corruption (Lawson 2002; Sives 1993). But the evolution of civil society is a long-term process. Voluntary associations, NGOs, and media outlets do not typically spring forth and become effective overnight. Thus, insofar as strong civil societies encourage better governance, we can expect these causal mechanisms to accumulate over several decades. Again, the age and historic strength of democracy would seem to matter.

Finally, older democracies should benefit from greater institutionalization in the political sphere. Although political institutionalization is difficult to define, there seems to be general consensus that procedures in a well-institutionalized polity are functionally differentiated, regularized (and hence predictable), professionalized (including meritocratic methods of recruitment and promotion), rationalized (explicable, rule based, and nonarbitrary), and infused with value (Huntington 1968; Levitsky 1998; Polsby 1968). Virtually all long-standing democracies fit this description. They feature highly developed, highly differentiated systems of governance, involving both formal bureaucracies and extraconstitutional organizations such as interest groups, political parties, and other nongovernmental organizations. Thus, the length of time a democracy has been in existence can serve as a rough indicator of its degree of institutionalization. By contrast, the length of time an authoritarian regime has been in existence may have little or no bearing on its level of institutionalization. Indeed, institutional reversals are common in authoritarian regimes, as in the latter days of the Soviet Union or in Iraq under Saddam Hussein.[7]

The reasons for this may stem directly from authoritarian systems of rule. Where power is personalized, as it is in so many authoritarian settings, the development of legal-bureaucratic authority is less likely and more tenuous. In particular, leadership succession is difficult to contain within regularized procedures and promises a period of transition fraught with uncertainties. Thus, even if a monarch or dictator adheres to consistent policy objectives during his or her rule, there may be little continuity between that regime and its successor. The hallmark of a long-standing democracy, by contrast, is its ability to resolve the problem of leadership succession without turmoil and without extraordinary discontinuities in policy and in political organization. The framework remains intact, and this means that the process of institutionalization may continue, despite the occasional bump in the road.

Some authoritarian regimes may be considerably institutionalized, as some of Latin America's military dictatorships and Mexico under one-party dominance have demonstrated. But the institutionalization of power can produce greater gains within a democratic setting than in an authoritarian setting. Institutionalization matters more under democracy. Consider the problem of establishing rule of law in a polity and resolving problems of coordination (for example, between different interests, different points of view, and different identities) (Hardin 1999). In the Mexican example, the tremendous power of the presidency under PRI rule undermined the legitimacy of other institutions and subjected them to the caprice of the president. And in military regimes there is even less need for highly institutionalized procedures for reconciling differences and establishing the rule of law. The sovereign may rule directly.

In a democratic setting, by contrast, resolving conflict is complicated and generally takes a good deal of time. Somehow, political actors must agree upon (or at least agree to respect) the imposition of society-wide policy solutions that involve uneven costs and benefits. In order to handle these quintessentially political problems, a democratic polity has little choice but to institutionalize procedures for negotiation among rival constituencies and organizations. Once these procedures are established (a process that takes time), they may be more effective in resolving differences and finding optimal solutions than would be fiats imposed from above. The notion of democratic overload is much more compelling when applied to new democracies than when applied to old. Democratization is often a boisterous, obstreperous affair. Established democracies, by contrast, tend to be more restrained, with the norm of incremental change more likely to be accepted.

Thus, given sufficient time, we can expect that democracies will be less likely to suffer from corruption and more likely to adopt measures to combat it than authoritarian governments. Arguably, the problem of overload arises not from institutional sclerosis (Olson 1982) but rather from insufficient institutionalization (Huntington 1968). If democracy survives its often tumultuous youth, it should contribute to cleaner government, even if no immediate improvement was registered in the initial transition from authoritarian rule. Democracy, in other words, is best considered as a stock, rather than level, concept. Two dimensions of democracy, history and degree, must be gauged together in order to explain a country's governance.

ECONOMIC POLICY AND POLITICAL CORRUPTION

Turning to the role of public policies in determining rates of corruption, what kinds of public policies are likely to be associated with higher or lower rates of corruption? Which specific policies matter most and how? While several public policies may play a role, I focus here on the possible effects of a handful of neoliberal economic policies, such as those that several Latin American countries have adopted since the 1980s. Do neoliberal policies deter political corruption?[8] If so, which policies matter most and how?[9]

To date, most empirical work on these questions is of the case study variety. Much of this research centers on neoliberal reforms of the past two decades. Manzetti and Blake (1996, 668) find that recent market reforms have changed, but not eliminated, the politics of corruption in Latin America.[10] The partial character of neoliberal reform in most African countries may have enhanced rent-seeking activity on the part of privileged actors (van de Walle 2001, 179–80; see also Lewis and Stein 1997; Reno 1995). Market reforms in communist and postcommunist countries have elicited similar comments from some observers of these cases (see Hellman 1998; White 1996). By contrast, other studies demonstrate support for the notion that neoliberal reforms ultimately reduce political corruption (Krueger 1993). Moreover, other work focused on socialist regimes supports the neoliberal argument (see Kramer 1989; Di Franceisco and Gitelman 1989; Liu 1989; Lu 2000; Riley 1998; Varese 1997).

Cross-national studies with larger samples are less common and have obtained mixed results on these questions. Tanzi and Davoodi (1997) find public investment (as an indicator of government intervention) to be slightly correlated with corruption but short of statistical significance at usual thresholds. Looking at industrial policies, Ades and Di Tella (1997) also find a weak connection between government behavior and aggregate system-level corruption (see also Elliott 1997; Shleifer and Vishny 1998). Sandholtz and Koetzle (2000) find a reasonably strong connection between economic freedom and clean government. Treisman (2000) and Blake and Martin (2006), however, find less consistent support for the influence of economic freedom in their respective examinations of somewhat larger data sets.

There are myriad public policies that might influence levels of political corruption around the world, but there is little theoretical work that delineates the ways in which this might occur. The task here is to identify a series of potentially important policies, assess their causal logic, and test their explanatory power empirically. The principal hypothesis is that market-oriented, neoliberal economic policies help reduce political corruption. In particular, I focus here on the impact of macroeconomic and trade policies. Do conservative fiscal and monetary policies, price stability, and trade openness contribute to lower levels of corruption? This section delineates the rationale for linking neoliberal policies and corruption.

According to the broad neoliberal hypothesis, less government involvement in the economy and in civil society should result in less corruption. Certainly, there would appear to be less opportunity for corruption, since political corruption can only occur in a policy area where government has substantive powers. Fully market-based systems, almost by definition, should be less prone to governmental graft, all else being equal. By the same token, widening the scope of the free market and enhancing its competitiveness should dampen at least some of the demand for political corruption, since corruption itself is often a response to blocked market transactions. By contrast, interventionist policies vest policy-making power in government bureaucrats to direct market relations, thus offering incentives to businesspersons to cultivate special relations with government officials, who in turn may depend politically on support from key interest groups and actors.[11] The complex nature of such intervention, and the need for rule interpretation, makes decision-making transparency difficult to achieve. Moreover, the concentrated nature of the private good, coupled with the diffuse nature of the public good, present difficult collective action and free-rider problems that translate into political incentives that augur poorly for the protection of the public interest. Such policies can also create powerful political constituencies for or against corruption.

Price stability is a critical and fundamental element of sound economic management for neoliberals. Without stable and relatively low rates of inflation, economic actors face tremendous uncertainty over relative prices and asset values. Real wages tend to deteriorate and prosperity suffers. In particular, high rates of inflation shorten actors' time horizons and increase their discount rate, potentially increasing the expected utility for politicians of corruption. As discussed above, while the private benefits of corruption will often be garnered in the short term, its public costs are borne out over a longer period. By the time the public costs of corruption become evident, its culprits will likely be long out of office in a context of high instability.

It is also possible that the policies that generate inflation themselves promote corruption. Loose, expansionary fiscal policies, for example, offer greater opportunities for graft by giving government bureaucrats access to greater volumes of government resources, the distribution of which may be influenced by bribes, kickbacks, and the like. Similarly, loose monetary policy expands the pool of resources available for political purposes through the printing of money. Relatedly, the printing of money can also be used to finance fiscal deficits.

There are good reasons to suspect that trade policies might be tied to political corruption (see, among others, Ades and Di Tella 1997c, 1999; Bhagwati 1982; Knack and Azfar 2000; Krueger 1974; Leite and Weidmann 1999; Sandholtz and Koetzle 2000; Smith 1939 [1776]; Treisman 2000). First, barriers to international market transactions can create material and bureaucratic incentives for corrupt behavior. Countries that erect high barriers to trade fight the natural propensity of individuals to truck and barter. By raising the price of goods above their market price, trade barriers may induce businesspersons to bribe their way to exemptions or special treatment (including high levels of effective protection). By the same token, trade restrictions are complicated to administer, involving an intricate set of rules and procedures that tend to inflate the size of the government bureaucracy and that must be delegated to bureaucrats to enforce. The combination of complexity, particularism, and delegation can encourage corrupt practices on the part of government officials. Rule-making powers of this nature, when coupled with the material resources of would-be international traders, can be a recipe for malfeasance. Conversely, to the extent that trade enhances competition in the domestic market and thereby reduces the profit margins for domestic producers, it leaves fewer resources available for extraction by corrupt officials (Treisman 2007, 236).

A second argument stems from the constituencies formed over time by closed-market policies. While an open-economy regime is likely to foster an outward-looking business class, a closed system is likely to foster an inward-looking, inefficient private sector whose prosperity rests on close ties to the state and rents provided by protectionist policies (see Thacker 2000a, 2000b; Ranis 1990). Groups dependent on protection from foreign producers and investors are unlikely to criticize corrupt practices by governmental actors upon whom their livelihood depends, or may even be beneficiaries of those practices themselves. Thus, a protectionist regime can buy political silence or even complicity on the part of middle-class groups who might otherwise participate in anticorruption campaigns. Closed-economy policies may hinder the formation of a constituency for political accountability amongst the business community and other elites.

Third, an outward trade orientation should enhance links to the international economy and foreign business groups, and from thence to "Western" notions of acceptable business and political practices, for the sake of business expediency, if nothing else. Even if no sort of cultural diffusion takes place between foreign and domestic groups, internationally oriented groups may find it in their material interest to adopt business and political practices consistent with those of their primary foreign trade and investment partners. An inward orientation, by contrast, may give business and government alike a more domestically oriented perspective, one relatively insulated from foreign influences. This is not likely a propitious political environment for fighting domestic corruption.

DATA

The empirical approach used here employs cross-national statistical analysis of the 1996–2002 time period. The dependent variable is the World Bank's measure of corruption control.[12] Independent variables include a level and stock measure (explained below) of the Polity2 variable from the Polity IV data set and measures of inflation, the ratio of money supply (M2) to international reserves, the budget balance (as a percentage of GDP), import duties (as a percentage of imports), and imports (as a percentage of GDP). All analyses include a wide variety of control variables. I use a between-effects estimator to generate empirical results.

The primary indicator of corruption used in this study comes from the World Bank's governance indicators, compiled by Kaufmann, Kraay, and Mastruzzi (2003) from a wide variety of international polls. The advantages of the World Bank measure of corruption control over others are its enormous breadth of coverage and the variety of sources employed in compiling the index, rendering it less susceptible to poll- or question-specific idiosyncrasies.[13] Higher scores indicate better perceived control of corruption, while lower scores suggest higher levels of perceived corruption.[14]

Among the many choices of measures of regime type, few examine long-term historical patterns. The best available choice for tracing such patterns is the Polity2 variable from the Polity IV index (Marshall and Jaggers 2000). This variable measures the extent to which democratic or authoritarian "authority patterns" are institutionalized in a given country. It takes into account how the executive is selected, the degree of checks on executive power, and the form of political competition.[15]

The level measure of democracy is simply the score a country receives on the Polity2 index in a given year. Similar to measures of capital stock, the stock measure of democracy captures the stock of democratic experience that a country has enjoyed over an extended period of time, as well as its depreciation over time. This measure sums each country's annual scores on the Polity2 variable from 1900 to the observation year, with a 1 percent annual depreciation rate. This means that a country's regime stock stretches back over the course of the twentieth century, but that more distant years receive less weight than recent ones. The year 1900 was chosen as a threshold that ushered in a period in which mass democracy became a world-historical phenomenon (no longer restricted to the United States and a few European states).[16]

Indicators of economic policy and outcomes include macroeconomic indicators, and measures of trade and trade policy. On the macroeconomic side, inflation measures annual changes in the price level, with data from the World Bank's (2003) *World Development Indicators*. M2/reserves expresses the ratio of money and quasi money (M2) to gross international reserves (World Bank 2003). The budget balance measures the net budget balance, including grants, as a percentage of GDP (World Bank 2003). Two indicators test the impact of trade and trade policy. Import duties as a percentage of the total value of imports provides one measure of the level of trade protection, and imports as a percentage of GDP serves as a summary measure of trade openness (World Bank 2003). Finally, a dummy variable coded one for all Latin American countries facilitates the analysis of the Latin American cases in a global context.

Control variables include a wide array of possibly confounding factors. Higher levels of GDP per capita (logged, World Bank 2003) should be associated with better corruption control. A dummy variable for Africa should correlate negatively with perceived corruption control. Western Europe should demonstrate better outcomes, while expectations about the Asia variable are more mixed. A history of socialist rule is often seen as conducive to corruption. Having an English legal origin is often thought to promote good governance (La Porta et al. 1999). To the extent that countries farther from the equator have better governance, latitude (absolute value, scaled to 0–1, logarithm, La Porta et al. 1999) should correlate with better corruption control. Ethnically fractious countries would be expected to do worse in combating corruption (Alesina et al. 2002). To the extent that having a large population (total population, logarithm, World Bank 2003) makes certain governmental tasks more difficult, population might be expected to diminish governance quality. Distance (in thousands of km) from the nearest financial center (Tokyo, New York, or London) is intended to capture the negative impact of geographic distance from the cores of the international economy. Oil (millions of barrels per day per capita) and diamond (rescaled to billions of metric carats per year per capita) production levels capture the resource curse (Humphreys 2004), which may hamper governments' ability to control corruption. The percentage of Protestants in the population should correlate positively with lower levels of perceived corruption (Gerring and Thacker 2004).

A time trend variable helps control for spurious correlation between any pair of similarly trended dependent and independent variables; this should be signed in whatever direction a given dependent variable is trended, on average, over time. A control variable that measures the average value of the dependent variable across all countries, weighted by the inverse of the geographic distance (in kilometers) of each country from the country in question, helps address spatial concerns (e.g., the neighborhood effect). Countries lying close to one another may display similar values for extraneous reasons (culture, geography, diffusion, and so forth). The inclusion of this variable in all regressions should help minimize possible spatial autocorrelation in the sample.

To minimize possible endogeneity between the dependent variable and some independent variables (as well as among some independent variables), GDP per capita and population size are measured in 1960 rather than on a contemporary annual basis. In the absence of valid instruments for these variables, this method helps alleviate concerns about potential reverse causality between corruption and prosperity and population growth. In other cases, all dynamic controls and independent variables are lagged by one year (except in the case of the geography-weighted dependent variable, which is contemporaneous). Other controls, such as region, socialism, legal origin, fractionalization, distance from the nearest financial center, and Protestantism are treated as constant through time. The chapter appendix lists descriptive statistics for the dependent and independent variables used in the analysis.

RESULTS OF THE GLOBAL ANALYSIS

This chapter employs between-effects regression on corruption data from 1996, 1998, 2000, and 2002. Because of the standardization technique used by Kaufmann et al. and the entrance of new countries into the data set over time, scores within countries are not directly comparable over time.[17] These two factors point to a multiyear cross-sectional analysis in lieu of a time-series—cross-section (or pooled or panel) design. The between-effects estimator used here averages the results from each separate cross-section. This provides the benefits of bringing as much data as possible to bear on the problem at hand without violating the highly questionable (in this instance) temporal assumptions of regression analysis.

Table 1.1 presents the results of the relationship between democracy and political corruption. The overall fit of the models is quite good, with F values significant at better than the 0.0001 level and adjusted R^2 values that suggest that the models explain roughly 65 to 70 percent of the variation in levels of perceived corruption around the world. Column 1 in table 1.1 presents a baseline model that includes all of the control variables but no measure of democracy. Columns 2 through 4 introduce level and stock democracy variables. Democracy level appears at first to have a positive relationship with better corruption control, significant at the 10 percent confidence level. The results for democracy stock are robustly significant

Table 1.1 **Democracy and corruption, 1996–2002**

Model variable	1 Base	2 Demo level	3 Demo stock	4 Combined	5 Inter-action	6 Latin America only	7 Not Latin America
Democracy level		0.017* (0.009)		−0.006 (0.010)			
Democracy stock			0.001*** (0.0002)	0.001*** (0.0003)	0.001*** (0.0003)	0.001** (0.001)	0.001*** (0.0003)
Latin America	−0.115 (0.183)	−0.180 (0.188)	−0.203 (0.171)	−0.158 (0.176)	−0.208 (0.172)		
LA*Democracy stock					0.0004 (0.001)		
GDP per capita (ln, 1960)	0.210*** (0.043)	0.195*** (0.043)	0.140*** (0.043)	0.139*** (0.042)	0.142*** (0.043)	0.518** (0.177)	0.135*** (0.044)
Africa	−0.073 (0.184)	−0.101 (0.189)	−0.081 (0.173)	−0.118 (0.177)	−0.083 (0.174)		−0.051 (0.181)
Western Europe	0.664*** (0.223)	0.676*** (0.224)	0.424* (0.215)	0.424* (0.217)	0.436** (0.216)		0.420* (0.221)
Asia	0.407** (0.171)	0.366** (0.175)	0.303* (0.164)	0.295* (0.165)	0.306* (0.165)		0.312* (0.168)
Socialism	−0.502*** (0.154)	−0.452*** (0.153)	−0.176 (0.158)	−0.143 (0.158)	−0.194 (0.161)		−0.185 (0.164)
English legal origin	0.093 (0.127)	0.073 (0.127)	−0.031 (0.120)	−0.030 (0.121)	−0.026 (0.121)		−0.006 (0.127)
Latitude (ln)	0.173** (0.068)	0.174** (0.068)	0.180*** (0.063)	0.191*** (0.064)	0.182*** (0.063)		0.172** (0.069)
Ethnic fractionalization	−0.354 (0.229)	−0.239 (0.227)	−0.186 (0.217)	−0.136 (0.214)	−0.191 (0.218)		−0.174 (0.234)
Population (ln, 1960)	−0.030 (0.032)	−0.011 (0.027)	−0.034 (0.030)	−0.022 (0.025)	−0.034 (0.030)		−0.036 (0.032)
Distance to nearest financial center	−0.029 (0.028)	−0.022 (0.028)	−0.015 (0.026)	−0.018 (0.027)	−0.015 (0.026)		−0.036 (0.030)
Oil production per capita	−0.206 (0.368)	0.130 (0.391)	0.369 (0.361)	0.392 (0.370)	0.346 (0.364)	−11.291*** (3.734)	0.426 (0.371)
Diamond production per capita	0.087** (0.043)	0.083* (0.043)	0.058 (0.041)	0.065 (0.041)	0.059 (0.041)		0.063 (0.042)
Protestant (%)	0.011*** (0.002)	0.010*** (0.002)	0.007*** (0.002)	0.007*** (0.002)	0.007*** (0.002)		0.007*** (0.002)
Geography–weighted dependent variable	0.050** (0.023)	0.036 (0.025)	0.035 (0.023)	0.030 (0.023)	0.036 (0.023)	0.236 (0.188)	0.032 (0.023)
Trend	−0.125 (0.162)	−0.004 (0.139)	−0.088 (0.152)	0.064 (0.131)	−0.091 (0.152)		−0.069 (0.160)
Constant	11.627 (16.291)	−0.519 (13.596)	8.506 (15.191)	−6.542 (12.805)	8.740 (15.233)	−3.886*** (1.253)	6.774 (16.098)
Observations	643	616	639	616	. 639	79	560
Number of countries	168	167	167	167	167	20	147
Adjusted R-squared	0.65	0.64	0.69	0.69	0.69	0.50	0.7054
Prob. > F	0.0000	0.0000	0.0000	0.0000	0.0000	0.0000	0.0000

Standard errors in parentheses. A between-effects estimator was used for these regressions.
* Significant at 10%. ** Significant at 5%. *** Significant at 1%.

at better than the 1 percent level of confidence. But when both variables are included together in the same estimation, results for the level variable lose significance, while those for stock remain virtually unchanged. In short, controlling for a country's history of democracy and authoritarianism (as well as a number of other control variables), its current level of democracy does not appear to have any significant relationship with its level of perceived political corruption.[18] Confirming some prior findings (e.g., Blake and Martin 2006; Gerring and Thacker 2004), democracy's beneficial effects on the quality of government appear to be time-dependent and best captured over the long term.

Results for control variables suggest that countries that are wealthy, Western European, Asian, Protestant, and far from the equator tend to exhibit lower levels of perceived corruption, all else being equal. The potential negative effects of socialist rule on corruption control drop out with the inclusion of the democracy stock variable.

Table 1.2 presents findings for the relationship between economic policy and political corruption. Again, the model fit is quite strong, with highly significant F values and high adjusted R^2 values. Column 1 replicates table 1.1's column 3 as a baseline model to which the economic variables are added. Macroeconomic policies appear to exert an important impact on corruption perceptions. I tested inflation, money supply, and budget balance simultaneously in an attempt to parse out the possible effects of inflation itself (e.g., time-horizon and discount rate effects) from the potential effects of its underlying macroeconomic policy causes (e.g., the effects of large fiscal deficits), as discussed above. Results suggest that inflation exerts a significant (at the 0.10 level) influence on perceived corruption, even controlling for the underlying policies that help determine the rate of inflation. This may be because of the shortening of time horizons and the raising of politicians' discount rates in an unstable, inflationary macroeconomic environment. Fiscal deficits are associated with higher levels of perceived corruption, independent of the rate of inflation, while the ratio of money supply to gross international reserves does not appear to exert any independent effects.

Two measures of trade policy and outcomes offer similar conclusions, as seen in columns 3 and 4 of table 1.2. Higher levels of trade protection, as measured by import duties as a percentage of the total value of imports, lower the perceived level of corruption control, while higher proportions of trade to GDP raise it. Societies with more open economies tend to exhibit less corruption, all else being equal. Finally, column 5 presents a combined model that includes both macroeconomic and openness variables jointly, along with all control variables that demonstrate a significant relationship with corruption scores.[19] Results for inflation, budget balance, and trade remain significant and their coefficients reasonably stable. Macroeconomically stable, open economies exhibit lower levels of political corruption, controlling for a host of other factors.

The results for control variables in table 1.2 show a positive association with corruption control for democracy stock, GDP per capita, Asia, latitude, and Protestant. Other controls occasionally but inconsistently attain statistical significance across various specifications.

A variety of other estimation procedures were employed to gauge the robustness of these findings. The between-effects estimator employed here offers many benefits, effectively allowing the analysis of multiple cross-sections jointly while avoiding many of the problems that would arise if the data set were treated as panel data. This allows the researcher to examine more data points while at the same time recognizing that the data do not represent a time series. I also ran several tests using more conservative techniques (with N ranging from 131 to 167) and found results highly consistent with those presented here. One set of tests ran four separate cross-sectional analyses (one for each observation year), with country-clustered standard errors on each of the models from table 1.1, column 3, and table 1.2, column 4. These eight additional tests revealed patterns quite consistent with those reported in the tables.[20] Only the cross-sectional analysis of data from the year 2000 for the imports estimation failed to reach the 10 percent level of statistical significance ($p < 0.13$), while most results met the 5 percent level. All signs and coefficients for the variables of interest were consistent with the present findings. A second test employed weighted-least-squares (WLS) analysis on a single cross-section on the average values for all variables from each of the four separate cross-sections. The WLS procedure used as a weight the inverse of the average standard error in the corruption score for each country to give greater weight to those countries with less variance among the different data sources employed by the World Bank to assign corruption scores. Again, results were highly robust, significant at better than the 1 percent level in both cases, with coefficients at least as strong as those in tables 1.1 and 1.2. A final set of tests combined these two techniques to conduct WLS analysis on each separate cross-section. Again, results were strongly robust. In sum, the results presented here do not depend on a particular estimation technique or method of compiling the different cross-sections.

Table 1.2 **Economic policy and corruption, 1996–2002**

Model variable	1 Base	2 Macro	3 Import duties	4 Imports	5 Combined	6 Interaction	7 Latin America only	8 Not Latin America
Inflation		−0.003* (0.001)			−0.003** (0.001)			
M2/reserves		−0.009 (0.006)						
Budget balance (% of GDP)		0.070*** (0.024)			0.044*** (0.017)			
Import duties (% of imports)			−0.017*** (0.005)					
Imports of goods and services (% of GDP)				0.007*** (0.002)	0.008*** (0.002)	0.008*** (0.002)	0.026** (0.010)	0.008*** (0.002)
Latin America	−0.203 (0.171)	−0.256 (0.226)	−0.406* (0.218)	−0.153 (0.159)	−0.136 (0.145)	0.047 (0.272)		
LA*Imports						−0.005 (0.005)		
Democracy stock	0.001*** (0.0002)	0.001*** (0.0003)	0.001** (0.0003)	0.001*** (0.0002)	0.001*** (0.0002)	0.001*** (0.0002)	0.002** (0.001)	0.001*** (0.0003)
GDP per capita (ln, 1960)	0.140*** (0.043)	0.251*** (0.086)	0.260*** (0.075)	0.156*** (0.041)	0.281*** (0.053)	0.151*** (0.041)	0.769*** (0.209)	0.146*** (0.042)
Africa	−0.081 (0.173)	0.060 (0.272)	0.209 (0.262)	−0.038 (0.169)		−0.027 (0.170)		0.023 (0.173)
Western Europe	0.424* (0.215)	−0.116 (0.468)	0.235 (0.241)	0.314 (0.202)		0.323 (0.203)		0.329 (0.204)
Asia	0.303* (0.164)	0.433* (0.237)	0.503** (0.212)	0.324* (0.166)	0.510*** (0.145)	0.324* (0.167)		0.344** (0.168)
Socialism	−0.176 (0.158)	0.134 (0.208)	−0.202 (0.190)	−0.248 (0.151)		−0.253* (0.151)		−0.272* (0.158)
English legal origin	−0.031 (0.120)	−0.047 (0.194)	0.068 (0.158)	−0.002 (0.115)		0.016 (0.116)	−0.997* (0.526)	0.064 (0.119)
Latitude (ln)	0.180*** (0.063)	0.161* (0.094)	0.031 (0.083)	0.179*** (0.061)	0.207*** (0.055)	0.180*** (0.061)		0.174*** (0.066)
Ethnic fractionalization	−0.186 (0.217)	−0.248 (0.293)	−0.402 (0.263)	−0.309 (0.198)		−0.302 (0.198)		−0.309 (0.210)
Population (ln, 1960)	−0.035 (0.030)	−0.037 (0.037)	−0.086** (0.034)	0.009 (0.032)		0.007 (0.0312)	0.190 (0.116)	0.001 (0.033)
Distance to nearest financial center	−0.015 (0.026)	0.003 (0.035)	−0.015 (0.033)	−0.019 (0.025)		−0.025 (0.026)		−0.052* (0.028)
Oil production per capita	0.369 (0.361)	0.331 (0.473)	0.347 (0.432)	0.327 (0.383)		0.333 (0.383)	−9.366** (3.451)	0.377 (0.386)
Diamond production per capita	0.058 (0.041)	−0.029 (0.061)	0.047 (0.052)	0.065* (0.037)		0.067* (0.037)		0.072* (0.037)
Protestant (%)	0.007*** (0.002)	0.007 (0.004)	0.008*** (0.003)	0.009*** (0.002)	0.009*** (0.002)	0.009*** (0.002)	0.032 (0.018)	0.010*** (0.002)
Geography-weighted dependent variable	0.035 (0.023)	0.003 (0.027)	0.028 (0.025)	0.020 (0.022)		0.020 (0.022)		0.015 (0.022)

(Continued on next page)

Table 1.2 *(Cont.)* **Economic policy and corruption, 1996–2002**

Model variable	1 Base	2 Macro	3 Import duties	4 Imports	5 Combined	6 Interaction	7 Latin America only	8 Not Latin America
Trend	−0.088	−0.135**	−0.057	−0.087	−0.150***	−0.098		−0.108
	(0.152)	(0.068)	(0.057)	(0.080)	(0.047)	(0.081)		(0.088)
Constant	8.506	12.540*	5.477	7.357	12.724***	8.463	−9.622***	9.678
	(15.191)	(6.711)	(5.519)	(8.043)	(4.582)	(8.140)	(2.683)	(8.814)
Observations	639	289	313	583	316	583	77	506
Number of countries	167	95	105	158	108	158	20	138
Adjusted *R*-squared	0.69	0.67	0.76	0.75	0.83	0.75	0.56	0.77
Probability > *F*	0.0000	0.0000	0.0000	0.0000	0.0000	0.0000	0.0000	0.0000

Standard errors in parentheses. A between-effects estimator was used for these regressions.
*Significant at 10%.   ** Significant at 5%.   *** Significant at 1%.

LATIN AMERICA IN THE GLOBAL CONTEXT

How does Latin America fit into these global patterns? Is it that different from the rest of the world? Despite popular perceptions to the contrary, Latin America is only slightly worse than the global mean in its levels of perceived corruption in the World Bank index (see appendix). The region demonstrates a higher level of current democracy and a slightly better historical measure of democracy stock. Inflation tends to be a bit lower in Latin America, and the budget balances of Latin American countries on average show somewhat smaller deficits. Import duties are slightly lower, but the region tends to rely less on imports. In short, in terms of its regional averages, Latin America does not particularly stand out from global trends.

Within the region, table 1.3 shows that Chile stands out as the country with the best record of perceived corruption control in 2001–2, while Paraguay registers the lowest score in the region. Costa Rica and Uruguay register the best annual democracy scores, while Venezuela and Ecuador score somewhat lower. Costa Rica also enjoys the longest history of strong democracy in the region, followed somewhat distantly by Colombia and Uruguay. Paraguay, Nicaragua, and Mexico round out the bottom of the regional trends in democratic stock. The most open economies in the region are the Honduran, Costa Rican, and Salvadoran, while Argentina and Brazil have the least import penetration.

Referring back to tables 1.1 and 1.2, we find that in only one model (import duties) does the coefficient for the Latin America dummy vari-

Table 1.3 **Corruption, democracy, and openness in Latin America, 2001–2002**

Country	Corruption control	Democracy level	Democracy stock	Imports/ GDP (%)
Argentina	−0.81	8	−23.70	10.16
Bolivia	−0.86	9	37.21	24.49
Brazil	−0.10	8	−9.95	14.40
Chile	1.51	9	119.85	32.66
Colombia	−0.55	7	233.89	19.04
Costa Rica	0.86	10	631.25	44.93
Ecuador	−1.04	6	119.03	34.19
El Salvador	−0.53	7	−114.78	42.88
Guatemala	−0.76	8	−113.49	27.97
Honduras	−0.80	7	110.40	54.99
Mexico	−0.25	8	−215.65	29.97
Nicaragua	−0.49	8	−223.39	N/A
Panama	−0.27	9	−46.85	34.87
Paraguay	−1.25	7	−257.46	38.23
Peru	−0.27	9	59.90	17.28
Uruguay	0.79	10	198.82	19.89
Venezuela	−0.97	6	130.66	17.56

able approach statistical significance. Controlling for other factors, therefore, Latin America's levels of perceived corruption do not appear to differ appreciably from global patterns. A range of other tests yields similar findings. It is possible that democracy's effect, for example, might be different in Latin America than elsewhere. Recent reports of societal discontent with democracy's material and other achievements in the region suggest that democracy may not have produced the same kinds of benefits in Latin America that it has produced elsewhere (see, among others, Graham and Sukhtankar 2004; Weyland 2004). An interaction term multiplying the Latin America dummy variable by democracy stock (LA*Democracy stock), however, did not approach statistical significance, suggesting that democracy's effects do not differ noticeably between Latin America and the rest of the world (table 1.1, column 5). A split-sample analysis of only Latin American countries shows very similar results for democracy stock, significant at the 0.05 level.[21] The same test of non–Latin American countries is quite consistent with both the Latin American and full sample results (see table 1.1, columns 6 and 7).

The same explorations of the economic policy results offer similar conclusions. An interaction term multiplying Latin America by imports does not approach statistical significance, and a split sample generates similar levels of significance for Latin America as for the rest of the world, though the coefficient for imports is higher for the Latin American cases.[22]

Finally, an analysis of the residuals from table 1.1, column 3, and table 1.2, column 4, can tell us how well the Latin American cases fit the models. In general, the region on average overperforms slightly, though not dramatically. That is, Latin American countries on average actually tend to have even lower perceived corruption than we would expect according to the models, but not by much. As seen in table 1.4, in only one case does a Latin American country fall more than one standard deviation off of the regression line: Chile has a significantly lower level of perceived corruption than the model predicts. All other cases' corruption scores fall within a single standard deviation of their predicted values. Table 1.5 shows the same patterns for the imports results, again with only Chile as a moderate outlier.

Table 1.4 **Latin American residuals for democracy estimates**	
Country	Democracy stock residual
Chile	1.71
Uruguay	0.83
Brazil	0.67
Costa Rica	0.54
Mexico	0.54
Nicaragua	0.44
Panama	0.39
Peru	0.34
El Salvador	0.04
Colombia	0.02
Guatemala	0.00
Ecuador	−0.16
Bolivia	−0.26
Honduras	−0.32
Paraguay	−0.49
Argentina	−0.50
Venezuela	−0.65
Region average	**0.18**

Table 1.5 **Latin American residuals for import estimates**	
Country	Imports residual
Chile	1.68
Uruguay	0.96
Brazil	0.73
Costa Rica	0.54
Mexico	0.50
Peru	0.48
Panama	0.48
Colombia	0.12
Guatemala	0.07
El Salvador	−0.06
Ecuador	−0.08
Bolivia	−0.10
Argentina	−0.38
Honduras	−0.43
Paraguay	−0.50
Venezuela	−0.51
Region average	**0.22**

The empirical results in this chapter corroborate prior findings that long-term democratic rule, macroeconomic stability, and trade openness are associated with lower levels of political corruption. Perhaps somewhat surprisingly, Latin America appears to fit these trends remarkably well. Despite its reputation as a region plagued by corruption and scandal, from a global perspective the causal dynamics of corruption in Latin America do not stand out from the crowd, either for better or for worse. Furthermore, the potential benefits of long-term democratic rule and stable, open economic policies appear as likely to help combat corruption in Latin America as elsewhere.

Whatever dissatisfaction may persist in the region about the prospects for democratic consolidation, neoliberal development strategies, and reducing corruption, the impact of the first two upon the third in Latin America appears to be no less—or more—than what we observe across the world more generally. Latin America's visible levels of corruption appear to be driven in good measure by incomplete democracies with short histories and by limited-to-intermediate levels of economic openness. In this regard, it may be no accident that the two Latin American countries with the greatest degree of corruption control in table 1.3—Chile and Uruguay—have some of the longest and deepest experiences with effective democratic rule in the region and have engaged in sustained economic opening over the last quarter century or more.

APPENDIX

Descriptive statistics for dependent and independent variables

Variable	Observations	Mean	Standard deviation	Minimum	Maximum
Corruption control	712	0.00	0.99	−1.89	2.58
Democracy level	665	3.07	6.70	−10.00	10.00
Democracy stock	696	34.00	288.02	−531.99	633.97
Inflation	584	24.30	130.31	−9.62	2671.79
M2/reserves	574	10.84	94.65	0.20	2207.39
Budget balance (% GDP)	348	−2.44	3.94	−25.80	14.70
Import duties (% imports)	258	8.13	9.09	0.00	59.94
Imports (% GDP)	617	45.32	24.71	1.35	162.29

Descriptive statistics for dependent and independent variables, Latin America

Variable	Observations	Mean	Standard deviation	Minimum	Maximum
Corruption control	80	−0.24	0.61	−1.22	1.55
Democracy level	77	7.37	2.00	1.00	10.00
Democracy stock	79	23.46	199.76	−308.50	633.97
Inflation	77	16.46	30.51	−1.21	235.56
M2/reserves	78	3.28	1.55	0.97	9.50
Budget balance (% GDP)	46	−1.71	2.20	−7.31	2.92
Import duties (% imports)	29	6.75	3.18	2.01	13.18
Imports (% GDP)	77	37.93	25.81	9.49	112.12

ALFREDO REHREN

2   The Crisis of the Democratic State

During the 1980s, most Latin American countries experienced third-wave democratization. Formal democracies were inaugurated through competitive elections and full-fledged respect for political freedoms.[1] However, many Latin American democracies subsequently showed creeping signs of political corruption, a malaise threatening democratic legitimacy. Democratic inauguration gave way to constitutional accusations and the impeachment of presidents Fernando Collor de Mello in Brazil and Abdalá Bucaram in Ecuador. In Venezuela, the corruption of the political class undermined a once stable democracy, brought the downfall of Carlos Andrés Pérez, and catapulted Hugo Chávez to power. Systemic corruption in Mexico unleashed unrestrained power struggles and political crimes within the PRI, undermining the party's ability to remain in power for the first time in seventy years. President Carlos Menem in Argentina was accused of corruption when he decreed most privatizations without congressional approval and impeded the intervention of the judiciary to investigate. President Alan García fled Peru on charges of corruption and after a landslide election; Fujimori eventually followed the same fate (Aguirre 2001; Bailey and Godson 2000; Flynn 1993; Galarza 1999; Morris 1999).

Despite the region's long history of corruption, democratization and neoliberal reforms in the eighties initially nurtured theoretically sound expectations that corruption would fall and become a thing of the past. The available data, however, suggest otherwise. Not only do the data fail to confirm much of a decline, but in many cases they show the exact opposite: an increase in corruption. But rather than seeing corruption as purely a legacy of the region's authoritarian past, this chapter explores how recent political and economic changes—couched within the context of historically weak institutions, *personalismo*, and a culture of secrecy—have helped forge new patterns and new forms of corruption. It examines how historic practices of clientelism—and its attendant corruption—have given way to new patterns of clientelism; how the neoliberal shrinking of the state has perhaps eliminated one type of corruption, but forced parties to rely even more on state resources from privatization to create new political linkages; and how the proliferation of elections has prompted new demands from parties and candidates for resources. The increase in corruption brought on by democratization and neoliberal reforms, in turn, threatens the foundations of democracy itself, undermining the public's perceptions of parties, politicians, and institutions. The challenges to these struggling democracies are clear.

THE ENTHRONEMENT OF CORRUPTION IN LATIN AMERICA

Despite some problems with measurement discussed by Morris and Blake in the introduction, the available data reveal high levels of corruption throughout Latin America. The 2002 Corruption Perception Index by Transparency International, for example, shows seven Latin American countries—Guatemala, Nicaragua, Venezuela, Bolivia, Ecuador, Haiti, and Paraguay—among the twenty most corrupt countries in the world. Despite minor improvements in the others, Haiti and Paraguay maintained similar positions during the 2003–2005 period. According to TI's 2003 Global Corruption Report and data from the *Latinobarómetro* poll, 71 percent of citizens in the region consider public officeholders in their respective countries as corrupt; only countries with a solid democratic path such as Chile, Costa Rica, and Uruguay fell below the 60 percent figure (Lagos 2001a, 313; 2003, 283). Data from the World Bank, in turn, place Argentina, Bolivia, Ecuador, Honduras, Paraguay, and Venezuela within the quintile of countries in the world with the least control over corruption in 2002 (Transparency International 2003b, 264–65; Kaufmann et al. 2003b). Evidence also suggests that matters have hardly improved in recent years. In the *Latinobarómetro* survey in 2002, 72 percent of respondents in seventeen countries of the region believed that corruption had increased a lot. In the 2003 Global Corruption Report, between 80 and 95 percent of those interviewed in Argentina, Bolivia, Colombia, Costa Rica, Ecuador, Guatemala, and Paraguay estimated that corruption had increased significantly in 2002.

Direct experience with corruption—as opposed to perceived corruption—is less frequently observed, though it too may be on the rise. Twenty-seven percent of those interviewed in 2002 recognized that they or a member of their families had been a victim of corruption. However, in some countries of the region, the percentage of members within a household who paid a bribe in any form during 2004 had increased over the prior year, especially in Mexico and Paraguay, where 31 percent and 43 percent of the population reported doing so (Transparency International 2003, 284; 2005b, 23; see also Seligson 2004).

Such evidence suggests that in spite of the advances in the democratization process, the adoption of the Inter-American Convention against Corruption in 1996, the measures agreed upon in the Presidential Summits of the Americas and the efforts of the World Bank, the Inter-American Development Bank, the establishment of country chapters of Transparency International, and, most recently, the 2003 Convention of the United Nations Against Corruption, corruption remains consistently high throughout the region and seemingly stubbornly resistant to change. From 1980 to 2005, the average corruption perception index for the region was of 3.6 (in TI's transparency scale, where 1 is the most corrupt and 10 the least corrupt). This regional average has varied little over two and a half decades, as indicated it table 2.1 and figure 2.1.

CONCEPTUALIZING CORRUPTION

Corruption can be understood as the abuse of public office for private gain.[2] Nye (1967, 67) defined it as "behavior which deviates from the formal duties of a public role because of private-regarding (personal, close family, private clique) pecuniary or status gains; or violates rules against the exercise of certain types of private-regarding influence." Van Klaveren (1978, 149–63) defined corruption from a behavioral perspective, underscoring how those occupying public positions illegitimately maximized individual income by manipulating the demand for public goods and services. In a much broader approach, Friedrich (1966, 74) identified corruption as favors conferred by public authorities induced by money or other stimuli that ran against the "public interest."

Table 2.1 **Corruption perception index for Latin America, 1980–2005**

Country	1980–1985	1988–1992	1996	1997	1998	1999	2000	2001	2002	2003	2004	2005	Average, 1980–2005
Chile	6.6	5.5	6.8	6.1	6.8	6.9	7.4	7.5	7.5	7.4	7.4	7.3	6.9
Costa Rica				6.5	5.6	5.1	5.4	4.5	4.5	4.3	4.9	4.2	5.0
Uruguay				4.1	4.3	4.4		5.1	5.1	5.5	6.2	5.9	5.1
Peru					4.5	4.5	4.4	4.1	4.0	3.7	3.5	3.5	4.1
Brazil	4.9	3.5	3.0	3.6	4.0	4.1	3.9	4.0	4.0	3.9	3.9	3.7	3.9
Jamaica					3.8	3.8			4.0	3.8	3.3	3.6	3.7
El Salvador					3.6	3.9	4.1	3.6	3.4	3.7	4.2	4.2	3.8
Argentina	4.9	5.9	3.4	2.8	3.0	3.0	3.5	3.5	2.8	2.5	2.5	2.8	3.4
Panama								3.7	3	3.6	3.6	3.5	3.4
Mexico	1.9	2.2	3.3	2.7	3.3	3.4	3.3	3.7	3.6	3.6	3.6	3.5	3.2
Colombia	3.3	2.7	2.7	2.2	2.2	2.9	3.2	3.8	3.6	3.7	3.8	4.0	3.2
Ecuador	4.5	3.3	3.2		2.3	2.4	2.6	2.3	2.2	2.2	2.4	2.5	2.7
Guatemala					3.1	3.2		2.9	2.5	2.4	2.2	2.5	2.7
Nicaragua					3	3.1		2.4		2.6	2.7	2.6	2.7
Venezuela	3.2	2.5	2.5	2.8	2.3	2.6	2.7	2.8	2.5	2.4	2.3	2.3	2.6
Bolivia	0.7	1.3	3.4	2.1	2.8	2.5	2.7	2	2.2	2.3	2.2	2.5	2.2
Honduras					1.7	1.8		2.7	2.7	2.3	2.2	2.6	2.3
Paraguay					1.5	2.0			1.7	1.6	1.9	2.1	1.8
Latin America	**3.8**	**3.4**	**3.5**	**3.7**	**3.4**	**3.5**	**3.9**	**3.7**	**3.5**	**3.4**	**3.5**	**3.5**	**3.6**

0 = high corruption; 10 = low corruption.
Source: Transparency International.

Heidenheimer perceptively argued that public opinion determined when an act was corrupt or not. He distinguished between black, gray, and white corruption, leaving open the possibility of conflict when the public's and the political elite's perception of corruption collided. As a result, elite/ public differences in the perception of corruption could lead to the erosion of the legitimacy of democratic institutions. As a result, Heidenheimer (1989, 2001) relates the study of corruption to sociocultural values across countries and over time. While the first two approaches mentioned above are formal and "market-centered," focusing upon the nature, content, and legality of the exchange, Friedrich's and Heidenheimer's perspectives bring corruption closer to the realm of democratic politics by focusing more on the public interest and public opinion.[3]

However, these perspectives on corruption fail to take into account the structural and institutional context within which corrupt exchanges occur (La Palombara 1994). Political economy views corruption as rent-

Figure 2.1 Corruption perception index (CPI) for Latin America, 1980–2005

Source: Transparency International (various years)

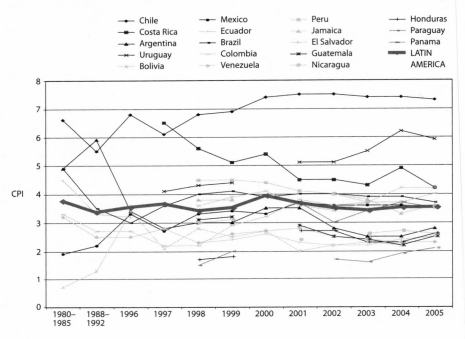

seeking and profit-seeking activities, bounded by the institutional linkages existing between politics and markets (Rose-Ackerman 1978). Corruption thus appears as an illegitimate and institutionally bounded exchange whereby bureaucrats, politicians, and businesses maximize benefits, power, or profits by thwarting the public interest. Current scandals of corruption around the world and in Latin America unfold within networks linking bureaucrats, politicians, and businesses within and across political institutions such as parties, bureaucracies, legislatures, judiciaries, and executives at different levels of government (Nielsen 2003, 125–49).

CLIENTELISM, POLITICAL PARTIES, AND CORRUPTION

Clientelism is a mode of political linkage built upon a patron-client relationship. Based upon asymmetric transactions, the patron controls power resources and functions as a *guardian* of his clientele, providing access to resources in exchange for personal loyalty and political support. This dyadic and particularistic relationship takes place between individuals of unequal power and status and is geared to benefit each by exchanging employment, contracts, and power positions in return for political and electoral support (Lemarchand 1981).

When political parties control the bureaucracy and behave as virtual patrons, dispensing public resources and positions in exchange for partisan allegiance, and eventually allow party members to enrich themselves, clientelism facilitates corruption. The Italian *tangentopolis* and many cases in Latin America demonstrate the strong linkage between political clientelism and corruption.[4] The tenuous line that separates clientelism from corruption indicates how the latter serves as an instrument of political clientelism, generating a "vicious circle" of "clientelism-corruption-clientelism" (Heywood 1997, 427).

Political clientelistic patterns, for instance, forced Italian politicians to search for increasing material incentives to invest in the struggle for political power. The need to buy more votes encouraged the search for funds through illegal means, prompting them to "become corrupted." By investing bribes to buy votes, corrupt politicians became more competitive and built, together with organized crime, parallel networks to the political parties. This pattern had a "perverse effect" on Italian democratic politics and constitutes a warning for Latin American countries where paternalistic, hierarchical, patronage, and clientelistic schemes are deeply ingrained (Colazingari and Rose-Ackerman 1998; Della Porta and Vannucci 1997).

Finally, the historical identification and dependency of Latin American parties on the state have created structural conditions favoring patronage and corrupt clientelistic practices. Parties have also traditionally recurred to interpersonal and family linkages embedded in the region's political culture, making *compadrazgo*, favoritism, and nepotism important components of corrupt clientelistic networks (see Lomnitz 1994; Maingot 1994).

THE TRANSFORMATION OF THE STATE: MARKET ECONOMICS AND CORRUPTION

The consolidation of capitalist democracies in the region implies the allocation of resources in society by market forces and competitive political forces seeking popular and electoral support. The privatization of state-owned enterprises that accompanied democratization effectively reduced the size and financial resources of the state. Such changes challenged certain traditional forms of corruption since few positions in the bureaucracy remained available to satisfy the massive clientelistic demands and patronage schemes of the past. This forced the state to become more selective and elitist. In addition, the concomitant rise of nongovernmental organizations and the strengthening of civil society reduced further the space traditionally reserved for the state in implementing social policy. State shrinking and greater social density redefined, from a structural perspective, the space for state action in Latin America.

The change in the nature of the state thus weakened the bases of traditional clientelistic patterns, forcing political parties to develop new forms of political linkages. The political handling of social programs such as CONASUPO and PRONASOL in the context of privatizations carried out by President Salinas de Gortari in Mexico, for example, attempted to maximize political support for the PRI in rural areas. The result was a form of semiclientelism keeping pace with traditional nonautonomous citizenship. In Argentina, President Menem used the resources coming from privatizations to strengthen his inner circle and the Peronist corrupt clientelistic machine working at provincial levels: a stronghold of *menemismo* (see Fox 1994; Gibson 1997; Saba and Manzetti 1997). Menem allowed provincial and local governments to contract loans, contributing thus to an increase in the national debt that would contribute to the severe financial crisis years later, prompting the downfall of President De La Rúa. The resources from privatizations were used by President Fujimori in Peru to finance massive social programs through individualized and fragmented assistance schemes in popular sectors, while the presidential entourage at the top bribed all opposition to the regime—legislative, judicial, military, and entrepreneurial—with the same resources. These components made Fujimori's neopopulist regime a mafia state (Aguirre 2001; Roberts 1995).

Clearly, corruption prospers in state-dominated and heavily regulated economies where organized groups with privileged access to government face structural conditions that create opportunities for rent-seeking behavior and grand corruption. State privatization schemes thus minimize the scope and dimensions of this form of corruption. However, since political parties in Latin America survive based exclusively on their dependence on the state, then privatizations did not have the expected impact on corruption. Instead, privatization actually increased corruption. Parties and partisan leaders found new sources of finance in governmental revenues coming from privatizations, contributing to presidential corruption. A privatized economy and "reduced administration" does not always mean a clean administration (Manzetti 1999; Manzetti and Blake 1996; Rose-Ackerman 1996).

The components and dynamics of neopopulist regimes, such as Salinas in Mexico, Menem in Argentina, and Fujimori in Peru, also created conditions for new patterns of corruption to take hold and grow uncontrolled. The personalization of power in leaders who stood above weak political institutions, appealing directly to a fragmented electorate, especially through television, increased the traditional autonomy and *caudillismo* deeply ingrained in Latin American presidentialism. Though popularly elected, once in power these leaders engineered diverse mechanisms to remain horizontally unaccountable to congress and the judiciary, freeing them to engage in corruption. Moreover, by subordinating fragmented political parties, factions, and movements to the leader's own political will and instilling a deep sense of personal loyalty, these leaders also weakened vertical mechanisms of accountability. Neopopulist experiences dovetailed very nicely with an emerging new form of democracy: *delegative democracy* (see Knight 1998; O'Donnell 1994; Weyland 1998).

In this context, presidents and their inner circles behaved with absolute impunity, manipulating corrupt clientelistic networks. This fed grand corruption. While publicly orchestrating the support of popular, disorganized sectors through semiclientelistic schemes, absolute discretionary presidential power was used to sell privileged information regarding privatizations and to pay off legislators and judges who opposed decisions coming from the executive.[5]

FINANCING LATIN AMERICAN POLITICS AND CORRUPTION

The obscure and opaque nature of political finances in the region—a virtual black box—mediates the relationship between corruption and political clientelism. It is a well-established fact that dues paid by militants cover neither the operating nor the electoral costs of parties and candidates. Throughout the world, legislation regulating the financing of parties and electoral campaigns is relatively easy to circumvent. This is particularly true in Latin America, where in most countries it is difficult to determine the extent of private contributions, the main donors, and how private or public funds, even from foreign origins, reach political parties or electoral campaigns. Incoming governments often feel pressed by in-

Table 2.2 **Electoral campaigns: Transparency measures by country**

Country	Any direct public funding? (1)	Any disclosure laws? (2)	Free TV time to candidates and/ or parties? (3)	Campaign transparency index (1) + (2) + (3)	Transparency perception index (average, 1980–2002)
Argentina	Yes	Yes	Yes	3	3.6
Bolivia	Yes	Yes	Yes	3	2.2
Brazil	Yes	Yes	Yes	3	3.9
Colombia	Yes	Yes	Yes	3	3.0
Costa Rica	Yes	Yes	Yes	3	5.3
Mexico	Yes	Yes	Yes	3	3.0
Ecuador	Yes	Yes	No	2	2.9
El Salvador	Yes	No	Yes	2	3.7
Guatemala	Yes	No	Yes	2	2.9
Paraguay	Yes	No	Yes	2	1.7
Uruguay	Yes	No	Yes	2	4.6
Chile	No	Yes	Yes	2	6.8
Honduras	Yes	No	No	1	2.2

Source: Pinto-Duschinsky (2002, 76–77).

terest groups, interests represented in partisan factions, national or multinational business, and foreign governments that may have contributed to their campaigns (Pinto-Duschinsky 2002).

By 2002, countries such as Argentina, Bolivia, Brazil, Colombia, and Mexico had adopted laws mandating public financing of electoral campaigns, free publicity on television, and transparency with regard to donations. Such moves rested on the notion that public funding increases the levels of transparency and reduces the opportunities for corruption. However, as shown in table 2.2, these countries suffered the highest degrees of corruption from 1980 to 2002. As the same table indicates, there seems to be no correlation between the calculated index of transparency for electoral campaigns and the transparency perception index of corruption for the same period.[6] These preliminary findings suggest a reexamination of the hypothesis that transparency and public funding of elections help control corruption in the region. On the contrary, comparative studies suggest that rather than decreasing corruption, public funding ensures a financial floor from which parties and candidates work to outdo their competitors by acquiring additional resources through corrupt networks (Heidenheimer 2002; Pujas and Rhodes 2002; Rhodes 1997).

In Chile, a country that historically has enjoyed a relatively clean record, citizens see campaign financing as nontransparent and a manipulation that favors interest groups and politicians. As a consequence, campaign financing fosters a lack of confidence and trust in elected representatives. A poll taken in December–January 2002, for example, found that 38 percent of those polled believed that "all political sectors have something to hide" regarding campaign financing. Out of two alternatives (totally 200 percent), 62 percent believed the most important source of campaign financing was "central or municipal governments"; 38 percent mentioned "interest group donations in exchange for future favors"; 23 percent tracked the source of money to "private funds belonging to candidates themselves"; and 48 percent believed campaign funds originated in "individual donations made by party militant or sympathizers (Centro de Estudios Públicos 2002).[7]

Recent corruption scandals in Chile unveiled the workings of partisan networks built to funnel public funds presumably into the 1999 presidential candidacy of Ricardo Lagos. Preliminary court evidence points to the importance of outsourcing mechanisms used by the Ministry of Public Works to transfer funds illegally to the campaign management staff of Lagos, a previous minister of Public Works himself (Rehren 2004, 14–15).[8] The 2003 anticorruption legislation granting public funding for electoral campaigns has already spawned several accusations against government candidates. Congressional candidates belonging to parties of the governing coalition have been charged with transferring funds, with the implicit support of governmental agencies, out of social programs to finance their campaign workers. Others have been taken to court for fraud for illegally presenting to the Electoral Commission receipts of nonexistent consultancies to justify their campaign expenses. In chapter 7, Adam Brinegar addresses the Chilean experience regarding these events in more detail.

CORRUPTION, POLITICAL PARTIES, AND DEMOCRACY

It has been underscored that "corruption in a democracy" is "corruption of democracy" because it conceals an exclusionary logic: "those who benefit from corrupt actions, decisions, or exchanges do so by excluding those who, under democratic norms, have a claim to inclusion" (Warren 2002, 2004). The elitist nature of Latin American democracies, together with the concentration of power in the executive, the personalization of presidential power and decreasing levels of political participation, contribute to low degrees of horizontal and vertical accountability and create the conditions for the expansion of corruption. Legislatures with low prestige and weak oversight powers and a corrupt judiciary with low levels of autonomy provide no effective counterweight to presidential power. The further inclination of presidents to strengthen the office and keep governmental affairs opaque has added to these conditions feeding corruption.

A culture of secrecy and lack of transparency in handling governmental affairs at all levels contribute to a lack of knowledge of the contextual surroundings in which decision making is made and public policy implemented. A good example is the low degrees of transparency in which budgeting practices are conducted, as shown by the Latin American Index of Budget Transparency (http://www.internationalbudget.org). This environment hampers citizens' ability to exercise control over government. In short, *delegative democracies* contain important components that favor corruption.

The absence of institutionalized party systems in Latin America has also helped feed corruption. Well-structured competitive politics ensures democratic legitimacy and control over corruption. A strong political opposition, as Johnston (2002a, 784) notes, "develops an interest in credible action against corruption, both in the political arena and through independent judiciary and investigative agencies. They can encourage, protect, and follow through on direct responses to corruption by citizens and civil society groups—building resistance to corruption in civil society." By contrast, when political parties are weak, internally divided along factional lines and have fragile links with civil society, they will always be exposed to the election of elites immersed in corrupt behavior. A weak judiciary and low degrees of institutionalization of party systems in Latin America cannot conduce to an effective control of corruption.[9]

The most important single factor underlying corruption in recent years has been the change in the nature of contemporary political parties since democratization. Most parties have become "enterprises" and their leaders have assumed leadership styles as *political entrepreneurs* whose basic motivation has been to win "material benefits—either from the salary and related perks of office or from involvement in various forms of corruption—as the principal motivation for political action" (Hopkin 1997, 260). Consequently, representatives—the *guardians of democracy*—look for reelection at any cost, thereby acquiring a natural penchant for corruption. They have the opportunities to abuse office because most of the time they are protected by immunity and the prerogatives of the position:

Table 2.3 **Perception of corruption by institutions in Latin America, 2003**

	Business licensing	Courts	Customs	Education system	Political parties	Utilities	Medical services	Immigration passports	Police	Private sector	Tax revenue	Other
Argentina	3.6	19.2	3.2	4.3	**58.2**	0.5	0.9	0.2	3.1	0.6	3.4	2.7
Bolivia	18.2	7.7	10.8	2.4	**34.8**	2.2	1.2	1.2	16	0.9	3.7	0.9
Colombia	2.4	2.4	3.4	8.8	**38.0**	8.1	8.8	1.0	8.5	1.4	12.9	3.4
Costa Rica	4.3	8.6	14	3.2	**29.0**	1.1	2.2	12.9	5.4	4.3	15.1	0
Dominican Republic	2.0	12.1	6.1	8.1	**25.3**	13.1	0	2.0	4.0	0.0	8.1	19.2
Guatemala	3.0	8.0	14.0	12.0	**27.0**	6.0	4.0	8.0	10.0	6.0	2.0	0
Mexico	2.9	6.6	3.3	8.7	19.9	9.0	3.5	1.4	**36.5**	0.8	6.1	1.1
Panama	3.0	15.0	6.0	2.0	**35.0**	10.0	3.0	3.0	11.0	2.0	2.0	8.0
Peru	2.6	**35.0**	3.1	2.3	15.9	10.0	2.0	3.1	10.0	2.3	9.7	4.1
Latin America	4.7	12.7	7.1	5.8	**31.5**	6.7	2.8	3.6	11.6	2.0	7.0	4.4
Total sample	7.0	13.7	4.2	7.5	29.7	4.1	8.4	3.3	11.5	3.1	5.2	2.2

Bold indicates most corrupt area for each country surveyed.
Source: Global Corruption Barometer, 2003; Transparency International.

"to the extent that elected representatives are immune from legal inquiry, they have more opportunity to either advance or abuse their designated function in representative democracy" (Wigley 2003, 24).

Data are quite clear in revealing that corruption is having a corrosive effect on perceptions of parties, institutions, and regimes. The increasing deteriorating image of political parties in the continent should not surprise scholars of Latin American politics. Data available from Transparency International through the Global Corruption Barometers confirm this trend. As shown in table 2.3, parties are perceived as the most corrupt institution in all the countries included in the 2003 survey, which asked 30,387 people in forty-four countries, "If you had a magic wand and you could eliminate corruption from one of the following institutions, which one would be your first choice?"

In eight of the ten Latin American countries surveyed, political parties formed the institutions citizens most wanted to clean up. Mexico and Peru distinguish themselves from the rest because institutions such as the police and the judiciary respectively are seen as the most corrupt. Notice that the concerns raised about Latin American political parties exceeded the average observed across all forty-four countries studied in this 2003 survey.

Faced with the deteriorating image of democratic institutions and politicians and crises of participation and representation, corruption poses a threat to democratic legitimacy and stability in the region in the medium term. Research conducted on the attitudes of individuals victimized by corruption toward democratic legitimacy concludes that "those who experience corruption are less likely to believe in the legitimacy of their political system and also are less likely to exhibit levels of interpersonal trust" (Seligson 2002, 429). Those who become elected to fulfill functions of political representation or those who are appointed in the bureaucracy manipulating their positions and resources to benefit themselves or to finance partisan machines, do away with the public trust bestowed upon them by the electorate and public opinion.

THE CHALLENGES AHEAD

Overcoming both old and new forms of corruption is no easy task, but the consequences of entrenched, systemic corruption are striking. The challenges are clear. Politicians today need to reconstruct new bases of support and political linkages, and a more efficient administration is crucial in the face of dwindling electoral support. With fewer resources to distribute, electoral support must depend more on the effective delivery of public goods and services to the community than on traditional clientelistic or market-oriented semiclientelistic schemes. To accomplish this, the bureaucracy must become a key institution in the delivery of better quality and less costly public goods and services to the citizenry rather than a political tool of the elite to garner support (see Geddes 1994, especially 131–39). State reform, the development of a bureaucracy based on merit and a more independent, modern, and efficient judiciary are all crucial components of any anticorruption strategy capable of controlling corruption and strengthening the deteriorated image of democracies in the region.

A free press has had perhaps the strongest impact on the airing of corruption scandals in the region, providing some checks on corruption. By further increasing the degree of press freedom, public opinion will be better informed of the actions and whereabouts of those responsible for governmental affairs, making them more accountable to the people. Although press freedom has increased according to measurements carried out by Freedom House in recent years, it has not been established whether such an improvement correlates with the perception of corruption, except in the more traditional democracies of Chile, Costa Rica, and Uruguay.[10]

Corruption has severe consequences for democratic legitimacy and stability. A society valuing personal success in the face of poverty and inequality of opportunities produces social discontent and a deterioration of public morality. Under such circumstances, corruption might be considered a means for the poor to achieve quick success by circumventing established practices and institutions. Moreover, when a society relies upon money to buy political power and influence, the poor are the most often manipulated by corrupt elites within or outside established democratic institutions. Representatives, bureaucrats, and the judiciary become questioned on the grounds of their democratic morality. The plight worsens if politicians do not reveal an ethical commitment and transparency in their public behavior.

A preliminary interpretation of the extent and causes of corruption in Latin America points to the predominance of grand corruption. This white-collar corruption is practiced by highly placed politicians and bureaucrats in the upper echelons of power with the exclusion of the great masses of the population. Those who wield political, bureaucratic, and economic power to build corrupt networks in order to maintain themselves in power or to increase their sphere of domination advance corruption. Globalized markets and politics seem to be contributing to an increase rather than a decrease in corruption in Latin America when external actors find propitious grounds for corruption within national political elites. In addition, low degrees of political transparency, weak anticorruption legislation, and nonenforced regional or international agreements make corruption a rampant phenomenon.

Politics has never been and probably will never be immaculate. But corruption has reached such unprecedented levels in recent years that it may damage the very moral foundations of politics (Sartori 1994, 161). In the near future the politics of corruption might well become the corruption of politics in Latin America. Only strong democratic institutions guaranteeing citizens access to government and a strong political opposition will make governments more accountable. The development of a tradition of administrative probity, solid business ethics, and a political culture committed to honesty, social solidarity, and public trust will forge a stronghold against corruption.

JOHN BAILEY

3 Corruption and Democratic Governability

Corruption regularly appears among the top five problems cited in opinion polls in most Latin American countries. Along with violence, crime, inequality, and institutional weaknesses, it figures prominently in contemporary scholarly work on quality of democracy as well. Researchers have made considerable progress in measuring aspects of corruption and in linking these to reduced support for regimes and policies as described in the introduction. But to this point, much of the work employs rather blunt categories and focuses on specific pieces of the broader problem complex, usually with little attention to how the pieces might fit together. We need to reframe the corruption-democracy problem by differentiating among types of corruption and the various ways in which these affect democracy—considered both as a regime as well as a set of component state institutions and processes.

In this chapter I explore the effects of corruption on democratic governability in Latin America, emphasizing the types of corrupt exchanges that affect different arenas of politics and policy making.[1] As I use the term, democratic governability encompasses not only how power is achieved and the rules of the game (democracy as regime), but also the exercise of power by state agencies acting within a le-

Georgetown's School of Foreign Service and its Center for Peace and Security Studies provided helpful support for this project. Enrique Bravo lent helpful research assistance, and Stephen Morris contributed helpful comments.

gal framework to address priority problems in a society (governability).[2] Democracy in the Schumpeter-Dahl conception focuses on processes that govern access to power and the accountability of governments to electorates (Dahl 1971, chap. 1). Apart from the protection of key civil rights, that approach has relatively little to say about the functioning of state institutions.[3] But coherent state institutions and policy-making capacity are keys to governability, understood as "the ability of a government to allocate values over its society, to exercise legitimate power in the context of generally accepted rules" (Bailey and Godson 2000, 7). Thus, we need to differentiate between the nature of the political regime (e.g., democracy, authoritarianism, totalitarianism, and the like) and the bureaucratic institutions, including courts and legal system, and policy processes that give the state the power to allocate values (Mazzuca 2000; O'Donnell 2001). Regime, in this sense, refers to the rules of the game about how power is acquired (e.g., popular election, lottery, inheritance, etc.) and how government relates to civil society. State refers to the administrative and judicial apparatus. Democratic governability thus encompasses not only how power is achieved and the rules of the game (democratic regime), but also the exercise of power (governability).[4]

To anticipate theoretical-empirical challenges, we need to assess which kinds of vulnerabilities are more important to the functioning of regime and state. Also, we shall find that mass publics attach diverse meanings to corruption and also tend to conflate the procedures and performance dimensions in a broad notion of democracy. This complicates our efforts to make democracy-corruption linkages.

I begin with definitional and analytical issues and proceed to examine the direct and perceived effects of corruption in relation to various arenas. My hypothesis is that some types of corruption are more important than others for democratic governability. Rather than developing new empirical findings, my goal is to sketch a map of the corruption-democracy landscape that marks the sites that merit priority exploration.

CORRUPTION: MEANINGS, TYPES, AND ARENAS

"Corruption" is a highly contested term, loaded with normative baggage. The concept does not travel well across different cultures, through time, or across different individuals and social categories. Following Michael Johnston (2002b), I find it useful to combine public-office and public-opinion approaches to defining corruption.[5]

Joseph Nye's oft-cited public-office-centered definition is a useful beginning point: "Corruption is behavior which deviates from the formal duties of a public role because of private-regarding (personal, close family, private clique) pecuniary or status gains; or violates rules against the exercise of certain types of private-regarding influence. This includes such behavior as bribery (use of a reward to pervert the judgment of a person in a position of trust); nepotism (bestowal of patronage by reason of ascriptive relationship rather than merit); and misappropriation (illegal appropriation of public resources for private-regarding uses)" (Nye 2002, 284).

Nye's approach emphasizes the public-private distinction that characterizes the modern, Western nation-state, which is the point of reference of most Latin American experience. The main benefit of this approach is its relatively narrow scope: we focus on government, public policy making, and public-private exchanges. A limitation is that formal-legal duties of a public office vary considerably across political units and over time. In the neoliberal era of state restructuring we find varieties of public functions (welfare, education, and law enforcement come to mind) delegated to private firms. Also, we will probably find gaps between formal-legal rules about corruption, the informal rules that hold among political activists and elites, and the meanings that mass publics attach to corruption.

To address these gaps, Michael Johnston suggests that we supplement the analytical definition by including perception and opinion: "A better approach is to use a formal analytical definition [in this case Nye's] to identify corruption, to posit social conceptions of corruption as an important factor affecting political response (or nonresponse) to corruption, and then to examine the divergence between the two outlooks. This strategy, rather than attempting somehow to merge two fundamentally contrasting conceptions of corruption preserves the differences between them, and focuses our attention upon those contrasts as interesting political question in their own right" (Johnston 2002b, 189–90).

Johnston's idea is helpful because we can return to Nye's definition and interpret his notion of "rules" broadly to include both the formal-legal and informal customs. That is, public actors may engage in behavior that is technically corrupt, but which they may view as ethically acceptable. The contrasts between social conceptions and laws might go the other way—that is, the public may interpret as corrupt the behavior of public officials that is technically lawful. Despite the utility of narrow definitions, if public opinion views some types of misbehavior in the private sector as "corrupt" this becomes a relevant datum. Further, perceptions of what constitutes trivial versus serious corruption vary over time and across groups and strata defined in different ways.[6] These perceptions, in turn, influence attitudes related to regime legitimacy and individual behavior (e.g., voting, obeying the law, and the like). In sum, it is the interplay between the analytical and opinion perspectives that opens up useful lines of inquiry.

Thus, via this research strategy we travel two paths. First, in an analytical sense we will explore the ways in which corruption negatively affects regime and state through a variety of linkages. Second, with a public opinion approach, we will investigate the ways in which perceptions of corrupt exchanges can undermine regime and state.

In terms of types of corruption, we might think of abuse of public office in two basic ways: bribery in various forms and at various levels (money, property, or some "good" is given or extorted in exchange for a publicly controlled good), and political transactions (duties are violated to exchange a public good for a resource that benefits the public official's power or influence).[7] The two ends may be served in the same transaction, or there might be separate acts and different motives.

We need to make two more sets of distinctions: where does corruption take place (in which "arena" of politics)? And, is the transaction voluntary or coerced? Figure 3.1 depicts three principal arenas. Much of the work on corruption, especially work done by international financial institutions and donor organizations, focuses on the "output" side of politics, the administrative-regulatory-judicial arena.[8] Characteristic of this arena, the public duties of officials are set out in laws, decrees, and codes with one or another degree of clarity and precision. The discretion granted to the public official ranges from virtually none (the toll for a two-axle vehicle is fifty centavos, exactly) to extensive (building permits should take into account the structure's aesthetic impact on the neighborhood). In all, the output side of politics is dense, complicated, and important; but it is only one of several arenas.

On the "input" side and in the "conversion" process (policy making within the "black box") we need to consider two key processes that are typically subject to corrupt exchanges. First, bribery and political corruption may influence the core input processes of democracy taken in the procedural sense. That is, corruption may influence access to the ballot, party competition, election processes, mass participation, and the menu of legal rights that these require.[9] Second, with respect to conver-

Figure 3.1 **Principal arenas of corruption**

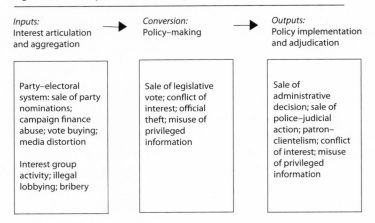

Inputs:
Interest articulation and aggregation

→

Conversion:
Policy–making

→

Outputs:
Policy implementation and adjudication

Party–electoral system: sale of party nominations; campaign finance abuse; vote buying; media distortion

Interest group activity; illegal lobbying; bribery

Sale of legislative vote; conflict of interest; official theft; misuse of privileged information

Sale of administrative decision; sale of police–judicial action; patron–clientelism; conflict of interest; misuse of privileged information

sion, both bribery and political corruption may influence rule-making aspects of public policy making. Policy makers may decide an issue in light of its impact on their personal finances or on their power resources (or both), rather than in light of legitimate constituency interests or the "public good" as decided through a deliberative process. Issues in this arena may be less relevant to grassroots-level corruption and more relevant to particular interests, especially wealthier individuals and groups (including organized crime).[10] Perceptions of corruption in this arena, however, may have important effects on attitudes at the grassroots level.

Finally, we need to examine the corrupt exchange itself. Two or more parties engage in a transaction in which something of value is offered or requested for something under public control. The exchange may be entirely voluntary on all sides, or one or another party might bring coercion to bear. One usually thinks of the government official as the extorter, but that role might also be played by the private citizen.[11]

With the groundwork laid, we can proceed to address the relationships between corruption and democracy as regime, policy-making processes, and policy implementation by state agencies. The orienting question is: What are the direct effects of corruption and of the perceptions of corruption on democratic governability? In mapping this, my approach is to provide examples of corruption in the various arenas and speculate about their direct effects on regime and state. With the arenas sketched, we can consider the effects of corruption as filtered through perceptions. An assumption is that the majority of the Latin American cases meet minimum standards of functioning polyarchy, operating in generally weak but coherent states.[12]

As to the limits of the analysis in this chapter, the issues of the pervasiveness of corrupt practices in a polity (contained versus systemic) and the long-term effects of path dependence deserve extensive treatment but can only be noted in passing. In chapter 1 of this volume, Thacker already has identified a dynamic of path dependence in which long-standing democracies' relationship with corruption differs from that found in democracies with shorter or erratic histories. In turn, several subsequent chapters in this book examine distinctions between contained and systemic corruption.

CORRUPTION AND REGIME: DEMOCRATIC PROCEDURES

The mainstream, procedural approach views democracy in terms of competing parties, periodic elections, and extensive participation. To these are added a series of requisites, such as control by elected officials over government, access to information, and the like. From an analytical perspective, it is evident that the forms of corruption that distort these fundamental processes are the most serious.[13] "Corruption . . . breaks the link between collective decision making and people's powers to influence collective decisions through speaking and voting, the very link that defines democracy" (Warren 2004, 328).

Beyond anecdotes, we do not know much about the prevalence of corrupt practices in gaining access to the ballot, influencing votes, or distorting information as provided by mass media.[14] Presumably, closed-list proportional representation systems, with nominations controlled by party leaders, would tend to centralize corruption. Primaries, especially open primaries, would act to decentralize corruption.[15] Open-list proportional representation general elections would also seem to decentralize corruption as several candidates compete to attract support from party followers. Given widespread poverty, income inequality, and increased funding flowing into more competitive elections, be these primary or general elections, one would expect that forms of bribery are increasing as well. Scattered examples of vote buying in the region suggest a mixed picture:

In Brazil's municipal elections in March 2001, for example, 7 percent of voters were offered money for their votes. Different surveys in Mexico place the frequency of vote buying at between 5 percent and 26 percent, while a 1999 Gallup survey in Argentina found that 24 percent of interviewees knew someone who sold his or her vote (Pfeiffer 2004, 76–77).

The anecdotes suggest that bribery takes place in the electoral arena, but we are only recently beginning to study whether and how it influences outcomes via studies that are national rather than cross-national (Cornelius 2002; Stokes 2005).

The overall costs of campaigning are generally rising throughout the region. Our knowledge about campaign finance is improving rapidly—for example, with respect to methods of calculating abuses of campaign finance rules. But the sources of the abuses—that is, those who are breaking the rules and what is received in exchange—remain hazy (Speck 2004). Also, we know a bit about incumbents' abuse of office to reward or threaten voters. With respect to distorting information or creating an uneven playing field, we know less about favorable deals that media outlets offer parties in exchange for special concessions. In sum, from an analytical perspective, corrupt practices that infect basic procedures of democracy as regime merit priority attention.

CORRUPTION AND POLICY-MAKING PROCESSES

In a single chapter I can only illustrate the vast arena of rule making with two typical examples. First, in divided government where the president's party lacks a majority in the assembly, the president can go beyond traditional pork or favors by resorting to direct cash payments to pass legislation. Consider in this vein the high-profile example of this dynamic in early twenty-first-century Argentina. Mario Pontaquarto, a former Senate clerk, claimed to have been dispatched in April 2000 by the government of Fernando de la Rúa (December 1999–December 2001) to bribe a number of senators into voting for a law that effectively reduced workers' employment rights; the law passed in May 2000. The total amount of the bribe was apparently five million Argentine pesos (the equivalent of US$5 million). The funds were allegedly siphoned from the state intelligence service's secret funds (TI 2005b, 97–98).

In a second scenario, legislators simply abuse their duties to pocket money through multiple schemes. One such example of legislative theft comes from Brazil. In 1993, in a bombshell interview with *Veja* magazine, a Brazilian congressional staffer alleged that members of Congress were systematically defrauding the Treasury by writing budget amendments that would benefit specific senators, deputies, and businesspeople. The budget scheme was allegedly run by a number of legislators whose short stature gave rise to the "dwarves" nickname used in the press. They allegedly defrauded the Treasury in two ways. First, legislators wrote budget amendments that benefited specific construction companies, in exchange for bribes and illicit campaign funds. Second, the legislators wrote budget amendments that transferred funds to "phantom" social organizations created by friends and family members and appropriated the transfers (Taylor and Buranelli 2007).

It is difficult to defend legislative theft as an expedient path toward the pursuit of productive public policies. However, with respect to the first scenario of divided government with weak party discipline, one could make a functionalist argument that vote buying may be necessary (or at least helpful) to rule making. Still further, the direct purchase of legislators' votes may be less expensive overall than the quantities of pork cum kickbacks needed to achieve legislative majorities. Elements of a counterargument, nonetheless, are more persuasive. First, legislative vote buying obviates the need to employ transparent arguments and to engage in negotiations to design good quality legislation that likely has consensual support from the voters who elected these legislators. Second, as the Argentine example shows, the use of money from the intelligence service's budget brings the state security apparatus (with its own methods and agendas) into the legislative arena.

CORRUPTION AND POLICY IMPLEMENTATION/ADJUDICATION

I sketch two overlapping arenas here. The first is a broad category of administration that runs the gamut from ordinary service delivery by street-level bureaucrats through the top levels of grand corruption. The second involves both rule implementation and rule adjudication: police and administration of justice.

ADMINISTRATIVE CORRUPTION

This form of corruption involves abuse of office in the quotidian operations of government in extracting resources, distributing goods and services, and regulating behavior. It can be quite significant, depending on the incidence and locus of the abuse. Most services the state provides have some rationale, but some might be considered more important than others. In terms of basic state functions and societal survival, one would assign priority to taxation and budget administration, national defense and public security, and the regulatory agencies that oversee public health and safety.

In terms of incidence, we might differentiate between overall levels of corruption. Corruption might be "contained" in specific offices or agencies, or it might be systemic—that is, present throughout the administration, from the ministers at the top to bottom-level support staff. There seem to be dynamics of vicious cycles and tipping points that can trap a system in high levels of governmental and societal corruption. Manzetti differentiates between systems of low corruption, with functioning checks and balances, internal constraints, and an exigent civil society versus those with high corruption, which is the case in most Latin American countries: "High corruption takes place when: (1) many checks and balances among the three branches of government and the institutional mechanisms to combat corruption are weak or not used; (2) there are not self-restraints in profiting from corruption as commissions reach extremely high levels; and (3) corruption is so widespread at any societal level has to be accepted and tolerated. . . . (M)any LDCs are likely to fall into the second model" (Manzetti 2000, 139).

One might add that there seem to be varieties of mechanisms that appear to reproduce Manzetti's scenario of high corruption levels, trapping governments and societies in a kind of low-level equilibrium of poor quality administration. Two examples serve to illustrate ordinary administrative corruption. The first example comes from municipal government in La Paz, Bolivia:

The city government was in effect a huge "construction company" that wasn't constructing much. The city owned tractors, trucks, and all kinds of construction machinery. There were 4,000 city laborers, who were paid meager, fixed salaries and were only coming to work an average of five hours a day. Machinery was also used for a similar amount of time, rendering it extremely inefficient given its high capital cost. But I found that the use of gasoline, oil and spare parts was abnormally high. Surely they were being sold in the black market, I thought, and soon this suspicion was sadly verified. New tires and expensive machinery parts such a fuel injectors, pumps, and Caterpillar parts were available for sale; and in exchange broken and used parts were "replaced" on the city's machinery. (Mayor MacLean-Albora quoted in Klitgaard 2000, 7)

A second example can be found in a nationwide milk distribution program in Peru analyzed by López-Cálix, Seligson, and Alcázar in this volume: "[Leakages] in Peru are significant and far more pervasive and extensive at the bottom of the [distribution] chain than at the top. From the entire amount of public funds intended for the Vaso de Leche program, barely 29 percent get to their intended beneficiaries. This does not mean that 71 cents from each dollar are fully lost in corruption costs. The rest of the resources leak away through a combination of administrative costs, ineligible products and beneficiaries, and other modalities. Results also challenge the predominant view of the last decade that organizations that are closer to the people they serve are inherently better in service delivery."

Woven into these examples are two points that merit attention. First, corruption is embedded in administrative systems marked by low pay and poor performance. Second, decentralization does not offer an automatic cure for corrupt practices.

POLITICAL MOTIVATIONS FOR CORRUPTION IN PROGRAM ADMINISTRATION

Apart from issues of theft and bribery, governments and political parties frequently use public programs as resources to generate support. Widespread poverty and weak institutions in the region create special problems of clientelism in the delivery of public goods and services that are supposed to be universally available and distributed according to neutral criteria. As discussed ably by Rehren in chapter 2, clientelism is a form of asymmetric relationship in which a patron provides goods or benefits in exchange for the client's support.

In a clientelist network, the patron can assume diverse forms: an individual, group, corporation, or—rather commonly—a political party. Argentina's Partido Justicialista (PJ) provides an interesting example of the reinforcement of clientelism in a context of neoliberal adjustment: "A 1997 survey of 112 PJ base units in the capital and Greater Buenos Aires found that 96 percent engaged in some form of social assistance, including food distribution, medical and legal services, child care, and programs for the elderly. Base units also implemented government social policies. In Buenos Aires province, for example, PJ activists participated actively in the Life Plan, which distributed a daily ration of eggs, milk, and other basic goods to nearly 400,000 people through a network of 10,000 block workers, or *manzaneras*" (Levitsky 2003, 28).

Clientelism typically hinders efforts to professionalize the public bureaucracy. It also undermines notions of citizenship, a status with legally established rights and duties. Citizens are likely to be more active, exigent participants in public life, while clients will tend to remain more passive and tolerant of corrupt practices. In chapter 4 of this volume, Manzetti and Wilson explore the relationship between clientelism, weak administrative institutions, and public support for the government.

In general usage, grand corruption refers to high-level officials pocketing money from kickbacks, theft, embezzlement, insider deals, and the like. Privatizations of public enterprises provide some of the most spectacular recent cases of grand corruption in the region. These corrupt privatizations tend to be massive and convoluted, highly visible and yet opaque events (see Manzetti 2000).

The more ordinary, recurring types of grand corruption provide simpler examples. One of the most visible cases of the early twenty-first century was the alleged embezzlement of 4.5 million *quetzales* (US$600,000) of public funds by Guatemalan President Alfonso Portillo, Vice President Juan Francisco Reyes, and his private secretary, Julio Girón. They have been accused of setting up thirteen bank accounts and four ghost companies in Panama to launder the embezzled funds (TI 2004, 197). The Bolivian defense minister in 2000, Fernando Kieffer, faces allegations that he "diverted international donations for the people of Aiguila and Mizqu who suffered an earthquake in 1998; that some of the money was used to buy an overpriced executive jet; and that he was behind the irregular purchase of Galil weapons for the army" (TI 2005b, 108). Nicaraguan President Arnoldo Alemán is alleged to have obtained roughly US$100 million in public funds via fraud, embezzlement, and misappropriation. At least one legislator, Leonel Teller, speculates that the figure involved may be closer to US$250 million (TI 2004, 222).

As the Guatemalan and Bolivian examples illustrate, grand corruption often involves transnational actors. This form of corruption could, at some point, undermine an entire government's finances. Grand corruption frequently triggers scandals, and the more typical effect is the devastating example it sets for all government employees and the citizenry at large. If top officials are shown to be corrupt and, even worse, to suffer no consequences, the lesson to all others is a negative one.[16] The inertia of the vicious cycle of corruption is thus reinforced.

CORRUPTION IN LAW ENFORCEMENT AND JUSTICE ADMINISTRATION

Law enforcement straddles rule implementation and rule adjudication, while administration of justice falls into the latter category. As armed agents authorized to use lethal force and operating generally out of public view, police officers *are* the law in a real sense, in effect "the state on the streets" (Hinton 2006). Police engage in many different types of activities, and I return to the discussion of types of corruption to reiterate a basic point. Transit police may prey upon the innocent, but many motorists are caught breaking the law. The subsequent exchange is usually one of bribe-seeking and bribe-offering. Other types of police, whether preventive (uniformed) or investigative (plain clothes), are notorious throughout the region for engaging in violent, abusive activities with virtually complete impunity, and for constituting key elements of organized crime. That is, active or retired (or purged) police officers are routinely found to be involved in a wide variety of violent racketeering, including extortion, kidnapping, drug trafficking, and "social cleansing."[17] In some activities, the police operate simply as uniformed criminals. In other activities, the police extort payments from victims. The exchange here is bribe-extorting and intimidated bribe-conceding.

The judicial system plays fundamental roles in democratic governability. It can provide for horizontal accountability—that is, guaranteeing the checks and balances needed to contain executive and legislative power. It constitutes the institutional framework and functioning agencies within which citizens can translate their abstract legal rights into practical action.[18] Most important, the courts are the "meta-institution" in the sense of applying the rules to other institutions and actors. If the courts do not work, there's little hope for the rest of the system.

In sum, police and courts play central roles in creating basic order and justice or the oft-cited rule of law, which is the bedrock of a democratic political system. With recent upsurge of criminal violence throughout much of Latin America, these roles are even more important. Corruption eats away at the willingness and capacity of these institutions to excel in these important roles.

These examples illustrate the various sites on a map of policy making and implementation. Here we are interested in the direct effects of corruption on democratic governability. The priorities flagged to this point include party-electoral functions, grand corruption, and police-judicial corruption. We turn now to look at the effects as mediated by perceptions.

EFFECTS OF CORRUPTION AS MEDIATED BY PUBLIC OPINION

The effects of corruption on democratic governability will depend in good part on how the populace evaluates what they perceive to be corrupt exchanges, assuming that evaluations influence opinions and behavior. What do we think we know about the corruption-democracy linkage in terms of perceptions? Findings to date generally point in the same direction. Perceptions of or (self-reported) experience with corruption are generally correlated with reduced support for (or less confidence in) democracy (understood as regime), incumbents, policies, or specific agencies. Canache and Allison, for example, use data from the 1995–97 World Values Survey and the 1997 Transparency International Survey. They find that citizens perceive corruption negatively and they connect those perceptions to their evaluations of political leaders and institutions. They find no evidence, however, that perceptions of corruption have soured mass opinion on democracy as a form of government (Canache and Allison 2003, 18–19). Seligson (2002) finds that self-reported experience with corruption (taken as forms of bribery) is correlated with reduced support for key institutions of government in four Latin American countries. Other researchers report that perceptions of corruption are associated with withdrawal and voter abstention. "In brief, perceptions of corruption can reinforce the existing distribution of political power by effectively removing from the political arena citizens who may have reason to challenge the system" (Davis et al. 2004, 701). A deepening of democracy leads toward the opposite result—the opening of channels through which discontented citizens can find effective voice through democratic participation.

These studies provide a useful point of departure. How might we reformulate the democracy-corruption relationship to examine the perception linkages in a more disaggregated way? We begin with the basic question: What do individuals perceive as "democracy" and "corruption"? What do the terms mean in everyday life, in different countries, and at different times? The little bit of survey material at hand suggests that mass publics conflate several attributes in their perceptions of democracy. With respect to Costa Rica, for example, Jorge Vargas Cullel (2004, 115) reports that about 30 percent of respondents in a 2001 national survey defined democracy in basically procedural terms, about 21 percent chose an "expanded definition" that included better representation and improved citizen control over the government, about 8 percent responded in behavioral terms (better leadership), another 10 percent emphasized economic progress and equality, and the remaining 31 percent mixed in elements from all the preceding definitions. Camp reports that surveys on Costa Rica, Mexico, and Chile suggest that most Latin Americans do not conceptualize democracy or have the same expectations from democracy as do North American theorists or citizens. "(W)hat most distinguishes the Latin American version of democracy from that of the United States is its emphasis on social and economic equality and progress" (Camp 2001, 9). The value of Camp's comparative approach is to remind us about the important national differences in conceptions of democracy. His findings suggest that of the three countries Costa Rica most nearly resembles the U.S. emphasis on democracy in political terms, while the other two emphasize government performance (Camp 2001, 15).

What meanings do mass publics assign to corruption? Based on data from Transparencia Mexicana surveys done in 2001 and 2003, Bailey and Paras (2006) found that Mexican respondents identified a wide range of different phenomena as corrupt. *Mordidas* (bribes) make up the most important category, and this meaning coincides with most scholars' definitions. But it is cited by only a fifth to a quarter of the respondents. Dishonesty, by either government or citizens, makes up the next largest category with 15 percent. Then there is a laundry list of items with no obvious logical connections, ending in a large "don't know" response. In sum, a respondent who cites "corruption" may have in mind bribery, dishonesty, failure to implement a program, poor quality administration, or something else. And the mix probably varies from one country to the next.

Where is "corruption" seen to exist? A 2005 survey carried out by Transparency International in fifteen Latin American countries asked about the degree to which corruption affects different spheres of life in the country.[19] The term "corruption" was undefined but was scored on a five-point scale from least to most present. Two sets of findings are pertinent. First, respondents make no sharp public/private distinctions. Corruption is seen in both society and government. Both the private sector (3.5) and communications media (3.3) fare rather poorly, with religious bodies seen as least corrupt (2.8). Second, the most corrupt public sectors are customs (4), legal system/judiciary (4.3), police (4.3), the legislature (4.4), and political parties (4.5) (Transparency International 2005a).

Noting the presence of corruption in different sites need not mean that those are considered the most serious. Transparency International's Global Corruption Barometer surveyed some 40,838 people in forty-seven countries in July 2002. The barometer tapped into the impacts of corruption on different spheres of life as well as perceptions of change over time. "The most striking finding came when respondents were asked from which institution they would choose to eliminate corruption first if they had a magic wand. The overwhelming first choice was political parties, followed by the courts and the police" (TI 2004, 288; Rehren presents similar data from 2003 in chapter 2). We will reconsider below this apparently strange assortment of actors.

In a survey done in Nicaragua that presented various situations of corruption, Seligson (1997, 9–12) found that respondents were most negative in their judgment of legislators who take bribes from private companies. Respondents were less critical about teachers accepting gifts, transit police soliciting bribes, or public employees accepting payments. They were least critical of a mayor who loans out the town's tractor to construct a baseball field. With respect to judgments about corrupt practices, respondents were most negative about businesses paying bribes and about students giving gifts, but were less so about using connections to get a job, paying bribes to transit police, or paying a bribe to get a birth certificate.[20]

Limited as they are, these bits of data suggest interesting possibilities for reformulating the democracy-corruption relationship in terms of perceptions. With respect to democracy as regime, respondents appear to be particularly negative about political parties. With respect to state institutions, they tend to focus on police and the courts.

Political parties play the central role of linking mass preferences to elite competition for control of government. Public estimation of parties is generally low across most countries. It is not obvious what precisely is perceived to be corrupt about the parties themselves. Probably more at issue is the perception of some mix of campaign finance abuses, forms of electoral fraud, campaign pandering and opportunism, and rhetoric that is considered to be deceptive.

The negative evaluation of the police is a recurring finding throughout most of the region. In chapter 5 of this volume, Blake examines further the relationship between confidence in the police and public attitudes toward bribe-taking. That the judiciary is also cited as a priority concern among government functions is a bit of a puzzle. Citizens come into daily contact with the police and thus have some basis for judgment. Yet, far fewer would seem to interact with judges and judicial proceedings. One possibility is that respondents are also including as part of the "judicial branch" (*poder judicial*) the offices of the *ministerios públicos* (roughly, prosecuting attorneys) and the *policía judicial* (investigative police). Citizens would have more possibilities of contacts with these offices in the course of filing complaints or of being party to a criminal investigation. In many countries in the region these two offices have ample track records of corrupt behavior.[21] Another possibility involves the upsurge of concern over criminal violence since the mid-1980s and the demonstrated inadequacy of the legal system to respond. "Corruption" here may be the respondents' way to condemn ineffectiveness, as well as to convey dissatisfaction with judges and court officials perceived to be on the take.

Rothstein (2005) makes a persuasive argument about why law enforcement and judiciary are critical to democracy in terms of linkages of perception. He suggests strong connections between law enforcement and social trust, a crucial element of democratic governability. In effect, police and judiciary have the critical task of tracking down and punishing those who have broken the rules. If they perform that task effectively and fairly, the broader community will more likely believe that offenders cannot get away with criminal activity. Thus, most people will refrain from criminal acts, and the basis of generalized trust is reinforced. Put negatively, where the police and judiciary are seen as ineffective or—worse—corrupt, people are less likely to trust others or to trust the broader political system.

As a category separate from functions (parties, law enforcement) I would also underline the importance of perceptions of grand corruption. Recall Seligson's findings (2001a) about the seriousness that respondents attach to corrupt behavior by legislators who accept bribes and by the business firms that offer them. These exchanges approximate our notion of grand corruption: misbehavior by high-level officials involving substantial sums. Perceptions of grand corruption also give us clues about an interesting puzzle in the democracy-corruption linkage. Self-reported experience with corruption (which runs in the 13–25 percentage range) is much less than perceptions of corruption in government as a whole or in specific institutions (which run in the 65–70 percent range).[22] Why do relatively few respondents say they experienced corruption yet so many express negative evaluations of distant actors and agencies? A three-part hypothesis can account for the disparity. First, respondents probably underreport their experience with corruption. Second, respondents base their views about distant institutions on media reports, which may or may not be accurate but which tend to emphasize incidents of grand corruption, often in the context of scandal. In many, if not most, cases, the reported incidents of grand corruption go unpunished, creating frustration about impunity. Third, respondents may be dissatisfied with government performance or about their particular circumstances and choose "corruption" as an all-purpose label to vent their negative feeling.[23]

RECASTING THE DEMOCRACY-CORRUPTION LINKAGES

Corruption is rightly seen as a prominent cause of low-quality democracy throughout much of Latin America. The scholarly and policy work in this field has progressed considerably over the past twenty years. It is useful to differentiate between democracy as regime apart from state institutions and the legal system in which the regime operates. It is also useful make some basic differentiations among arenas of policy making and to consider the nature of corruption as it operates in these sites. Further, we need to posit analytical linkages between corruption and regime and state in ways that set orders of priority among functions and processes. Finally, apart from the direct linkages, the perceptions of corrupt exchanges constitute an important set of mediated linkages. A challenge inherent in examining perceptions is that the terms "democracy" and "corruption" in daily usage can be complex, vague, multidimensional, or confused.

Space limitations excluded discussion in this chapter of the mixes and interactions of different types of corruption. Do scandal and grand corruption, for example, magnify negative perceptions of ordinary corruption? Nor was the broader context considered. For example, is corruption viewed less negatively in an economy experiencing solid growth and low inflation? Is the problem less serious early in a fixed term than later?[24]

I have ventured some speculations about which types of corruption operating in particular arenas might be more important to the operations of democracy and state institutions. These particular guesses might prove wrong as our understanding of the origins and maintenance of democracy advances. Even so, I think the rationale behind the speculations remains sound: We need to unpack and disaggregate the broad concepts that we have employed up to this point in order to analyze more effectively their interrelationships.

LUIGI MANZETTI AND CAROLE J. WILSON

4 Why Do Corrupt Governments Maintain Public Support?

Since the early 1990s there has been a growing awareness world-wide of the pernicious consequences that political corruption has on economic growth and public support for democratic institutions. In some cases, people's outrage has resulted in the impeachment of presidents (Brazil, Peru, Ecuador) and the resignation of prime ministers (Italy, Germany, Japan) or their outright demotion (the Philippines, Indonesia, Georgia). Although the international press has highlighted such events as landmarks in the fight against corruption, much less attention has been paid to the fact that to this day a score of politicians with tarnished reputations still succeed in winning office at the highest levels. A typical example is Italy's Silvio Berlusconi, who, despite a score of judicial inquiries accusing him of a wide range of crimes, was elected prime minister in 1994 and 2001. Unfortunately, as much as Berlusconi's story may be an extreme case, it is far from an isolated one.

Why do citizens support corrupt governments and their leaders? Our hypothesis is that people in countries where government

This is a revised version of an article first published in *Comparative Political Studies* 40, no. 8 (2007): 949–70. Reprinted with permission. The authors' names are listed alphabetically. We are grateful for the helpful comments of our friends and colleagues, including Giacomo Chiozza, Herbert Kitschelt, Guillermo Rosas, Kurt Weyland, and J. Matthew Wilson, as well as those of the reviewers.

institutions are weak and patron-client relationships are strong are more likely to support a corrupt leader from whom they expect to receive tangible benefits. Using a cross-national analysis of citizens in fourteen countries, we find statistical evidence consistent with our hypotheses as people are more likely to support the government if the government is ineffective, a measure, we argue, that indicates the ability of government to use the state apparatus for building clientelistic relations. This has significant implications for democratic accountability and good governance. Further, this study brings empirical evidence to descriptive analyses that underscore the importance of political clientelism in regime support. It also complements the more recent statistical analyses on the role of institutions by using survey data to demonstrate that support for corrupt governments at the individual level is likewise dependent on the strength of political institutions.

LITERATURE REVIEW

From the 1960s until the late 1980s, the so-called functionalist theory dominated much of the academic debate on political corruption. It viewed corruption as a necessary evil to cut bureaucratic red tape, redistribute resources, and sustain socioeconomic development in countries whose governments opposed communism (Goldsmith 1999; Heidenheimer 1970; Huntington 1968; Leff 1964; Nye 1967; Waterbury 1976). However, the end of the cold war, which had provided much of its rationale, made the functionalist perspective obsolete, and it quickly fell out of favor.

During the past decade there has been a resurgence of studies on corruption. This is in part due to a change in perception in the United States and other major industrial countries during the early 1990s. The collapse of the command economies in the former Soviet bloc, combined with the abandonment of import-substitution industrialization in many developing countries, created a historic opportunity for the promotion of trade liberalization and privatization around the globe. However, this required that capital and portfolio investments, coming primarily from the industrialized countries, be safeguarded from old-styled government corruption. In other words, the changed geopolitical and economic conditions made it imperative that corruption be substantially reduced. It is not by chance that by the mid-1990s the World Bank and the International Monetary Fund, heavily influenced by the United States, began to include anticorruption clauses in many of their loan agreements.

The World Bank has increasingly paid a lot of attention to the effects of corruption in the past ten years, particularly in developing and post-communist countries. Many of the World Bank–sponsored studies in this regard fall under the general theme of "good governance." The underlying assumption of the World Bank studies is that much corruption stems from poor government administration, particularly when it comes to the realm of economics. What follows is that a good deal of corruption could be curbed by promoting well-meaning administrative reforms. To this end, World Bank economists have developed much-needed cross-national data sets to test a series of hypotheses (Kaufmann 1997; Kaufmann, Kraay, and Mastruzzi 2003; Kaufmann, Kraay, and Zoido-Lobaton 1999; Kaufmann and Wei 1999).

Political scientists have generally focused on the causes and effects of corruption, usually regarded as a dysfunction in democratic systems. High levels of corruption undermine both interpersonal and government trust, preventing collective action and the development of civic behavior (Mishler and Rose 2001; Morris 1991). This, in turn, may have dire consequences for the survival of a political system, an issue particularly troublesome for new democracies (Montinola and Jackman 2002; Rose-Ackerman 1999; Theobald 1982; Tulchin and Espach 2000). Some recent studies have looked closely at the relationship between corruption and system support. In their study of Central and Eastern Europe, Rose, Mishler, and Haerpfer (1998) found that high levels of corruption negatively affected support for the democratic system and conversely increased the acceptance for authoritarian alternatives. In his analysis of Bolivia, El Salvador, Nicaragua, and Paraguay, Seligson (2002) also found even stronger statistical evidence that corruption undermines the political legitimacy of democracy and negatively affects interpersonal trust in particular and civil society relations more generally. In a subsequent study using a broader country sample, Anderson and Tverdova (2003) confirmed earlier findings that in countries experiencing high levels of corruption people display more negative attitudes toward civil servants than in industrial nations. Yet more interesting, they found that in such countries, negative evaluations are unlikely to be shared by government supporters, which may explain the ability of tainted administrations to retain power in the face of scandals and poor performance.

While many such studies have made a very important contribution in identifying both country-specific as well as cross-national factors that fuel corruption or citizens' alienation from the political system, they tend to ignore that many corrupt leaders are elected despite their reputation. In brief, much literature on the subject, when it comes to democratic systems, overlooks the fact that corruption may be related to the nature of the electoral process (Leftwich 1995); see also the discussion by Rehren in chapter 2 of this volume. This may be because many scholars believe corruption to be, by nature, antithetical to democracy and when it occurs, it is an anomaly rather than the norm (Elliot 1997). However, the corruption scandals that shook the political establishment in France, Italy, Germany, and Japan in the 1990s show that seasoned democracies are deeply affected by this phenomenon, which by no means should be identified with developing or postcommunist countries alone.

CORRUPTION, CLIENTELISM, AND GOVERNMENT SUPPORT

There are plenty of anecdotal accounts of people's continuing support for governments tainted by corruption, but there has been little empirical hard evidence. In this analysis, we will examine these claims more systematically. To avoid confusion, we will briefly set forth definitions of these phenomena and later show how they are related to our hypothesis.

Corruption manifests itself in many forms, which unfortunately cannot be described in detail here. However, in general terms, corruption represents an illegal transaction where public officials and private actors exchange goods for their own enrichment at the expense of society at large. On the one end of the spectrum, we may have government officials abusing their position of power to force citizens and businesses alike to pay bribes in order to receive public goods. The most extreme form of this type of corruption is the so-called kleptocracy, where political leaders, usually autocrats unrestrained by checks and balances, openly use government institutions to enrich themselves in any way possible.[1] At the opposite end of the spectrum, we have private citizens and companies who become the perpetrators of corrupt activities by dispensing bribes to officeholders to turn to their advantage the content of decrees, parliamentary votes, bureaucratic regulations, and judicial decision. Such illegal activities may be initiated to either change existing policies or to shape future ones.

For its part, clientelism is usually defined as an informal relationship between two actors enjoying asymmetrical socioeconomic power where the "patron" has the upper hand since he/she controls the kind of resources that his/her "clients" pursue but often cannot receive otherwise. Thus, it is a system that often establishes a relationship of domination and exploitation that perpetuates the lock on power of resourceful political leaders (Kitschelt 2000). Clientelism also entails reciprocity in the form of self-regulating and mutually beneficial exchanges of "favors" of unequal magnitude (i.e., clients may receive jobs, contracts, permits, pensions, cash payments, and other more basic goods in return for votes). As a political phenomenon, clientelism is based upon informal but widely accepted cultural and behavioral norms. Traditional patterns are based upon personalized relationships grounded in loyalty and deference, whereas more modern types can be more "anonymous" and orchestrated by party machines dispensing patronage on behalf of the patron (Kitschelt 2000).

There exists substantial theoretical and empirical evidence showing clientelism entrenched in polities where resources are scarce and controlled by deep-seated political cliques. This situation leads people to willingly exchange their votes for whatever favors they can muster (Bratton and van de Walle 1994; Brusco, Nazareno, and Stokes 2004; Clapham 1982; Dhillon and Wantchekon 2003; Eisenstadt and Lemarchand 1981; Estévez, Magaloni, and Díaz-Cayeros 2002; Fox 1994; Kitschelt, Mansfeldova, and Markowski 1999; Leftwich 1995; Lemarchand 1972; Lizzeri and Persico 2001; Luttmer 2001; Malesky 2001; Roniger and Gunes-Ayata 1994; Schmidt, Guasti, Land, and Scott 1977; Scott 1972b; Theobald 1982).

Some scholars have focused on whether different types of electoral systems may be more prone to corruption than others, although the evidence is often contradictory. One school of thought contends that party lists typical of large voting districts in proportional representation systems are more likely to be associated with corruption than in electoral systems where districts are smaller and politicians compete against one another. The theory behind this argument is that in smaller districts voters have a greater ability to hold individual candidates accountable, which helps in deterring corruption (Mitchell 2000; Persson, Tabellini, and Trebbi 2003). A second school of thought puts forward a more nuanced explanation contending that what matters is whether the electoral system creates incentives for politicians to pursue a "personal vote," which is more likely to induce less accountability, more rent-seeking strategies, and possibly more corrupt behavior (Ames 1995b; Cain, Ferejohn, and Fiorina 1987; Carey and Shugart 1995; Fiorina and Noll 1978; Samuels 1999).[2]

Another set of recent studies have tried to explain the strategies behind the electoral success of politicians who rely on extensive and well-organized clientelistic networks. Medina and Stokes (2002), for instance, theorize that incumbents who exercise monopoly control over political and economic resources are quite successful in keeping the status quo, establishing credible threats against clients who may defect to the challenger, and thus significantly reducing electoral competition. Moreover, since poverty fuels the demand for clientelistic handouts, politicians have an interest in perpetuating economic stagnation and preventing the development of redistributive policies on more impersonal, merit-driven bases that escape their control.

In similar vein, Wantchekon (2003) found that in Benin incumbent candidates' winning electoral strategy disregards making promises on programmatic platforms. Instead, they make clientelistic appeals that are perceived as more credible than what challengers have to offer: They provide part of the promised favors *prior* to an election. Brusco, Nazareno, and Stokes (2002), confirming earlier work on the same theme, showed that in Argentina clientelistic networks are particularly successful in mobilizing the votes of the poor and less educated through the delivery of handouts. In a follow-up study on Argentina, Stokes (2005) showed how politicians are not only quite successful in obtaining people's votes in return for tangible handouts but also have very effective means to monitor their clients' votes at the ballot box, thereby deterring their defection. Equally important, Stokes (2005) found that clientelistic party machines in Argentina do not favor, as previously assumed, die-hard supporters (whose vote they will get anyway), but rather concentrate on people whose vote is in doubt, as they have no strong ties to the machine itself.

There is also substantial agreement in the literature that clientelism is most likely to be pervasive and strong in polities where poverty abounds. Kitschelt (2000) noted how the poor and uneducated, as opposed to more affluent and educated citizens, are less interested in politicians who promise public goods (as opposed to individualized ones) in the long term. Nor are the poor that concerned with the downside of their client status. They have basic needs that must be dealt with immediately. Having been neglected for generations, they know that expecting government institutions to help them is simply unrealistic since institutional channels do not work and they are usually controlled by the political bosses who run clientelistic networks, which brings them back to square one. This explains why clientelism can be strong and alive even in the presence of competitive elections. As long as large numbers of poor exist who can fall prey to electoral machines, clientelistic politicians' prospects to stay in power will be good.

This observation brings us to the next point. There is an increasing body of literature showing empirically that clientelism and weak government institutions are strongly related. What defines "strong" government institutions then? Strong institutions are usually identified with legal systems that uphold the rule of law and property rights, with administrative bureaucracies that deliver public goods and services in an efficient, impartial, and timely manner, with limited and predictable business regulations, and with low levels of political and administrative corruption (Knack and Keefer 1995; Mauro 1995; Easterly and Levine 1997; Kaufmann, Kraay, and Zoido-Lobaton 1999). Strong government institutions also have effective checks and balances in place that keep elected officials accountable for their actions and ensure a fair degree of transparency in the policy process.

Conversely, clientelism thrives when government institutions are weak and unable (or unwilling) to provide public goods they are meant to do on paper (Shefter 1977), political accountability is low, and the policy process is shielded from public scrutiny. This situation allows clientelistic networks to step in and replace government institutions as the only source of basic goods for deprived communities. Indeed, as Stokes (2005) noted, clientelistic politicians have a vested interest in keeping government institutions cumbersome, corrupt, and ineffective since this situation enhances their legitimacy status with poor voters as the true problem-solvers. In a recent cross-national analysis, Keefer (2005) found empirical evidence suggesting a strong association between weak government institutions and patronage politics in young democracies. Weak government institutions are unable to provide public goods based upon fair and rational criteria because they tend to be captured by power groups that use them to dispense favors and create rent-seeking favoring their clients. Thus, in such a context, politicians do not make credible pre-electoral promises based upon a clear program, and voters are all too aware that such promises will not be honored. Consequently, the only credible promises are those where politicians build a reputation for targeting what are in principle public goods only to political clienteles in exchange for votes. This pattern seems particularly relevant to the young democracies of Latin America.

It is this relationship between the inability of government institutions to deliver public goods, on the one hand, and the ability of clientelistic networks to take advantage of such a situation, on the other, that is fundamental in explaining why people tend to support corrupt governments. We argue that weak government institutions allow corrupt politicians to take control of government resources and turn the delivery of public goods into "private" favors by providing patronage to their clientelistic networks. Put differently, we contend that corrupt governments, in spite of their bad reputations, may survive because they are able to buy off voters (or at least enough voters) through clientelistic networks. If corrupt governments are better able to provide favors, citizens may support such governments because of the incentives they supply, even if (and, in fact, because) they are corrupt.

Examples of this kind of a situation are numerous, and some politicians have been candid enough to admit it. A notorious case is that of Adhemar de Barros, one of Brazil's most important politicians from the 1930s to the 1960s, whose supporters were fond of saying, "Rouba, mas faz!" or "He steals, but delivers!"(Rosenn 1971, 523). Another case closer to home is that of former Louisiana Governor Edwin Edwards, whose supporters in the 1991 gubernatorial elections proudly displayed bumper stickers stating "vote for the crook: it's important!" (Lee Hancock, *Dallas Morning News*, September 5, 1997).[3]

In a political scenario of this kind, as noted by some of the scholarly work mentioned above, clientelism becomes the winning electoral strategy in the hands of corrupt politicians.[4] Thus, the strength of democratic institutions measures the opportunity structure for politicians to engage in client-patron behavior and the returns to them for such behavior.[5] Our theoretical model makes a contribution to the current scholarly debate regarding the puzzle of why people support corrupt governments. It does so by integrating recent insights from the clientelism and good governance literature into a single, unified model of popular support. The difficulty in testing our argument is that there are simply no cross-national data to measure directly the level of patronage provided by politicians. However, the strength of democratic institutions provides a way to measure indirectly the concept of clientelism and patronage politics. There is a very high correlation ($r=0.88$) between corruption, as measured by the 1995 Transparency International Index and our measure of strength of democratic institutions (see below). We argue that is because where democratic institutions are strong, corrupt behavior by politician for the distribution of patronage through clientelistic networks is costly. Where democratic institutions are weak, patronage politics is cheap. This provides the central hypothesis we wish to test in this chapter: *Support for governments perceived as corrupt is inversely related to the strength of government institutions.*

Because weak government institutions provide an institutional context that enables clientelistic politics, we argue that those living in such contexts are less likely to punish governments that they perceive to be corrupt. Conversely, where government institutions are strong, we observe the enforcement of the rule of law and property rights by a competent judiciary, a government bureaucracy that delivers public goods in a professional and impersonal manner, efficient business regulations, and accountability and transparency standards scrutinizing officeholders' behavior. As a result, opportunities to amass large clienteles through the manipulation of government are constrained, and the private distribution of goods is relatively costly for both politicians and citizens. This situation makes it difficult for corrupt politicians in countries with strong democratic institutions to "buy" support through clientelistic networks. In such institutional contexts, corrupt politicians are more likely to be punished by the public.[6]

ANALYSIS OF GOVERNMENT SUPPORT AND CORRUPTION

To test the hypothesis that support for governments perceived as corrupt is inversely related to the strength of democratic institutions, we use individual-level data from the 1995 wave of the World Values Study (WVS) combined with national-level data (Inglehart et al. 2000). Our sample includes fourteen countries (all countries in the WVS with data for the included variables): Argentina, Australia, Brazil, Chile, Finland, Germany (East and West Germany are sampled separately), Mexico, Norway, the Philippines, Spain, Sweden, Taiwan, the United States, and Venezuela.[7] These countries include several different regions of the world and represent very different levels of development and types of political systems.

The dependent variable in the analysis, government support, is based on the question, "How satisfied are you with the way the people now in national office are handling the country's affairs?" Possible responses were "Very Satisfied," "Fairly Satisfied," "Fairly Dissatisfied," "Very Dissatisfied," and "Don't Know." For ease of exposition, we choose to dichotomize the responses by grouping the respective "very" and "fairly" categories into "Satisfied" (coded as 1) and "Dissatisfied" (coded as 0).[8] Forty-two percent of the sample expressed satisfaction with their government.

Because we are interested in determining why individuals choose to support (or not to support) corrupt governments, we compare the effect of the strength of democratic institutions on government satisfaction at different levels of perception of corruption. For the purpose of the analysis that follows, we use a subjective definition of corruption. Definitions of corruption vary from one scholar to another. Further, individuals perceive the same actions of government officials in different ways, some categorizing an act as corrupt and others finding such an act appropriate or at least licit (see the discussion by Bailey in the prior chapter on definitions and perceptions).[9] Because of this, we respect the survey respondents' own definition of corruption. Therefore, if a respondent indicates that there is a high level of corruption in his or her country, we assume that this reflects particular acts that the respondent has witnessed or otherwise acquired information about and deems as corrupt. Regardless of the definition, our interest is in why individuals continue to support governments they perceive to be corrupt. The mechanism of that perception itself, and why some individuals perceive more corruption than others is beyond the scope of this analysis, although it is likely that such perceptions may be filtered through partisanship and/or may be dependent on political information and attribution processes. We define the levels of perceived corruption on the basis of responses to the following question: "How widespread do you think bribe-taking and corruption is in this country?" Response choices were the following: (1) Almost no public officials are engaged in it (5 percent); (2) A few public officials are engaged in it (42 percent); (3) Most public officials are engaged in it (30 percent); and (4) Almost all public officials are engaged in it (21 percent). This measure of perceived corruption is treated as an interval level independent variable in the analysis.

The key independent variable in our hypothesis is strength of democratic institutions. To operationalize this variable, we chose the 1996 Government Effectiveness measure created by Kaufmann, Kraay, and Mastruzzi (2003). This measure "combines responses on the quality of public service provision, the quality of the bureaucracy, the competence of civil servants, the independence of the civil service from political pressures, and the credibility of the government's commitment to policies" (4). We believe that it is precisely the weakness of these aspects of democratic institutions that are indicative of clientelistic politics. For our sample of countries, the government effectiveness measure ranges from -0.69 to 1.77, with Venezuela having the least effective government and Norway the most effective. The mean level of government effectiveness in the sample is 0.92.

We expect this government effectiveness to be negatively related to our dependent variable, government support, for those who perceive high levels of government corruption. That is, as government effectiveness increases, we expect the likelihood of supporting the government to decline among those who perceive high levels of government corruption. This is the expected direction for the interaction term between government effectiveness and perception of corruption in our model.

In addition to government effectiveness, several other variables may provide explanations for why corrupt governments receive support and need to be controlled for in our model. First, support may be contingent on economic satisfaction. If citizens are satisfied with their economic condition, they may support the government regardless of its nature. Support may be dependent on subjective evaluations of personal economic circumstances (pocketbook) or objective national conditions (sociotropic). Second, some scholars suggest that some groups may be more tolerant of corrupt behavior because of cultural norms and expectations (Beck and Lee 2002; Schulte Nordholt 2000; Wertheim 1970). If this were the case, then we would expect that those who find corruption justifiable are more supportive of governments even if they are perceived to be highly corrupt. Finally, we control for education in the model. Education may influence government support by affecting the perception of corruption and the ability of individuals to attribute corruption to the government.[10] Variable wording and coding for these alternative explanatory variables are included in the appendix.

To estimate our model we use probabilistic regression (probit), since our dependent variable is dichotomous. The estimation results are displayed in table 4.1. The first column of numbers reports the untransformed probit coefficients followed by the standard errors. We report the clustered standard errors that take into account the fact that our observations within countries are not independent. The statistical significance of the noninteracted variable (economic satisfaction, inflation, and education) can be observed in the usual manner by noting the size of the standard error in relation to the size of the coefficient. As expected, both pocketbook and sociotropic economic evaluations (economic satisfaction and inflation) have statistically significant effects on support for governments, although education is not significant in the model.

The calculation of the statistical significance of the interaction terms and their constituent parts is not straightforward, since their effects are conditional upon the values of the component parts of the interactions (Norton, Wang, and Ai 2004). We therefore compute the marginal effects

Table 4.1 **Probit results for government satisfaction**

Independent variables	Coefficient	Clustered S.E.	Marginal effects when corruption is at its minimum***	Marginal effects when corruption is at its maximum***
Corruption	−0.20**	0.08	−0.11**	−0.09**
Government effectiveness	0.15	0.27	0.02	−0.09*
Government effectiveness × corruption	−0.11	0.07		
Economic satisfaction	0.07**	0.01		
Inflation	−0.01**	0.003		
Tolerance of corruption	−0.004	0.04	0.002	0.01**
Tolerance × corruption	0.01	0.01		
Education	0.01	0.01		
Constant	0.08	0.34		
N	16025			
Log likelihood	−10250.02			

$*p < 0.05$. $**p < 0.01$ in a one-tailed hypothesis test. ***$\frac{dy}{dx}$ holding corruption constant at the specified value, marginal effects have been calculated using the delta method with the *predictnl* command in Stata 8.2.

(the slope of the function with respect to x) of the interacted variables when all other variables are held constant at their means and corruption is held constant at its minimum and maximum values.[11] These results are presented in the third and fourth numerical columns of table 4.1. Here we see that the overall effect of corruption is significant and negative, indicating that rising corruption has negative consequences for support.

Government effectiveness also has a significant impact on the dependent variable, but only in the presence of high corruption. The marginal effect of government effectiveness is not significant when corruption is low, but it is negative and significant when corruption is high. Thus, government effectiveness does not affect satisfaction when the perception of corruption is low, but it does have an effect when perception of corruption is high. This supports the key hypothesis developed in this chapter. Those who perceive high levels of corruption are significantly less likely to "punish" the government in countries where government effectiveness is low than in countries where government effectiveness is high because they are likely to be beneficiaries of patronage.

The relationship between support and corruption in the presence of low levels of government effectiveness is evident in the predicted probabilities in table 4.2.[12] When government effectiveness is at its minimum and the respondent perceives a high level of corruption, the predicted probability of indicating satisfaction with the government is 0.43. This probability declines significantly to 0.20 when effectiveness is at its maximum. This demonstrates that weak democratic institutions allow corrupt governments to garner political support. Citizens in countries where government effectiveness is at its lowest are almost as likely to be satisfied with a government they perceive to be highly corrupt as they are dissatisfied (no significant difference in the probabilities). However, in the most effective countries, in the presence of high perceived corruption, the probability of satisfaction substantially decreases to 0.20. Note, however, that when citizens perceive corruption to be high (most or almost all government officials engaged in it), they are inclined to punish the government, but they do so more vigorously when government effectiveness is high (bottom two rows of table 4.2).

Our hypothesis about the role of patronage politics and government effectiveness in support of corruption survives even when controlling for differences in norms and expectations about corruption. We do find evidence that those who are more tolerant of corruption are more supportive of government even when the government is perceived to be highly corrupt. Table 4.1 shows that the marginal effect of tolerance of corruption is positive and significant when corruption is high. This indicates that those who are more tolerant of corruption are slightly more supportive of government when corruption is high. While its effect is statistically significant, it is smaller than both the economic variables and government effectiveness.[13]

Table 4.2 **Predicted probabilities of support for government**

Level of corruption (government officials involved)	Government effectiveness		
	Minimum	Mean	Maximum
Almost none	56	59	60
A few	52	48	47
Most	47	37	32
Almost all	43	27	20

Cell entries are the probability of observing an outcome *Support* when all variables are held constant at their means, but the values of corruption and government effectiveness (and therefore the interaction term) are varied. The probabilities are calculated using *Clarify* in Stata 8.2.

IMPLICATIONS

Why do some corrupt governments persist in democratic polities? We have argued that corrupt governments can retain voters' support by manipulating government institutions to benefit their clientelistic networks. In these circumstances, the programmatic distribution of public goods is supplanted with clientelistic machines that distribute such goods based on personalized exchanges. The extent to which corrupt governments are supported by their citizens depends then on their ability to dispense such patronage. Our analysis shows that political support for corrupt governments declines considerably if these governments are unable to capture the state apparatus to reward political loyalties and dispense tangible benefits. In countries where there are strong democratic institutions in place, there is considerably less tolerance for corrupt governments since citizens perceive the higher opportunity costs of clientelism and its association with corrupt leadership. These findings support Kitschelt (2000), according to which more affluent societies develop party organizations that foster programmatic coherence that ensure that citizens can depend on predictable policies for the distribution of public goods independent of the government in office and its client-patronage network.

The implications of these findings are distressing for countries with weak democratic institutions. Given that the weakest democratic institutions yield the highest likelihood of support for corrupt governments, it is not likely that political reform candidates in these countries will garner considerable support, as earlier theorized by Calvo and Murillo (2004), nor is there an incentive for incumbents to reform their institutions as postulated by Stokes (2005). If incumbents are corrupt, their best strategy to maintain support is to continue to pursue clientelistic politics, which perpetuate poverty, high income inequalities, and political dominance. A case in point is Argentina. As a result of the 2002 crisis, the number of poor in that country more than doubled compared to a decade earlier, encompassing half of the entire population. However, despite the fact that the Justicialist (Peronist) Party was in charge during the 1990s, and was largely responsible for the economic debacle of 2002, its dominance of Argentine politics is just as strong today, if not stronger. This is because there are more impoverished people who depend upon food, jobs, clothing, housing, and unemployment compensations controlled and dispensed by the clientelistic networks of that party, thus reinforcing its dominance at the ballot box. This is consistent with Stokes's (2005) argument that poverty feeds into well-organized clientelistic party machines, creating a perverse cycle that is highly detrimental to democratic consolidation and good governance.

Change for the better, therefore, will only occur slowly and most likely over a long period of time. Administrative and economic reforms will not yield the expected results if they are implemented by corrupt leaders. This helps to explain why the market reforms that the World Bank and the IMF financed in many developing and postcommunist countries in the 1990s failed: They targeted macroeconomic and some legal reforms but left untouched the core of the problem that was ultimately political (Shleifer and Vishny 1998). Worse yet, such reforms were often entrusted to corrupt leaders who relied on strong clientelistic machines. In fact, some high-profile presidents who were hailed as great reformers and who had received large-scale World Bank and IMF assistance were accused—after they retired—of engaging in large-scale corrupt activities (e.g., Alberto Fujimori, Carlos Menem, Carlos Salinas, and Boris Yeltsin), which Bailey categorized as grand corruption in chapter 3. Not surprisingly, none of these leaders made tangible efforts to change political institutions rooted in old clientelistic traditions, which, in turn, continued to foster corruption and rent-seeking behavior under new forms. This sad observation leads us to conclude that if multilateral aid does not scrutinize how governments operate politically and spend their borrowed money, foreign assistance may actually help the very people that market reforms would like to see out of power. In chapter 6 of this volume, López-Cálix, Seligson, and Alcázar examine some new auditing techniques employed in the Public Expenditure Tracking Survey in Peru's milk distribution; this sort of approach illustrates one path toward tracking the possibility that public funds may not be used optimally toward their stated aims.

Conversely, in countries with strong democratic institutions, corrupt governments are not likely to receive much political support. Citizens favor programmatic politics, and even corrupt governments will find it difficult to exploit democratic institutions to deliver enough patronage to "buy" considerable political support. The certainty of functioning democratic institutions and fair policies for the distribution of public goods makes the costs of supporting corrupt governments high.

As our analysis shows, at the extremes it appears that those countries with the weakest democratic institutions are likely to continue to support the status quo, even if there is considerable corruption. Those with the strongest democratic institutions are likely to support more honest governments. It is in the middle, however, that policy makers, politicians, and voters face important choices. It is in these countries that issues of institutional reform and candidate integrity resonate with voters, and where policymakers are faced with challenges to insulate the state apparatus from the government itself. While it is not certain that a given polity will support or reject a corrupt government, the strength of democratic institutions certainly provides an explanation for why corrupt governments are often permitted to exist, and even thrive, in some democratic nations.

While this analysis addresses one piece of the puzzle regarding the complex interaction between public support, government institutions, and corruption, there is considerable work to be done. For scholars and policy makers to provide recommendations to countries struggling with issues of corruption and political reform, the challenge remains to collect better data over longer periods of time, as stressed by Blake and Morris. Once this challenge is met, empirical analyses can yield even more precise and theoretically stronger insights regarding the linkages between corruption and public support within democratic and democratizing polities.

While the crux of this chapter has focused on perceptions of corruption and government effectiveness, we do also find that citizens' tolerance of corruption has a significant effect on support for corrupt governments.

APPENDIX: VARIABLES

ECONOMIC SATISFACTION (WORLD VALUES SURVEY)

How satisfied are you with the financial situation of your household? If "1" means you are completely dissatisfied on this scale and "10" means you are completely satisfied, where would you put your satisfaction with your household's financial situation?

INFLATION (ANNUAL PERCENT CHANGE)

World Economic and Financial Surveys

The World Economic Outlook (WEO) Database, September 2000, http://www.imf.org/external/pubs/ft/weo/2000/02/data/

TOLERANT OF CORRUPTION (WORLD VALUES SURVEY)

Someone accepting a bribe in the course of their duties

| Never | Always |
| justifiable | justifiable |

1 / 2 / 3 / 4 / 5 / 6 / 7 / 8 / 9 / 10

What is the highest educational level that you have attained? (Use functional equivalent of the following, in given society)

1. No formal education
2. Incomplete primary school
3. Complete primary school
4. Incomplete secondary school: technical/vocational type
5. Complete secondary school: technical/vocational type
6. Incomplete secondary: university-preparatory type
7. Complete secondary: university-preparatory type
8. Some university-level education, without degree
9. University-level education, with degree

CHARLES H. BLAKE

5 Public Attitudes toward Corruption

Corruption has become an increasingly visible political issue in Latin America in the contemporary era. During the 1990s and the early twenty-first century, corruption scandals culminated in the premature end of some chief executives' mandates—including Fernando Collor de Mello in Brazil, Fernando de la Rúa in Argentina, Alberto Fujimori in Peru, Jamil Mahuad in Ecuador, and Carlos Andrés Pérez in Venezuela. Past presidents from the same time period faced formal corruption investigations in Argentina, Bolivia, Chile, Costa Rica, Ecuador, Guatemala, Haiti, Nicaragua, Paraguay, Peru, and Venezuela. More recently, corruption allegations have prompted cabinet changes in the Ricardo Lagos government in Chile (discussed in chapter 7 of this volume by Adam Brinegar) and in the Lula da Silva government in Brazil (examined in chapter 8 by Matthew Taylor). Persistent and widespread corruption accented by high-profile scandals in almost every country of the region can undermine the public's confidence in democratic institutions and faith in democracy itself. The perception and reality of corruption can also affect the prospects for investment and economic development.[1]

Faced with mounting pressures at home and abroad, governments across the ideological spectrum in Latin America have launched anticorruption programs in response. Often rooted in international approaches and funding (Husted 2002; Manfroni and Werksman 1997;

Zagaris and Lakhani 1999), many countries have made changes to their legal and regulatory systems designed to combat corruption. At the international level, most countries in the Western Hemisphere have signed and ratified both the 1996 Inter-American Convention against Corruption and the 2003 United Nations Convention against Corruption. Within individual countries, penalties for corrupt behavior expanded and new regulations broadened the scope of activities formally identified as corrupt. Many of these same countries have created new policies to enhance the detection of corruption. Often major organizational reforms formed a part of these reforms. Between 1994 and 2003, Argentina, Bolivia, Brazil, Chile, Ecuador, Guatemala, Mexico, Panama, Peru, and Uruguay established new anticorruption agencies and every single country in Latin America created new auditing agencies or reformed existing agencies.

From the outset of this reform process, several analysts have noted that new structures and initiatives are at best a necessary, yet by no means a sufficient, step to reducing the prevalence of corruption. Writing on international support for reforms promoting the rule of law around the globe, Carothers (1998, 96) asserts, "The primary obstacles to such reform are not technical or financial but political and human. . . . Western nations and private donors have poured millions of dollars into rule-of-law reform, but outside aid is no substitute for the will to reform, which must come from within." O'Donnell (2004b, 48) takes this point further by noting the reciprocal linkages between the creation of new government agencies charged with providing horizontal accountability and the ability and willingness of groups and individuals outside of government to hold government officials accountable: "On one hand, an alert and reasonably well-organized society, and a media that does not shy away from reporting cases of encroachment and corruption, provide crucial information, support, and political incentives for the often uphill battles that agencies of horizontal accountability may wage against powerful transgressors. On the other hand, the perceived availability of this kind of horizontal agency may encourage undertaking actions of vertical societal accountability."

Accordingly, in the early twenty-first century, increasing numbers of anticorruption campaigns have followed the recommendations of Carothers (1999) and others (Johnston 2005a, 2005b; Peruzzotti and Smulovitz 2006), calling for an integrated approach that combines governmental changes with the incorporation of civil society organizations and educational institutions into a broad-based framework of reform that targets the prevailing political culture in and out of government. Inside government, reformers try to transform a subculture of impunity into a setting more apt to produce accountability.

In turn, reforms aimed at civil society try to strengthen interest groups dedicated to fighting corruption while they try to reshape public opinion regarding the acceptability of corrupt behavior. Indeed, many case studies on corruption dynamics in Latin America and around the world emphasize the importance of reducing public tolerance of (and complicity in) corrupt behavior. For instance, Bilikisu Yusuf (quoted in Maier 2000, 303), a Nigerian anticorruption activist, asserts: "It's not enough for us to say, 'Ah, the leadership is corrupt, government is corrupt.' We have not internalized the message of probity, accountability, and transparency. If we are going to hold people to account and really make meaningful change in Nigeria, we must first begin with ourselves."

Regarding Argentina, Sturzenegger (2003, 230) writes, "Parecería que muchos argentinos, resignados a que el sistema sea corrupto, hubiesen decidido aprovecharse de él en la medida de lo possible, en una sociedad que de repente se ha transformado en un salvése quien pueda" [It would seem that many Argentines, resigned to the idea that the system is corrupt, have decided to take advantage of the system whenever possible in what has abruptly transformed itself into an every-man-for-himself society].[2]

Despite interest in public attitudes toward corruption, to date there has been almost no systematic, cross-national research into the determinants of citizens' tolerance of corruption (Moreno 2002). Instead, past research has focused mainly on two related issues—citizens' perceptions of corruption and the effect of perceived corruption levels on citizens' attitudes and behaviors.[3] This chapter constitutes an initial inquiry into the dynamics of citizens' tolerance of corruption.[4] Under what conditions are citizens more likely to believe in a "zero tolerance" stance toward corrupt activity?

CONFIDENCE IN ENFORCEMENT MECHANISMS AND THE PUBLIC REJECTION OF CORRUPTION

Citizens do not form their attitudes toward corruption in a vacuum. People's evaluations of the likelihood of enforcement—via detection, investigation, and adjudication—form crucial influences on their own thinking about corruption. Where a circle of impunity is perceived within the government, citizens find it harder to maintain an outright rejection of corruption because such a position seems like folly.

While many different government agencies play a role in the dynamics of accountability, when citizens consider government probity regarding bribe-taking and other issues they are perhaps most likely to think about the enforcement mechanisms closest to the people—the police. Contact with the police constitutes many citizens' only experience with government officials charged with enforcing the rule of law. Bayley (1985, 129) highlights still further the influence that the police can have over people's perceptions of government: "A government is recognized as being authoritarian if its police are repressive, democratic if its police are restrained. It is not an accident that dictatorial regimes are referred to as 'police states.' Police activity is crucial for defining the practical extent of human freedom."

When the police seem inept or corrupt, this hampers the ability of citizens to maintain high levels of confidence in the rule of law.[5] Writing on the dynamics of police corruption in Europe and North America, Punch (2000, 322) clarifies the stakes bluntly:

Police officers are the state made flesh. As law enforcers and problemsolvers they are the most direct representatives of the state for citizens given their visible, uniformed, 24-hour presence on the streets and their crucial involvement in social intervention and law enforcement. If they are corrupt, and if citizens lose confidence in them, then this undermines the legitimacy of the state. More than any other officials their integrity is a vital barometer of a healthy society. This can be seen in some of the transient states of Eastern Europe where weak governments, economic malaise and rising crime put pressure on the police to be tough while they are chronically under-resourced; they are not only corrupt but also human rights are widely abused by the police—this, in turn, weakening their and the state's legitimacy.

Latin America joins Eastern Europe as a region in which relatively few people have confidence in the police. A 2005 study by Transparency International in fifteen Latin American countries revealed that the police joined the judiciary, the legislature, and political parties as the groups that citizens judged most corrupt (Transparency International 2005a).

Because the police play such a critical role in shaping public opinions about the rule of law—and about government more generally—public attitudes toward the police can have a powerful relationship on one's thinking about corruption. If citizens perceive the police as protecting certain criminals or as eliciting bribes themselves, it becomes harder to develop and retain a consistent rejection of corruption. If those seen as central

Table 5.1 Corruption attitudes and confidence in the police

	Believe bribe-taking can never be justified (%)	Feel confidence about the police (%)
North Africa and the Middle East	94.2	70.4
Asia	83.9	53.0
North America and Oceania	82.1	76.5
Latin America	76.8	37.4
Sub-Saharan Africa	76.2	55.6
Western Europe	76.0	70.6
Eastern Europe and the former Soviet Union	66.9	43.1

Source: European Values Study Group and World Values Survey Association (2005).

to law enforcement are corrupt, why should one reject corrupt activity? Conversely, when one believes that the police force tends to enforce the law in a largely even-handed manner, then a firm rejection of corruption is easier to maintain.

Aggregate, cross-regional data can be used to illustrate the potential relationship between confidence in the police and tolerance of corruption. Table 5.1 uses data from the European and World Values Surveys for 1999–2002 (European Values Study Group and World Values Survey Association 2005) regarding public attitudes toward bribe-taking and confidence in the police. Latin American respondents express the lowest level of confidence in the police and a somewhat below-average rejection of bribe-taking. Residents of post-Soviet and East European countries manifest the most tolerance of corruption and a similarly low level of confidence in the police. There is not a firmly consistent pattern in these regional data, but these data suggest that confidence in the police is worthy of further study as a potential determinant of individuals' attitudes toward corruption.

Some might contend that both low confidence in the police and intolerance of corruption can be influenced by one's past experience with police corruption. In particular, one might consider the potential impact of a "shakedown" from a corrupt police officer who tries to procure a bribe by accusing people of offenses that they have not committed. Citizens who have experienced a shakedown tend to have less confidence in the police; they might also exhibit less tolerance of corruption than people who have not lived through a shakedown. One might ask, then, is the proposed relationship between police confidence and attitudes toward corruption the spurious by-product of the shakedown phenomenon? This seems unlikely because there are several factors that influence a citizen's confidence in the police (e.g., perception of its response time, of its ability to solve crimes, of its ability to mediate disputes, of its ability to deter and prevent crime, etc.) and, similarly, several distinct factors that influence one's tolerance of corruption. As a result, the police shakedown scenario is not an antecedent variable driving a spurious association between police confidence and tolerance of corruption. Instead, even for citizens who have experienced shakedowns, police confidence remains an intervening variable affected by past negative experiences with police corruption. For all other citizens, police confidence (or a lack thereof) emerges from other sources. Regardless of the causal roots of one's (dis)trust of the police, it is reasonable to assume that it has a causal impact on the tolerance of corruption. In the World Values Survey data used in this analysis there is no measure of past personal experience with police corruption. Thus, in the study in this chapter there is no path to examining its potential role as an influence on either confidence in the police or in attitudes toward corruption. It remains a matter for future research.

ADDITIONAL INFLUENCES ON PUBLIC ATTITUDES TOWARD CORRUPTION

Confidence in the police may influence tolerance of corruption, but it is not the only potential factor affecting people's thinking on this matter. Case study research into the causes of corruption provides one starting point for theorizing about the causal dynamics of corruption attitudes. From the 1990s forward we have seen a dramatic increase in scholarly and governmental attention to corruption dynamics in the form of single country studies, comparative case studies, and cross-regional collections of case studies.[6] In turn, a smaller but similarly growing body of quantitative cross-national research at the aggregate level has also identified factors that could conceivably influence individuals' attitudes toward corruption.[7]

Perhaps the most consistent finding across both case studies and quantitative inquiries into corruption dynamics is that affluence affects the prevalence of corruption (Blake and Martin 2006; Goldsmith 1999; Kpundeh 1995; Sandholtz and Koetzle 2000; Treisman 2000; Williams 1987). Affluence limits the prospects for corruption through its impact on government and on civil society. On the one hand, affluence changes the context in which government officials carry out their tasks. Kpundeh (1995, 67) states this point most directly: "Low salaries encourage corrupt behavior."

Beyond the halls of government, affluence transforms societies by creating more space for citizens to become concerned about issues beyond their own survival and material well-being (as chapters 2 through 4 of this volume have discussed). Poverty forces most citizens to focus on basic survival concerns that form a fertile breeding ground for clientelist politics and weaken the prospects of citizen activism to prevent corruption. Past research on clientelism has documented this causal chain in multiple situations within and outside Latin America (Brusco, Nazareno, and Stokes 2004; Clapham 1982; Eisenstadt and Lemarchand 1981; Fox 1994; Kitschelt, Mansfeldova, and Markowski 1999; Lemarchand 1972; Roniger and Gunes-Ayata 1994; Scott 1972b; Schmidt, Guasti, Land, and Scott 1977; Theobald 1982). In turn, affluence has been associated with the rise of more programmatically coherent political parties that focus more on public goods and less on clientelist exchange (Kitschelt 2000). Research on postmaterialism suggests that affluence changes not only parties' interaction with citizens but also citizens' attitudes themselves. Freed from worrying about their immediate survival, citizens are more likely to adopt postmaterialist values that can include a concern for public goods and the broader context of life (Inglehart 1981, 1990, 1997).

Two potential hypotheses stemming from these past findings will be examined in this study. First, income may be negatively related to tolerance for corruption: the more income one earns, the less likely one will tolerate corruption. Second, overall life satisfaction similarly may be negatively associated with tolerance of corruption: the more satisfied people are with their own lives, the less likely they will tolerate corruption. This second variant on the postmaterialist thesis enables us to examine the possibility that differences in a person's overall sense of well-being can affect the prospects for postmaterialism across different income (and educational) strata within a society (Inglehart and Welzel 2005).

Some have theorized that women are more concerned about probity in public affairs than men. In a quantitative analysis of corruption dynamics, Swamy and Knack (2001) found that female participation in the workforce, in the legislature, and in ministerial posts are each associated with lower levels of corruption. This suggests the following hypothesis: women are less likely to tolerate corruption than men.

In a study of Chile, Costa Rica, and Mexico, Power and Clark (2001, 59–63) found that age was negatively associated with acceptance of anti-civic behaviors such fare-jumping on public transportation, running traffic lights, and inventing false excuses. According to Power and Clark, at least two potential theoretical linkages join age to attitudes toward corruption. On one hand, there could be a generation gap in which older respondents were socialized differently than younger respondents. On the other hand, there could be a life-cycle dynamic at work that affects people over time: the older citizens become, the more they see the damage done by corruption in different situations. In this study, we will examine the following hypothesis: the older one is, the less likely one will tolerate corruption.

Research on political efficacy and political participation suggests that education empowers citizens to view politics in a more engaged and critical manner (Dalton 1996). In addition, research into the emergence of postmaterialist values suggests that exposure to higher levels of education promotes the emergence of concerns beyond survival itself (Inglehart 1997). Presumably, the greater political efficacy and postmaterialist concerns among those with higher education would make them tend to be less tolerant of corrupt behavior than citizens with less education. In this study we will examine the following hypothesis: people with some higher education (beyond the secondary level) will be less tolerant of corruption than citizens with a secondary or an elementary education.

Putnam's work on social capital in Italy (1993) argues that interpersonal trust generates political engagement and horizontal networking within civil society that breed productive societal dynamics in the political and economic realms. Subsequently, Lagos (1997, 2001b) argued that interpersonal trust promoted confidence in government institutions among Latin American respondents. In turn, Moreno's (2002) cross-national analysis found an aggregate-level, bivariate relationship between an index of attitudes toward corrupt activity and the prevailing level of interpersonal trust in each country. Extrapolating from these findings, one could hypothesize that people with considerable interpersonal trust will be less tolerant of corruption than those with lower levels of trust.

ANALYSIS

In this empirical analysis, seven independent variables held to reduce tolerance of bribe-taking will be examined—confidence in the police, income, life satisfaction, age, female, university-level education, and interpersonal trust. The variables in this model of tolerance of corruption will be studied using the European and World Values Surveys Integrated Data

File for 1999–2002 (European Values Study Group and World Values Survey Association 2005).[8] For the variables under examination, data are potentially available for sixty-nine countries within the data set. To deal with concerns about the reliability of survey responses given under repressive conditions, Belarus, China, Egypt, Iran, and Vietnam have been excluded because Freedom House (2001) characterizes their political environments as not free (rather than free or partly free) during the year in which the WVS was conducted in each country. Responses given under repressive conditions—particularly responses about political issues and governmental authorities—can be unreliable, as respondents may not trust in the confidentiality of their participation in the survey. Including these five nondemocratic countries in this analysis would not change the logit results in the statistical analysis that follows.[9]

DATA

The dependent variable (attitudes toward bribe-taking) is a dichotomous variable derived from Variable F117 in the WVS. Respondents were asked if it were ever justifiable for someone to accept a bribe in carrying out their duties; the 10-point response set ranged from "Never" to "Always." On this dummy variable, respondents that replied "Never" were coded 0, while all responses accepting possible justifications (responses 2–10) are coded 1. Some may wonder why corruption attitudes are being treated as binary here. First and foremost, a binary measure is adopted because I want to understand what makes some people completely intolerant of bribe-taking (and not what causes variation along an artificial 10-point interval scale that some or perhaps many readers may view as ordinal). From a permissiveness perspective, the key distinction resides in the decision to tolerate corruption under some to many circumstances—as opposed to expressing no tolerance whatsoever. In addition, empirically in this data set, there is almost no variation observed over the upper half of the scale.[10] Accordingly, both theoretically and empirically, the crucial cross-national variation occurs in the percentage of the population that believes that bribe-taking is never justifiable.

RESULTS

The logistic regression results for the sixty-four countries are presented in table 5.2.[11] In accord with the argument presented earlier, confidence in the police is strongly associated with low tolerance of bribe-taking. Women are less tolerant of corruption than men. Age is also negatively

Table 5.2   **The dynamics of public tolerance of bribe-taking**

Variable	Coefficient	Variable	Coefficient
Confidence in the police	−.217***	Female	−.187***
	(.067)		(.026)
Income	−.001	Age	−.318***
	(.051)		(.005)
Life satisfaction	−.069	Interpersonal trust	.005
	(.056)		(.069)
University schooling	−.093	Constant	.069
	(.070)		(.234)
Model χ²	**110.33*****		
probability > χ²	**.000**		
N	**80838**		

Unstandardized logit coefficients with robust standard errors in parentheses.
* Denotes significant at .05 level.   ** Denotes significant at .01 level.
*** Denotes significant at .001 level.
Source: European Values Study Group and World Values Survey Association
(2005).

associated with acceptance of bribe-taking: the older one is, the less likely one will agree that bribe-taking can be justified under some circumstances. None of the other variables under analysis (income, life satisfaction, education, and interpersonal trust) have a statistically significant association with attitudes toward bribe-taking.

The calculation of predicted probabilities provides another way of representing the relationship between each of these factors and the dependent variable; these probabilities were estimated using the techniques developed by King, Tomz, and Wittenberg (2000). This technique calculates the predicted probability for respondents with stated values on each of the independent variables while holding the other variables constant. Respondents expressing confidence in the police were 16 percent less likely to express tolerance than the baseline respondent. Respondents aged fifty-five and over were 24 percent less likely to tolerate corruption than other respondents. Women were 12 percent less likely to express the opinion that bribe-taking could be justified under some circumstances than the baseline respondent.

Do public attitudes in Latin America mirror the broader cross-national trends identified in these sixty-four countries? There are ten Latin American countries under analysis—Argentina, Brazil, Chile, Colombia, Do-

Table 5.3 **The dynamics of public tolerance of bribe-taking in Latin America**

Variable	Coefficient	Variable	Coefficient
Confidence in the police	−.021	Female	−.134**
	(.061)		(.052)
Income	−.373*	Age	−.351***
	(.179)		(.005)
Life satisfaction	−.200***	Interpersonal trust	.105
	(.030)		(.147)
University schooling	−.080	Constant	.717
	(.141)		(.493)
Model χ²	455.90***		
probability > χ²	.000		
N	14467		

Unstandardized logit coefficients with robust standard errors in parentheses.
* Denotes significant at .05 level.   ** Denotes significant at .01 level.
*** Denotes significant at .001 level.
Source: European Values Study Group and World Values Survey Association (2005).

minican Republic, El Salvador, Mexico, Peru, Uruguay, and Venezuela—comprising well over half of the regional population. The results for Latin America alone are presented in table 5.3.

While the relationship observed between police confidence and tolerance of corruption is in the hypothesized direction, the observed relationship is not statistically significant. Similar to the broader pattern identified earlier, women are less tolerant of corruption than men and age is negatively correlated to acceptance of bribe-taking. In addition, income and life satisfaction also manifest negative associations with the dependent variable. Interpersonal trust and university-level education remain insignificant.

Again, predicted probabilities were calculated to estimate the effect of the significant independent variables on attitudes toward corruption. High-income respondents were nearly 19 percent less likely to express tolerance for corruption than the baseline respondent across these ten Latin American countries. Those with high life satisfaction were 13 percent less likely than the typical respondent to tolerate bribe-taking. People aged fifty-five and over were only 15 percent likely to tolerate corruption. Women were 12 percent less likely than the baseline respondent to express the opinion that bribe-taking could be justified under some circumstances.

Why is confidence in the police a significant determinant of individual attitudes toward corruption in a cross-regional analysis spanning sixty-four countries but not across these ten Latin American countries? One potential explanation lies in the stark difference between confidence in the police in Latin America and the confidence prevailing across the other fifty-four countries examined in these data. Across these ten Latin American countries, an unweighted average of 37.4 percent of the population has confidence in the police—ranging from a low of 12.1 percent in the Dominican Republic to a high of 55.1 percent in Chile. Peru, Argentina, and Mexico have levels of police confidence from 16 to 30 percent while the other five countries (Brazil, Colombia, El Salvador, Uruguay, and Venezuela) fall between 41 and 53 percent. In stark contrast, the average level of police confidence in the other fifty-four countries under examination is 57.8 percent. Put differently, the Latin American country in which citizens demonstrated the highest level of confidence in the police (Chile) had less confidence in its police force than the average country among the other fifty-four countries studied from across the rest of the world. In societies in which most citizens lack confidence in the police, the impact of holding confidence may be blunted by the prevailing societal trend. People willing to express some confidence in the police may limit the importance that they attribute to their own confidence because they know that many fellow citizens doubt the police's probity and effectiveness.

A competing explanation of Latin American exceptionalism is suggested by recent research into the dynamics of postmaterialism. Inglehart and Welzel (2005, 38) argue that one's sense of security can trump other influences on core values, "The feeling that the world is secure or insecure is an early-established and relatively stable aspect of one's outlook." Perhaps the relatively stable dynamics of socioeconomic inequality in Latin America outweigh the relevance of more situational evaluations of police performance and honesty. Many wealthy and middle-income Latin Americans feel relatively secure (and empowered), and this status encourages them to express a rejection of corruption regardless of their evaluation of the police.

This potential explanation might account for not only the insignificance of police confidence in Latin America but also for the statistically significant role played by income and life satisfaction as influences on tolerance of corruption. As noted earlier, in Latin America respondents with high incomes and with high life satisfaction were much more likely to express zero tolerance toward bribe-taking than respondents with low and intermediate levels of income and life satisfaction. These dynamics in ten Latin American countries are congruent with the individual level analysis of the relationship between clientelist scenarios and political support in Manzetti and Wilson's analysis in chapter 4 of this volume. Conversely, in the larger data set (in which there are many more affluent countries present), income and life satisfaction were not significantly related to attitudes toward corruption.

As noted at the outset, this study constitutes an initial inquiry into the understudied issue of public (in)tolerance of corruption. Future research can attempt to explore the potential explanations for Latin American exceptionalism noted above. Furthermore, additional surveys can expand the comprehensiveness of countries examined inside and outside of Latin America. If the recent wave of research on corruption, the rule of law, and the quality of democracy in Latin America is any indication (e.g., Diamond and Morlino 2005; Domingo and Sieder 2001; Mainwaring and Welna 2003; O'Donnell 2004b; O'Donnell, Vargas Cullell, and Iazzetta 2004; Philip 2003; Schedler, Diamond, and Plattner 1999; Ungar 2002), further inquiry into the issues explored in this chapter is likely to occur.

In large measure, this recent wave of research responds to scholarly and public concern that democracy in Latin America has stagnated, if not regressed, from the 1990s forward into the twenty-first century. It is entirely possible that these fears are justified and that the nondemocratic "brown spots" highlighted by O'Donnell (1994) have expanded in the years that have passed since he coined the term "delegative democracy." However, in my view, it is also important to recall that no democratic regime emerged fully born.

Around the world, democratic regimes have evolved in an ebb-and-flow manner over decades. Taking this longer view, citizens interested in the reduction of corruption over time might take heart from the observation made by Caiden, Dwivedi, and Jabbra (2001, 236): "long established democracies [have] also [gone] through difficult transitions and suffered for generations from continued wide-spread corruption until new generations grew out of corrupt habits, new leaders and institutions managed to get a handle on corruption, and a new civic culture gradually brought a new moral basis to governance." These trends remind us that systemic corruption has normally been reshaped and reduced by sustained effort inside and outside of government.

Historically, people have often reduced corruption in the course of doing other things—usually, while defending themselves against official abuse or the unfair advantages of others. The process was sustained not so much by a vision of good government, but by the self-interests of people who saw a less corrupt system as both necessary and possible. Today's high-corruption societies cannot afford to wait and see whether such outcomes eventually occur. Modern corruption can be deeply entrenched domestically and integrated into powerful international economic and political networks. The pace of change in the world economy and the harm corruption does to growth mean that a society not making progress against corruption is vulnerable to forces beyond its control, and is missing opportunities that will not last forever. The challenge is to build an anti-corruption force rooted in society, possessing real influence, and sustained by credible incentives, and to build it quickly. (Johnston and Kpundeh 2005, 150)

In short, the passage of time alone is not a remedy. To transform corruption dynamics, one needs not just to transform attitudes but also to engender new behavioral patterns and incentive structures that reduce the space for corruption. While change takes time, the stakes in an increasingly fast-paced and interconnected world are arguably higher than ever.

PART II   **NATIONAL CASE STUDIES**
OF CORRUPTION

JOSÉ R. LÓPEZ-CÁLIX, MITCHELL A. SELIGSON,
AND LORENA ALCÁZAR

6   Local Accountability and the Peruvian Vaso de Leche Program

Decentralization has become a dominant mantra in many development programs throughout the world. The reasoning seems sound enough. The larger the government unit, the more remote it is from popular control, the less accountable it will become. To solve the problem, decentralization is advocated by many policy analysts as the best way of putting control (back?) into the hands of the people, where public officials will be held accountable, and where public funds have the greatest chance of responding to local needs and local conditions. Moreover, at the local level, where citizens can observe the actions of public officials firsthand, corruption can be difficult to hide and relatively easy to control. This logic goes even further: take public programs out of the hands of public officials and turn them over to local civil society organizations, which, having a popular base of support, will be the most efficient, transparent, and noncorrupt administrators of public services.[1]

In many developing countries in recent years, as states have shrunk under pressure from neoliberal restructuring (as well as the already noted thesis that local is better), civil society organizations

We would like to acknowledge the work of Erik Wachtenheim for his important contributions to the research that led to this study.

have become the repository of many services that were once run by the state. The classic work by Putnam (1993), which is often cited as the key study to demonstrate the importance of cultural values in promoting democracy, is equally a landmark work about the importance of local government (in the particular case of Italy, regional government) and the role of civil society organizations in "making democracy work."

Those who promote decentralization and civil society organizations are not without their critics. Two main lines of criticism have emerged. First, local governments have fewer resources to institute controls over public spending and to carry out effective audits (López-Cálix and Melo 2004). Second, civil society organizations can often be highly undemocratic and promote the worst form of discrimination, as has been illustrated by Armony (2004) with the examples of civil society organizations promoting the rise of Nazi control in Germany as well as segregationist groups in the American South promoting lynchings of Blacks. In contemporary Guatemala, local civil society organizations have been linked to the wave of vigilante attacks that have become regular occurrences in that country (Seligson 2005).

One of the problems in the literature attempting to determine which side of this debate is closer to the truth is that much of it is qualitative in nature, where anecdotal illustrations of the pluses and minuses are deployed as evidence. On the other hand, the quantitatively based literature suffers from serious limitations of scientific control. That is, much of that work involves cross-sectional studies in which the level of centralization/decentralization is contrasted. The problem is that the controls are often too limited to rule out alternative explanations. Longitudinal studies suffer from the same problem; the macroeconomic and other conditions under which the newly decentralized government or civil society organizations are operating differ in many ways from their more centralized predecessor arrangements. As a result, one cannot be sure that it is decentralization rather than some other variable that is responsible for producing the outcome.

This study seeks to avoid the weaknesses of prior work. Rather than comparing across space or across time, with all of the inherent limitations in establishing effective control variables, this study examines a single country, Peru, and a single time period, 2002, and focuses on a single program, the Vaso de Leche (glass of milk). It draws upon a detailed study of public expenditures that enable us to trace the use of public funds from their inception in the budget process down to the consumption of the glass of milk inside households, and in so doing take note of the points in the system in which the loss of the milk occurs. We do not need to make any questionable assumptions about control variables, since we are not varying the place or the time in which the study is being conducted.

The focus of the chapter is on "leakages" in the administration of public funds. "Leakage" is defined as the portion of public funds that do not reach their ultimate targeted beneficiaries, but instead is diverted for other purposes, including private gain or other potentially legitimate but clearly unintended purposes. This particular study of leakages is different from the study of corruption per se. Studies of corruption examine the bald diversion of public funds and the taking of bribes by public officials that are both clearly illegal and fraudulent in intent (Rose-Ackerman 1999; Seligson 2002; Treisman 2000). Research on leakages, instead, begins by asking the question, "Why do public expenditures often not produce concomitant increases in social outcome indicators?" While there are many factors that go into the answer to that question, only recently has it been appreciated that part of the explanation lies in the fact that institutional factors, as well as local organization constraints, or private gain prevent some portion of public funds from reaching their intended targets. This "leaking away" of public funds in Peru is the subject of the present investigation. We study it using the World Bank's Public Expenditure Tracking Surveys (PETS) we carried out for this research.

Work on leakages of public expenditure is to date only in its pioneering stage worldwide. Our research builds on the seminal work developed by the World Bank in Africa, more particularly in Uganda (Reinikka and Svensson 2001, 2004). That research found that only 13 percent of the nonwage expenditures made by the central government were received by the local schools. This research on Peru deepens the approach followed in the Uganda study, however, mainly because it is able to trace linkages at *each* level in the chain from the first emission of public funds at the central level down to the consumer at the level of the household. The Uganda study looked only at the national/individual leakage and thus was unable to attribute leakages to each stage in the chain. As a result of our more comprehensive and disaggregated focus, surprising findings presented here emerge, especially because it is possible to identify and quantify the specific steps where the main leakages occur. Moreover, the Peru PETS, because it pinpoints the locus and key causal factors responsible for the leakages, gives policy makers clear direction for dealing with the problem.

To anticipate our findings: leakages in Peru are significant and far more pervasive and extensive at the *bottom* of the chain rather than at the top. From the entire amount of public funds intended for the Vaso de Leche (VdL) program, barely 29 percent get to their intended beneficiaries. The rest of the resources get leaked away. The results challenge the predominant view that organizations that are closer to the people they serve are inherently better in service delivery. Conventional wisdom assumes that the local and nongovernmental "agent" is more accountable than the national and public "principal."

FUNDING TRANSFERS FROM CENTRAL TO LOCAL GOVERNMENT: LEAKAGE PROBLEMS

In Peru, public resources are distributed by two mechanisms: those that are centrally allocated and administered through branch offices of the central government and those that are transferred to local governments (municipalities). The education budget is an example of the former, while the VdL program is an example of the latter. In both cases, there is a considerably long chain of intermediaries between the original central government budgeting office and the intended recipient. The findings presented here focus on the latter mechanism: public resources that are transferred to local governments (municipalities).

It is difficult to overstate the importance of central government revenue transfers to municipal governments. For the districts outside of Lima, transfers represent, on average, 72 percent of municipalities' total income. Among the districts of the poorest stratum, they can represent in excess of 90 percent of municipalities' total income. The central government's main transfers include the Fondo de Compensación Municipal (FONCOMUN) and VdL for all municipalities, and Canon Minero and Canon/Sobrecanón Petrolero for provinces and districts in regions where mining and petroleum products are extracted or the mining and petroleum company headquarters are located. In 2001, these four major central government transfers totaled 1.9 billion *soles* (roughly US$560 million). The largest of the four transfers is the FONCOMUN, which accounts for 1.4 of the 1.9 billion *soles* in 2001 (in some districts it represented upward of 90 percent of total income).

The second largest central government transfer is the VdL transfer, which totaled US$97 million in 2001. By law, approximately 7 percent of public social spending in Peru is dedicated to nutrition programs. Much of this effort involves the VdL program. These funds form part of the overall transfers of central government resources to local governments, 100 percent of which in turn are supposed to be delivered to local milk committees and from there on to households and individuals. This transfer, unlike the others, is earmarked specifically for use in the purchase of VdL products. This program is very important: the municipalities in our survey (described below) reported a total of 645,346 beneficiaries; or, expanding this to the national population equals 3,693,406 (2,207,209 being children up to age six) which would suggest coverage of 92 percent for children between the ages of birth and six years.

How meaningful are these transfers to the individual Peruvian? On a per capita basis, FONCOMUN transfers—the largest of the programs—average $8.57 in Lima per year and $18.61 per year in the rest of the country (see table 6.1). In a country in which the GNP per capita (PPP terms) was in the neighborhood of $2,080 at the time of our study, the largest of the transfers (FONCOMUN) amounts to no more than four-tenths of a percentage of GNP per capita. A similar comment applies to the canons. Yet, these calculations understate the effects since the funds are designated for the poor—not the entire population—and therefore the poor are to receive (at least in theory) a higher share of them on a per-capita basis. Moreover, the incomes of the poor average less than that national GNP per capita, which, after all, is the mean of all income. Indeed, in any Latin American country, where income distributions are almost always highly skewed, the income of the poor is only a small proportion of that of the national average. Finally, the cash value of those funds is not the only factor to consider as the transfer provides, in theory at least, key nutritional supplements for children, whose nutritional status during childhood could impact their future health, intelligence, and productivity. Unfortunately, the antipoverty funds face a number of problems in their administration.

Poverty fund administration is affected adversely by one of the most serious long-term problems faced by local governments in Latin America, which is the consistent inconsistency in the reliability of central government transfers. In many countries, such transfers result in almost constant arrears. While volatility is not directly a leakage-related issue, it does make planning difficult.[2] More directly, volatility produces suffering when milk and other foodstuffs are not delivered on time. In Peru, the new financial management system is now in place and volatility has been minimized but not eliminated. Our sample found that in the worst case, volatility for the VdL transfer, outside of Lima, can exceed 15 percent.

Overall, the municipal officials included in our survey claim to have a reasonable understanding of the various transfer programs while in fact they do not. For example, the survey found that 90 percent of the municipalities in the Lima area and 79 percent in the rest of the country claimed to know the allocation criteria used for the FONCOMUN program. Yet, the survey also found that when questioned, only 11 percent of the municipal officials in Lima—who had earlier in the interview claimed to have knowledge of the criteria—actually did. In the rest of Peru, surprisingly, the knowledge was higher among those who claimed to know, as 67 percent actually did. As for the amount of transfers expected from FONCOMUN, the knowledge base is more reasonable, as only 5 percent in Lima and 15 percent in the rest of Peru claimed not to know. In poor and rural areas outside Lima, however, this percentage of uncertainty increased to nearly one-third. In the case of Canon/Sobrecanon Petrolero transfers, there is considerable uncertainty as to the expected amounts, with the

Table 6.1 **Per capita transfers to municipalities in 2001 (U.S. dollars)**

	FONCOMUN	Canon Minero	Canon/Sobrecanon Petrolero	Vaso de Leche
Peru	15.35	1.20	12.51	3.73
Lima	8.57	0.09	NA	3.99
Urban	8.33	0.09	NA	4.00
Rural	25.24	0.19	NA	3.33
Number of observations	177	171	NA	177
Rest of Peru	18.61	1.89	12.51	3.60
Less poor	14.38	1.55	10.97	2.96
Poor	18.94	2.07	11.16	3.54
More poor	22.54	1.99	19.47	4.35
Urban	15.46	1.54	10.22	3.14
Rural	22.73	2.25	17.37	4.21
Small	31.97	1.84	48.15	4.37
Medium	20.05	1.77	19.40	4.13
Large	16.28	1.92	10.62	3.39
More accessible	17.33	1.81	9.81	3.39
Less accessible	23.72	2.15	20.90	4.47
Nonprovincial capital	16.98	1.48	11.95	3.73
Provincial capital	21.60	2.69	13.09	3.41
Number of observations	1,641	1,296	142	1,641

Source: World Bank 2002.

Table 6.2   **Municipalities unaware of transfer dates (%)**

	FONCOMUN	Canon Minero	Canon / Sobrecanon Petrolero
Lima	40		
Urban	42	N/A	N/A
Rural	38	N/A	N/A
Number of observations	**20**	**N/A**	**N/A**
Rest of Peru	33	35	40
Not Poor	27	29	2
Poor	49	63	94
Extremely poor	38	30	40
Urban	61	87	35
Rural	28	28	47
Small	30	30	38
Medium	39	36	31
Large	45	62	44
More accessible	18	21	15
Less accessible	66	66	64
Nonprovincial capital	34	33	41
Provincial capital	28	50	29
Number of observations	**99**	**74**	**32**

Source: World Bank 2002.

majority outside of Lima not knowing. Knowledge of the date of arrival of the transfers was another matter. In Lima, 40 percent of the municipalities did not know, and in the rest of Peru the results were only marginally better (33 percent did not know). Similar percentages are found for FONCOMUN and Canon Minero (table 6.2).

LEAKAGES IN THE VASO DE LECHE PROGRAM

The approach taken to the measurement of leakages in this study has been to employ survey instruments at each level in the process of transference of government funds from the central authority down to the household. Measuring leakages in transfers to subnational governments, local organizations, and program beneficiaries is not an easy task, however, because it confronts two central problems. First, none of the parties affected by the leak have an interest in having it revealed. Second, leakages can occur at so many levels that tracing them all requires a complex methodology. Those are the two challenges that this report faced and we believe, to a considerable degree, overcame.

The core of our methodology was to collect data at each stage in the transference of public funds from the top of the chain, the central government, to the bottom of the chain, the beneficiary. In order to gather data on each of these levels, the study carried out in Peru involved an extensive amount of fieldwork based on a series of questionnaires.

The project began with a pilot study in Lima, Peru. The objectives of the pilot included an assessment of the duration of the fieldwork and a test of its effectiveness for the purposes of the study (for example, to explore whether the information collected in the fieldwork would be sufficient to rigorously estimate leakages). The pilot consisted of twenty districts from the department of Lima (out of a total of 177 districts). Each district included a survey for its municipality; a survey of between three to five VdL mothers' committees within each municipality;[3] and a survey of a sample of beneficiary households (four per VdL committee).[4]

Based on the experience of the Lima sample, and with guidance from the National Institute of Statistics and Information (INEI), a national sample selection methodology was agreed upon. We stratified the sample into Lima/Callao, as it is the capital of the country, and other major regions of the country. In that stratification the departments selected were Ancash, Arequipa, Cajamarca, Cusco, Loreto, and Piura. We then substratified those departments into their municipalities and selected a total of one hundred municipalities in which the surveys were carried out. The sample is self-weighting, making it easy to work with when complex multivariate techniques are employed.

Our method of stratifying the municipalities was focused on poverty since the VdL program was meant to deal directly with poverty. In order to carry out this stratification, we developed a database consisting of the entire universe of districts in Peru, excluding Lima and Callao (a total of 1,651 districts). The Ministry of Economy and Finance's (MEF's) continuous index of poverty, FGT2, was used to calculate poverty population deciles.[5] The deciles were arranged into three groups such that group 1 consisted of deciles 1 to 3, group 2 of deciles 4 to 7, and group 3 of deciles 8 to 10. These three groups approximate the categories of "not poor," "poor," and "extremely poor" and were used to stratify the districts of our subpopulation into three strata. The three strata represent 14 percent, 41 percent, and 45 percent of the districts in Peru (excluding Lima and Callao), respectively. In order for the sample to be self-weighted fourteen, forty-one, and forty-five municipalities (for a total of one hundred) were chosen from each stratum respectively (from the subpopulation of six departments). The selection for each stratum was done using probability proportional to size (PPS) relative to district population.[6] Once the above procedure was carried out, individual municipalities were selected according to PPS criteria, using a complete listing of all districts selected that were ordered within the stratums by geographic order to allow a systematic selection that ensured geographic heterogeneity.

Within each municipality, the field teams obtained from the local government a roster of all of the VdL committees that at the time of the survey were beneficiaries, and systematic sampling was used to select four of those from each municipality, unless there were fewer than four in a given municipality, in which case all committees were selected. The only restriction was that if travel time to a given committee would have required more than twenty-four hours, a substitute was used. This means that the sample slightly underrepresented remote areas within the neighborhoods of the selected committees; the field team selected four households from the beneficiary lists that are maintained by each committee. Recalls were not made, but the next household on the list was used as a substitute when blanks were encountered.

The survey was conducted February 3–17, 2002. Within each municipality we interviewed the mayor, obtained municipal-level data from him or her, and also obtained the municipal roster of committees participating in the VdL program. We met with at least one committee member and interviewed that individual with our survey instrument, and in that interview we obtained a current list of individual beneficiary households. We used that list to systematically select four households in each committee catchment area, using a survey instrument intended for households.

In sum, the study employed data from surveys in a sample of 120 municipalities out of the 1,828 municipalities in Peru. It is in tracing the flow of funds in the VdL program that the survey research attempts to make its most innovative contribution. Using survey data at the level of the municipality, at the level of the local milk distribution committees, and, finally, at the level of the beneficiary household, it was possible to trace the flow and leakage of central funds from the top of the chain to the last link at the bottom. The methodology is very complex, not only because it involves multilevel comparisons but also because the input itself is transformed from cash to commodities as the funds move from the top to the bottom, and as the commodity itself actually becomes commodities, since the program is not limited to milk or milk products alone, despite its name. The product is then transformed at the household level, as the food products are mixed with other foods before being served. Yet, despite this complexity, it has been possible to determine the relative magnitude of leakages at each level.

The VdL program targets children seven years old or younger, as well as pregnant and nursing mothers, and, as a secondary priority, children seven to fourteen years old. The transfer criteria from the central government to the municipality are based on per-capita poverty formulas. At the municipal level, the local government is required, via special committees set up for the purpose, to use 100 percent of the funds for milk products, which must be overwhelmingly produced nationally. These committees are nearly ubiquitous, with 98 percent of the urban municipalities and 95 percent of the rural municipalities having them, according to the survey. The products are purchased via competitive bidding, which is supposed to help ensure employment of the lowest price criterion. However, the study found that while bidding was predominant, 19 percent of the products were purchased through other mechanisms, and some excessively high prices were also found.

As mentioned before, despite its name, the program called the "glass of milk" in fact includes milk, milk products, or milk substitutes, and other products such as oatmeal, quinoa, and other grains. This shift from milk to other products produces the unfortunate effect of reducing both the protein and calcium intake of the beneficiaries, since milk and milk products contain the highest levels of these nutrients in comparison to grains. The fieldwork determined that only 15 percent of all municipalities distribute milk alone, with the vast majority "diluting" the milk with the distribution of cereal, a combination of milk and cereal, or distributing cereal only. Once these products are purchased, they are transferred to the next level down in the chain: to the local committees or clubs comprising mothers, which are neighborhood or village-based volunteer groups. These local groups are then required to distribute the "milk" on some sort of regular cycle (daily, weekly, monthly, bimonthly) depending on local circumstances, based on the legal criteria mentioned above, as well as locally determined criteria for need. Within the recipient household, the "milk" is required to be fed to the children and mothers for whom it was designated. As the fieldwork for this project determined, much of the above is more theoretical than real.

Leakages in the VdL program occur at many levels, but measurement of these leakages is an extremely complex task. We explain our methodology in detail in the appendix. Perhaps the major complexity emerges from the law itself. According to the law, the foods must be distributed to beneficiaries in prepared form. This could mean, for example, mixing of powered milk into a cereal or other cooked product. It would be virtually impossible for any study to then measure with exactitude how a given amount of milk input arrives in the stomach of the beneficiary. But, more important, from a practical point of view, distribution committees often cannot reasonably prepare the food since the beneficiaries are preschool children whose parents cannot transport them on a daily basis to a central distribution point. Consider the mother who is nursing two preschoolers and whose partner works outside the home. She cannot reasonably be expected to visit a central kitchen each day to feed her children. Moreover, and more important according to our findings, the overhead costs of preparing the food, including distance, time, materials, and spoilage for unconsumed food, deter many committees from attempting to follow the law. As a result, 60 percent of the committees in the sample do not prepare the food and distribute it unprepared. For the purposes of the study, however, this is a plus, since it allows us to more precisely measure the distribution, since we can more easily count cans of milk, pounds of cereal, etc.

"MILK" LEAKAGE STAGE 1: CENTRAL GOVERNMENT TO MUNICIPALITY

While we had expected the largest leakages at this level, in fact we found virtually none. The leakage here represents 0.06 percent in Lima and 0.02 in the rest of Peru, all of which could be determined by rounding and recording errors. Thus, at the top level, where one often assumes the greatest level of corruption (and therefore the greatest leakage) the leakage is virtually nonexistent.

"MILK" LEAKAGE STAGE 2: UNACCOUNTED FOR CONVERSION OF TRANSFER TO PRODUCTS

Once the transfer reaches the municipality, the funds are converted to products to be given to the local committees. From the municipal level onward, the transfer of resources for the VdL program becomes in-kind transfers such that no subsequent stages of execution receive money but rather receive the transfer in-kind. Our fieldwork team was instructed to get prices and quantities of VdL product purchases made by the municipality in December 2001 and to verify this information via signed contracts, purchase orders, or receipts. The quantities were in most cases obtained from the municipality's distribution roster (*padrón municipal*), which includes the amounts allocated and distributed to each mothers' committee within the municipality's jurisdiction. This leak was defined as the percentage of the amount transferred to the municipality from the central government for the month of December 2001 that is unaccounted for by the total expenses of the municipality for that month (in terms of products purchased for the VdL program).[7]

Private gains are not the only possible reason for these leaks. One explanation for the leakages at this stage could be a diversion of VdL funds to cover the program's operating expenses (personnel, bookkeeping materials, transportation costs, and warehousing costs). Although prohibited by law, this kind of leak is not a result of a corrupt act. Indeed, the leakages at this stage are found more significant in small, rural, and less accessible districts. In many cases, it was found that in small rural districts there are severe budget as well as personnel limitations that make the operating costs of the program very high. Moreover, given the large and organized network of VdL mothers representing a unified and powerful faction of the constituency that exerts considerable pressure on mayors, it comes as no surprise that there may exist many cases in which the municipality supplements the central government transfer with municipal resources. Indeed, we find that often leak #2 turns out to be negative (the municipality spent more in December 2001 than was allocated to it by the MEF), although operationally leakages were truncated at zero.

"MILK" LEAKAGE STAGE 3: TRANSFER FROM THE MUNICIPALITY TO THE LOCAL COMMITTEES

Leakages found at this stage were more significant. In Lima, they averaged over 10 percent but were far lower—only 2.6 percent—in the rest of Peru (table 6.3). However, within the greater Lima area, rural communities have higher leakages than urban areas, a pattern that is also found in the rest of Peru. Every municipality has an allocation formula, based almost entirely on the size of the target population, that each VdL committee services. Thus, criteria of *relative* poverty do *not* play a role here, only the number of poor people. The roster of beneficiaries is centralized at the municipal level and provides detailed information on the quantities distributed to each committee within the district. This leak was defined as the percentage of the amount listed in the municipal roster not accounted for by the VdL committee and estimated using municipal and committee data computed at the committee level.

A clearer picture of the magnitude of the leakage problem that occurs

Table 6.3 **Leak #3: Municipality to local committees (%)**

Lima		Rest of Peru *(cont.)*	
Urban	6.83	Small	2.83
Rural	18.77	Medium	4.23
Number of observations	37	Large	2.25
Rest of Peru	2.59	More accessible	2.31
Less poor	0.54	Less accessible	3.70
Poor	5.67	Nonprovincial capital	3.10
More poor	5.22	Provincial capital	1.97
Urban	1.26	Number of observations	320
Rural	4.52		

Lima 10.06

Source: World Bank 2002.

Table 6.4 **Leak #3: Worst offenders**

VdL district committee	Leakage (%)	VdL district committee	Leakage (%)
Lima		**Rest of Peru *(cont.)***	
1	84.5	11	38.9
2	57.4	12	34.8
3	48.2	13	34.0
4	44.8	14	34.0
5	43.8	15	31.8
6	24.4	16	29.4
Rest of Peru		17	28.6
1	63.7	18	27.8
2	55.1	19	27.2
3	53.2	20	26.7
4	49.6	21	25.4
5	47.4	22	24.3
6	47.2	23	23.5
7	41.7	24	23.0
8	40.1	25	22.6
9	40.0	26	22.3
10	40.0	27	20.7

Source: World Bank 2002.

in the transfer from local government to civil society is obtained by examining the worst offenders. The national averages hide some very important information (table 6.4). There are twenty-seven districts/VdL committee pairs (about a tenth of the total surveyed) with leakages in excess of 20 percent and ten pairs that exceed 40 percent. In the case of such top-ranked worst offenders, the beneficiaries receive thirty-six cents of every dollar without taking into consideration all the leakages in prior segments of the chain of distribution.[8] A possible explanation of these very high leakages is that in some cases municipalities may make changes to the allocations to every committee, keeping one product already assigned for later distribution. Such informal arrangements significantly diminish transparency of the program and should be prohibited.

"MILK" LEAKAGE STAGE 4: COMMITTEE TO BENEFICIARY/HOUSEHOLD

Direct beneficiaries are those effectively used to define the amount of the rations to be distributed by the committee. Estimation of this leakage was done by calculating the monetary value of each product (using municipal price figures) and adding these up.[9] This allowed a comparison of the monetary value of the amount of all the products received by the VdL committee per direct beneficiary with the monetary value of the amount received by the individual households per beneficiary (excluding the committees that distribute prepared products). The first variable was obtained from the quantities declared by the mothers' committee representative in the VdL committee survey (in the four committees surveyed in each municipality). The second variable would be obtained from the quantities declared by the direct beneficiaries' household representative in the beneficiaries' household survey (in the four households surveyed for each VdL committee).

The leakage at this level is quite high. On average, over a quarter of the product is lost at this stage in Peru outside of the Lima area (table 6.5). Leaks are markedly more serious in urban districts (34 percent), in provincial capitals (40 percent), and in large districts (29 percent).

"MILK" LEAKAGE STAGE 5: WITHIN THE HOUSEHOLD
(DILUTION OF THE RATION)

This leakage was estimated using household-level data based on a customized survey at that level. As a final stage of the research effort, the fieldwork team visited four households per committee in order to quantify the amounts of the in-kind VdL transfers that actually reach the intended direct beneficiaries. The leak attributed to "beneficiary dilution" is defined at the household level as one minus the percentage of household members who consume VdL products, who are official direct beneficiaries (table 6.6).

Results make clear that, upon reaching the households, there is considerable dilution. On average, target beneficiaries receive only 41 percent of the ration that arrives at the household (not taking into account all

Table 6.5 **Leak #4: Vaso de Leche program (% at household level)**	
Total	26.70
Not poor	26.67
Poor	19.21
Extremely poor	32.19
Urban	34.53
Rural	25.01
Small	24.41
Medium	22.83
Large	29.63
More accessible	25.71
Less accessible	28.32
Nonprovincial capital	22.72
Provincial capital	40.31
Number of observations	**488**

Source: World Bank 2002.

Table 6.6 **Leak #5: Beneficiary household level (%)**	
Total	58.89
Not poor	59.93
Poor	57.89
Extremely poor	59.15
Urban	59.26
Rural	58.70
Small	59.01
Medium	61.46
Large	57.90
More accessible	60.75
Less accessible	56.11
Nonprovincial capital	58.69
Provincial capital	59.32
Observations	**985**

Source: World Bank 2002.

the losses associated with earlier leakages). This dilution effect occurs because in most cases the beneficiaries do not receive their rations directly from the committee, but because the children receive the rations filtered through their mothers (and in some cases the father), who pick up the total rations allocated to the household for later distribution.

"MILK" LEAKAGES ACROSS ALL STAGES OF THE TRANSFER PROCESS

In sum, the survey reveals that targeted beneficiaries get on average twenty-nine cents of each dollar initially transferred by the central government (see fig. 6.1). The survey surprisingly indicates the leak is much higher in the bottom (VdL committees and households, leaks 4–5) levels rather than in the top (central government and municipalities, leaks 1–3) levels of the ladder. Indeed, most of the leakage occurs during the last phase of the process, at the household level.

This finding challenges the predominant view that local, private organizations are more accountable in managing resources than official organizations. Leaks clearly affect the poorest, urban, and provincial municipalities more than others. Leakages are also larger in rural areas than in urban when the focus is on leakages 1–3, but urban leakages are higher in leakages 4, 5, and 6. Accessibility of the town and municipal vs. principal capital have no consistent pattern across the leakage types (table 6.7).

Figure 6.1   **How milk disappears in the Vaso de Leche program**

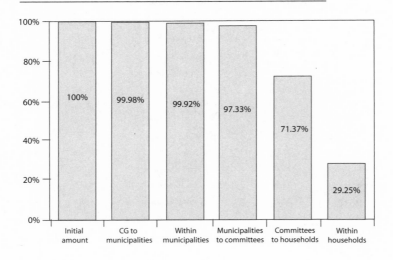

Table 6.7   **Summary of Vaso de Leche leakages (%)**

	Leak 1	Leak 2	Leak 3	Leak 4	Leak 5	Combined
Total	0.02	0.63	2.59	26.70	58.89	70.84
Not poor	0.00	0.13	0.54	26.67	59.93	70.81
Poor	0.00	1.36	5.67	19.21	57.89	68.34
Extremely poor	0.12	1.30	5.22	32.91	59.15	74.39
Urban	0.00	0.42	1.26	34.53	59.26	73.77
Rural	0.05	0.85	4.52	25.01	58.70	70.70
Small	0.11	0.05	2.83	24.41	59.01	69.94
Medium	0.00	0.59	4.23	22.83	61.46	71.68
Large	0.00	0.84	2.25	29.63	57.90	71.29
Accessible	0.00	0.54	2.31	25.71	60.75	71.67
Remote	0.09	0.82	3.70	28.32	56.11	69.98
Municipal	0.04	0.87	3.10	22.72	58.69	69.35
Provincial capital	0.00	0.21	1.97	40.31	59.32	76.25
Number of observations	**95**	**76**	**320**	**488**	**985**	**985**

Source: World Bank 2002.

IMPLICATIONS

A major lesson to learn from the VdL experience is that a social program, with a presumed high degree of participation of community leaders grouped in a committee, can be inefficient and unaccountable to both its agents (constituent beneficiaries) and to its principal (municipal authorities). In the process, efforts to realize the original goal of the program can be frustrated.

In the short term, suggested priority actions should focus on amending regulations to enforce accountability to the municipalities and committees: (1) review VdL regulations, particularly regarding products to be distributed and the form of distribution, so as to make the list of selected milk derivatives shorter and more homogeneous, and thus raise chances of improving the nutritional impact of the program; (2) establish a proper registry of VdL beneficiaries, if possible supported by SIAF (Integrated Financial Management System); (3) undertake information campaigns and training sessions to VdL committees and individual beneficiaries to raise their awareness of new information available and the rules; and (4) undertake surprise audits of worst offenders (municipalities and committees) in the near term, so as to eliminate excessive overpricing and major deviations. The implementation of the above actions requires a significant overhaul of the system and should be accompanied by the design of a new comprehensive framework for food supplementary programs in Peru.

The survey findings do send up an important warning signal: leakages in Peru are significant and far more pervasive and extensive at the bottom of the chain than at the top. From the entire amount of public funds intended for the VdL program, barely 29 percent get to their intended beneficiaries. This does not mean that 71 cents from each dollar are fully lost in corruption costs. Instead, many resources get leaked away through a combination of administrative costs, ineligible products and beneficiaries, and other modalities.

The survey results also challenge the predominant view of the last decade that organizations that are closer to the people they serve are inherently better in service delivery. This prevalent assumption has justified bottom-up programs, with a specific and strong emphasis on nongovernmental organizations and local participation. The core of the theorizing and research was that local organizations could overcome one of the central weaknesses of official institutions in developing countries—namely, their lack of accountability. Citizens who could directly observe, talk to, and even argue with those providing them key services would be able to hold those individuals and institutions accountable for their actions. In contrast, remote, faceless central governments are seen as beyond citizen reach and thus dominated by self-serving, rent-seeking elites. Our research shows that we should not assume that the relationship between accountability and development is always linear and positive. Problems are especially acute when asymmetric information, poor transparency, or low management capacity occurs at different levels—that is, beneficiaries, intermediate or final, have limited access to know how many resources they should receive from authorities and what procedures they should employ. In this scenario, citizens so dominate some development programs at the local level that they may divert resources from their original purpose, without being held accountable or sanctioned for doing so, because the principal agents—the official authorities, central or municipal in this case—do not know about it and may vitiate, even nonvoluntarily, the effects of these development programs. We find that citizens placed in direct control of a development program may, like the official authorities they are supplanting, distort its goal or become rent-seekers benefiting not the collectivity but their own interests, even though following their own rules is presumed to benefit their own community. The evidence amassed in this study enables us to compare diversions (referred to here as "leakage") of public resources for private gain or for a distorted purpose at each level of the public assistance "food chain." We also find that the lower we go down the chain, the *greater* the diversion.

These results merit a caveat. It could be argued that the larger size of leakages found at the end of the ladder may be due to measurement errors associated with the more dispersed nature of the evidence supporting them (written records in leakages 1, 2, and 3 versus a combination of written records and interviews in leakage 4 and a survey alone in leakage 5). Repeated use of this auditing technique in tracking transfers would give us a better sense of whether these household survey results vary widely across repeated applications to the same program. In turn, it should be noted that our findings regarding the level of leakage prior to the household level is similar to previous findings on international experience.

In sum, what we have is a classical setting of asymmetric information (and influence) between successive stages of a so-called principal-agent problem. Depending on the level, the principal might be the official authorities, and the agents might be the committees; or, in a given community, the principal might be the committee and the agents might be the beneficiary households. In both cases, the agents may behave in such a way that they divert resources from the principal's original intentions, since they have little knowledge of the original transfer received by the principal, and are neither accountable, nor sanctioned because of the diversion of resources. Thus, agents lack information about the exact amounts and management of resources by the principal and, conversely, the principal lacks the capacity to assess and held them accountable for such diversion. If more programs were subject to the sort of oversight accounting used in this study, improved information could help to reduce these information asymmetries, thereby helping the programs to become more effective in reaching their goals.

APPENDIX: TECHNICAL DEFINITIONS OF LEAKAGES IN THE VASO DE LECHE PROGRAM

LEAK 1: FROM THE CENTRAL GOVERNMENT TO THE MUNICIPALITIES

Leak 1 is defined as the percentage of the transfer reported by the MEF that is unaccounted for by the municipality. We compare the amount the MEF reports as outgoing with the amount the municipality reports to have received. This leakage is estimated with municipal-level data from December 2001.

$$\text{Leak}^1 = 1 - \left[\frac{\text{Amt. Municipality Reported}}{\text{Amt. MEF Reported}} \right]$$

LEAK 2: WITHIN MUNICIPALITY

Leak 2 is defined as the percentage of the amount transferred to the municipality "i" from the central government for the month of December 2001 that is unaccounted for by the total expenses of the municipality for that month (in terms of products purchased for the VdL program). Leak 2 is zero if the municipality spends the entirety of the resources available in December 2001 under the VdL program on products to be distributed by the program. This leakage is estimated based on municipal-level data.

$$\text{Leak}^2_{MUN} = 1 - \left[\frac{\sum_i (\text{Quantity}_i \times \text{Price}_i)}{\text{Transfer Amount}_{MUN}} \right]$$

LEAK 3: FROM MUNICIPALITY TO VDL COMMITTEES

Leak 3 is defined as the percentage of the amount listed in the municipality not accounted for by the VdL committee. This leakage is estimated using municipal and committee data and is computed at the committee level. This leakage indicates how much is lost in this segment of distribution but does not allow one to attribute it to one of the two parties involved at this stage. In other words, we estimate the leakage from the municipality to the individual VdL committees, but we do not know if the leakage is a result of misappropriation or inefficiencies of the municipality, the advisory committee, or both.

$$\text{Leak}^3_{\text{COM}} = 1 - \left[\frac{\text{Amount Received}_{\text{COM}}}{\text{Amount Listed in Municipal Roster}_{\text{COM}}} \right]$$

LEAK 4: FROM VDL COMMITTEES TO BENEFICIARIES/HOUSEHOLDS

Leak 4 is the loss due to the difference between what VdL committees receive according to beneficiaries registered and what they actually distribute to households. The estimation of the leakage at this level is done by calculating the monetary value of each of the products (using municipal price figures) and adding these up. This allows a comparison of the monetary value of the amount of all the products received by the VdL committee per beneficiary with the monetary value of the amount received by the individual households per beneficiary (excluding the committees that distribute prepared products). The first variable is obtained from the quantities declared by the mothers' committee representative in the VdL committee survey (in the four committees surveyed in each municipality). The second variable is obtained from the quantities declared by the beneficiaries' household representative in a beneficiary household survey (on four households surveyed for each VdL committee).

$$\text{Leak}^4 = 1 - \left[\frac{\left(\dfrac{\sum_i (\text{Quantity}_i \times \text{Price}_i)}{\text{Beneficiary}} \right)_{\text{HH}}}{\left(\dfrac{\sum_i (\text{Quantity}_i \times \text{Price}_i)}{\text{Beneficiary}} \right)_{\text{COM}}} \right]$$

LEAK 5: INSIDE THE HOUSEHOLD

Leak 5 is attributed to beneficiary dilution at the household level. It is defined as one minus the percentage of household members who consume VdL products and are direct beneficiaries. This leakage is estimated using household-level data.

$$\text{Leak}^5_{\text{HH}} = 1 - \left[\frac{\text{Beneficiaries}_{\text{HH}}}{\text{Consumers}_{\text{HH}}} \right]$$

ADAM BRINEGAR

7 Evaluating Citizen Attitudes about Corruption in Chile

In 2002 and 2003, a series of corruption scandals erupted in Chile—
including the bribery of legislators and government officials to obtain licenses for vehicle refitting plants, *sobresueldos* (overpayments)
to public officials, and the use of the Public Works Ministry (MOP)
to raise campaign funds. These events unfolded in the least corrupt
country in Latin America, according to Transparency International's 2005 Bribe Payer's Index (BPI) (see fig. 7.1). While the scandals
were relatively minor by Latin American standards—involving sums
of just $13,500 and $20,000 compared to $5 million in a Senate brib-
ery scandal in Argentina (see Bermúdez and Gasparini 2001 on the
Argentine scandals)—they nonetheless caused a major political up-
heaval in Chile. The ruling coalition, the Concertación, had held
power since the return to democracy in 1989, but its preeminence
had been challenged in the presidential and legislative elections held
between 1999 and 2001. This political backdrop fanned Concertación concerns about the potential effects of the scandals on their
ability to win the 2004 municipal and 2005 presidential and legislative elections.[1] In response to the scandals, both the left and the right
in January 2003 agreed to a package of anticorruption reforms that
included the professionalization of the civil service and campaign finance reform.[2]

For analysts of public opinion, the corruption scandals provide a rich opportunity to refine theories on the roles of partisanship, information, and economic performance on citizen attitudes about corruption. Recent analyses of public opinion and corruption have found that government affiliation (Anderson and Tverdova 2004; Davis, Camp, and Coleman 2004; Seligson 2002) and political information (Blais et al. 2005; Canache and Allison 2005; Zaller 1992) influence citizens' attitudes about corruption, especially their perceived level of corruption in the government. These studies, however, do not fully untangle the effects of partisanship on the corruption reform process or attitudes about the perceived level of corruption, reform, and vote choice. Also, in terms of vote choice, extant studies do not generally test for the mediating role of other issues, such as economic performance, which may be especially salient in developing countries because of the preeminence of public policy issues other than corruption, such as poverty and unemployment. Vote choice analyses also have largely focused on the direct effect of corruption on vote choice and not evaluations of the government's response to scandal (Blais et al. 2005; Peters and Welch 1980).

Finally—and importantly for understanding the effects of scandal on public opinion—the information theory of corruption's political dynamics is actually composed of two separate arguments that have not been analyzed together. One argument claims that citizens can better predict the amount of perceived corruption in government if they are more politically informed, which Canache and Allison (2005) find for Chile in their analysis of data from the World Values Survey. A second argument asserts that citizens will be more likely to hold politicians accountable for corruption scandals when they are better informed (Blais et al. 2005).

In Chile, these two perspectives were at odds with each other because of the country's relatively low levels of corruption—which was publicized heavily in the news media and understandably championed by members of the Concertación—and the equally heavily publicized scandals. This begs the question: Does a country's internationally low level of corruption—or the perception of citizens about low levels of corruption because of elite discourse—mitigate accountability? One of the major arguments in favor of cross-national surveys of corruption is that they change the elite discourse in countries that are highly corrupt in favor of greater accountability; elite discourse has been found to play a major role in shaping public opinion attitudes (Zaller 1992). But could these surveys also negatively affect the elite discourse in countries that are less corrupt?

Chile is remarkable for its relatively low levels of corruption in terms of both its income bracket (Treisman 1998) and for the Latin American region as a whole (see fig. 7.1). Yet, Chile is rarely studied by contemporary scholars of political corruption, with a few notable exceptions (Rehren 1996, 2000; Montinola 1996). Prior to the 1980s, however, Chile received substantial attention from scholars of bureaucratic politics because of the centrality of clientelism to Chile's pre-1973 political parties (Valenzuela 1977). Clientelism has traditionally been seen as the primary engine of corruption in Chile, arising first out of the oligarchic politics of the 1891–1924 period and then the highly competitive, populist, and electorally fractious politics of the post-1924 era. In the earlier period, clientelism was selective and focused on providing jobs to the incipient middle class and families of the political elite. The state was also relatively small with just 26,000 bureaucrats in 1925, and corruption—while heavy—mostly centered on the areas of currency exchange, credits, and tariffs. By 1970, partly as a consequence of more mass-based politics, the bureaucracy had swelled to 300,000 workers (Rehren 2000).

While the bureaucracy remained relatively competent, political parties managed to penetrate the state considerably, allowing them to use the bureaucracy for political advantage. A 1965 survey of 575 bureaucrats in twelve ministries found that political parties were perceived to be a more important influence than the central government on the bureaucracy (Petras 1969). Political parties were able to maintain their influence despite the president holding the power to nominate officials through an informal norm called the "*pase de partido*," which allowed parties to choose some of the nominees for public posts (Rehren 2000). At the same time, some notable reforms emerged out of Chile's competitive party system, including the creation of the famous *controlaría general de la república* (comptroller general of the republic), which provides, among many other functions, ex-ante- and ex-post-review of the legality of government actions (Valenzuela 1977).

While clientelism and its attendant corruption were important in gaining political support, Chile substantially benefited from a cultural norm against ostentatious displays of wealth and the general reluctance of presidents to steal from office for personal wealth (Allende 2003). Former dictator Augusto Pinochet, however, eventually was found to have violated this prohibition. A U.S. Senate investigation in 2004 revealed that

Source: Data are from Transparency International press releases (see http://www.transparency.org/surveys /index.html#cpi). Not all countries have full time-series data.

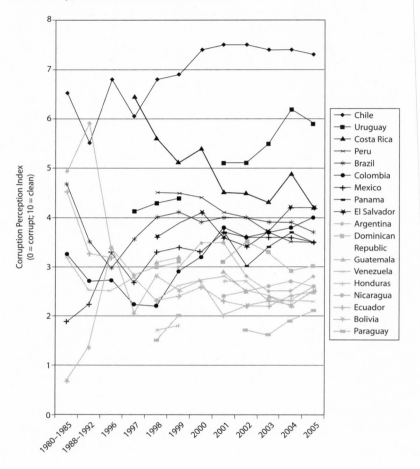

Pinochet had deposited $8 million in proceeds from off-budget spending and kickbacks on arm sales into a secret bank account at Riggs Bank in Washington, D.C.

Although Pinochet may have used the state for corrupt purposes, clientelism went into sharp decline after 1973, owing to neoliberal reform (Rehren 2000) and the suspension of normal party politics. After redemocratization, clientelism was not restored to pre-1973 levels for several reasons. Chile's new electoral system favors the development of more programmatic parties (Montinola 1996). In addition, the continued influence of neoliberalism limits the scope for clientelist activity. Critically, a constitutional provision prohibits politicians from increasing the president's budget. More generally, the weakness of Congress limits its ability to perform casework (Siavelis 2000). In addition, Pinochet introduced a more comprehensive merit-based civil service reform than was possible in the fragmented pre-1973 political system, further increasing the quality of the Chilean bureaucracy (Geddes 1994). Hence, somewhat paradoxically, Chile's low corruption levels may be a function of both its long republican tradition—which led to the establishment of effective government institutions, like the comptroller general—and neoliberal authoritarian legacies, which have reduced opportunities for corruption and clientelism since re-democratization. On the other hand, the reduction in clientelism in Chile may have made it more difficult for the legislature to perform its proper oversight role of the executive (Siavelis 2000), thus constraining its ability to ensure horizontal accountability.

The decline of clientelism also fed into a widespread belief that Chile's corruption problem was minor. This belief was supported further by Chile's relatively privileged position on cross-national rankings of corruption, political risk, and international competitiveness, such as the Growth Competition Rankings of the World Economic Forum, in which Chile ranked 22nd out of 119 countries in 2005 (Lopez-Carlos, Porter, and Schwab 2005). To a certain extent, elite discourse about corruption in Chile was probably influenced by the actual long-term decline in corruption, but the international rankings helped reinforce the idea and provided a counterpoint to corruption charges. Nevertheless, corruption scandals in the 1990s and 2000s revealed that corruption in Chile—especially corruption involving political parties—is still thriving, albeit significantly less than in other countries in Latin America.

CORRUPTION SINCE RE-DEMOCRATIZATION

From substantive analysis of press accounts of corruption scandals in Chile,[3] corruption was much less prevalent than in other Latin American countries from re-democratization in 1990 to the 2003 reforms, but corruption was nonetheless important for rewarding supporters and funding political campaigns. Government supporters were awarded with high-level patronage jobs and often paid under-the-table *sobresueldos* to increase their salaries. Former President Ricardo Lagos himself received an extra $1,300 a month when he headed the Public Works Ministry.[4] Some businesses were extorted for bribes to be used for party activities; over-charging on public procurement contracts was also apparently used by the Concertación to fund political activities. Millions of dollars in credits granted by the Agricultural Development Institute, for example, were found to be illegal, and Lagos was accused of irregularly acquiring $11 million in education materials when he was education minister under former President Patricio Aylwin.[5] The center-right coalition was unable to take advantage of corrupt opportunities at the national level but benefited from their close association with business interests and the lack of campaign finance regulations. Hence, the Alianza frequently outspent the left in elections, leading to several failed attempts by the center-left to pass campaign finance reform, the most notable being in January 2001. In the 1990s, corruption scandals at the municipal level were widespread, with the *controlaría* making 241 charges of corruption in 1993 and 1994 (Rehren 1996). Rehren found through an analysis of these scandals that private businesses were implicated more frequently and substantively in corruption scandals than in the pre-1973 period.

Despite its relatively clean image internationally, political scandals have meant that Chile since re-democratization has been a hotbed of corruption allegations and anticorruption reforms. As Davis, Camp, and Coleman demonstrate, anticorruption reform in Chile is exceedingly partisan—perhaps the most partisan in the region, theoretically because of the polarization of the political system (Davis, Camp, and Coleman 2004). Chile's high level of partisanship, however, eventually gave way to consensus over reforms in 2003 after a series of widely publicized corruption scandals.

THE CORRUPTION SCANDALS OF 2002–2003

In 2003, the time period under study, the Concertación was deluged by a rash of corruption scandals. Caso Coimas (or "Bribery Case") involved six Concertación deputies and three government officials accused of receiving bribes in the allocation of licenses to operate vehicle-refitting plants in the state of Rancagua. Beyond the embarrassment to the Concertación, the case had immediate effects on the balance of power in the House of Deputies, as the six deputies had their parliamentary rights stripped on November 11, 2002, creating a temporary 57–57 balance in the lower house of the legislature. Eventually, three participants—Christian Pareto, Jaime Jiménez, and Eduardo Lagos—were declared ineligible for public jobs for six years and sentenced to fifty days in jail on a suspended sentence.

At the same time, the long-standing practice of *sobresueldos* became public. Former President Eduardo Frei even admitted to using the wage supplements. The *sobresueldos* originated from secret reserved funds in the budget and—much more problematically—from GATE, a front company set up by officials at the Ministry of Public Works (MOP) to pay wage supplements and to fund campaign activities. In addition to Caso Coimas and MOP-GATE, another prominent scandal involved Vínculos Para Invertir (Inverlink), a financial company that bribed officials at the state development agency, CORFO, to acquire and trade illegally certificates of deposit. Also, a secretary at the Central Bank sent confidential financial data to Inverlink, a scandal that resulted in the resignation of the Central Bank head, Carlos Massad.

In response, President Ricardo Lagos in November 2002 announced a series of executive and legislative measures to reduce corruption, which included increasing official salaries (thus ending *sobresueldos*), improving the auditing of public contracts, obligating judges and legislators to declare their finances, establishing transparency and limits on campaign finance, regulating lobbying, and strengthening the role of the comptroller general (Valdés-Prieto 2002). Subsequently, on January 30, 2003, a new package of forty-nine reforms was agreed to by both the Concertación and the Alianza. This package included a massive reduction in the number of patronage jobs appointed by the president, reducing them from three thousand to just six hundred. By the end of 2003, many of the most important anticorruption reforms—campaign finance reform, new rules for public contracts, and civil service reform—had been passed. Thus, two trends—low corruption cross-nationally and a relative upswing in the number of scandals in the 1990s—shaped the debate about corruption in Chile in 2002–3.

PUBLIC OPINION AND CORRUPTION IN CHILE

Public opinion about corruption in Chile is partisan, but it has not been a major political issue for the public since re-democratization. Figure 7.2 depicts the priority citizens have placed on corruption in Chile since 1992 compared to unemployment and poverty, using surveys conducted by the Centro de Estudios Públicos. Citizens were asked to prioritize the most important issues from a list of fifteen issues, and the total mentions were added to provide the data in the figures. At no point has more than 18 percent of the public included corruption in their assessment of Chile's

Figure 7.2 **Priorities of the Chilean public, 1992–2005**

Note: The data were compiled from public opinion studies conducted by the Centro de Estudios Públicos, beginning in December of 2002. Respondents were asked, "Which are the three problems that the government should dedicate its greatest effort to solving? Indicate only 3." The percentages in the table are a summary of the total number of mentions each issue received.

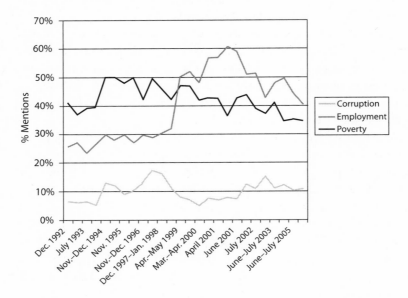

major priorities. However, the priority of corruption almost doubled between June 2002 (when 7.4 percent of the public prioritized corruption) and June–July 2003 (when it peaked at 15.5 percent). In general, the priority of corruption appears to follow scandal, with the other noticeable peak occurring in June 1997 after a prior, smaller bout of corruption scandals. Still, even during times of scandal, Chileans clearly prioritize other issues much higher than corruption.

In terms of voter preferences, from the perspective of the Concertación, popular support for the center-left fell from July 2002 to December 2002 from 43 percent to 35 percent, according to data from the Centro de Estudios de la Realidad Contemporánea (Latin American Monitor February 2003). This suggests that the Concertación may have been harmed by the scandals. As I mentioned earlier, the perception of potential damage worked to motivate a series of reforms designed to reduce the likelihood of future scandals.

In this section I shed light on the distinctly Chilean political dynamics of corruption by analyzing how the issues of partisanship, relatively low corruption, and different elite discourses on corruption affected citizens' attitudes about the priority of corruption, the level of corruption in government, reform, and vote choice during the 2002–2003 scandals. The analysis finds that partisanship indeed colored attitudes about reform and the priority of corruption but not the level of corruption in government. In terms of vote choice, attitudes about corruption did not directly affect vote choice but were mediated by economic performance and evaluations of the government's and opposition's response to scandal, suggesting the need for analysts of corruption to construct more sophisticated analyses of voter preferences. The latter finding also means that there is indeed a small electoral payoff associated with strong anticorruption actions (see Geddes 1994). On the other hand, given the complexity of reforms, citizens may not be able to induce politicians to develop strong reforms. Scandals in the mid-1990s, for example, resulted in higher levels of citizen interest in reform than in 2002–3, but the reforms—which did not fix campaign finance or professionalize the civil service—were weaker, with the most notable reform being a freedom of information act in 1999.[6]

THEORIES AND HYPOTHESES

The public opinion literature generally points to three major factors to explain differences among citizen attitudes about corruption: partisanship, information, and economic performance. The partisan argument (Anderson and Tverdova 2003; Davis, Camp, and Coleman 2004; and Seligson 2002) is that government affiliation strongly affects individual attitudes about corruption. We would thus expect that citizens will be more likely to prioritize corruption if they are members of the opposition than members of the government. In addition, opposition partisans will likely view corruption to be more important than incumbent partisans. Incumbent partisans should also be more likely to view anticorruption reforms as being adequate and, in general, should be more likely to accept the government's response to reform as appropriate.

In turn, information shapes perception in ways that can affect corruption attitudes.[7] In terms of the information theory, one argument claims that citizens will prioritize corruption higher and believe corruption is more strongly present in the government when there is scandal, *if* they pay attention to the news (Blais et al. 2005). Another argument is that informed citizens are likely to perceive less corruption when there is less corruption (Canache and Allison 2005), presumably because of the publication of cross-national studies on corruption or other salient elements of elite discourse.

In Chile, the effects of information may be more ambiguous on the priority of corruption, because Chile is a low corruption country. In effect, citizens may not prioritize corruption even if they are well informed, because they understand that corruption in Chile is minor compared to other countries. However, well-informed citizens may still believe that corruption is more important than less-informed citizens because of scandal. Politicians in Chile are well aware of the different frames. In the same article, Christian Democrat Alejandro Foxley (of the ruling Concertación coalition) argued that his party ought to propose a corruption reform agenda with the aim of specifically improving Chile's transparency scores, while UDI Senator Evelyn Matthei (of the opposition Alianza) argued that Chile should compare itself over time because of the increase in corruption in Chile over the past ten years (*El Mercurio,* October 21, 2004). Thus, if more-informed citizens prioritize corruption less in Chile and are less likely to believe that bribery is widespread in government, we would expect that the actual level of corruption frame has more resonance than the decline frame. On the other hand, if more-informed citizens prioritize corruption more in Chile and are more likely to believe that bribery is widespread in government, we would expect that the decline frame holds more resonance than the actual level of corruption frame. A lack of significance would indicate that the frames negate each other.

Given the importance of economic performance in most models of vote choice (Zaller 2002), it is also possible that citizens have different attitudes about corruption when they perceive the economy to be weak. This tests another argument made by international organizations dedicated to fighting corruption—that providing specific information about the reduction in corruption may result in citizen action (Kaufmann 2005). Respondents who are aware of the consequences of corruption may believe that corruption is a bigger problem and may be more likely to vote against the government. Hence, economic performance is theoretically likely to have a mediating effect on attitudes about corruption. Another consideration in terms of vote choice is how perceptions of government response to scandal affect voting behavior, which allows politicians the opportunity to take reform actions and for citizens to react to their performance. A positive relationship between perceptions of government performance to scandal and vote choice would indicate that politicians ought to be responsive to citizens, even if they have some latitude in the "quality" of reforms.

Given the literature on public opinion and corruption, we thus make the following hypotheses:

H1: Opposition party status, more information (following the scandal frame), and lower perceptions of economic performance will increase respondents' priority of corruption.

H2: Opposition party status, more information, and lower perceptions of economic performance will increase respondents' perception of bribe-taking within the government.

H3: Government party status and positive perceptions of economic performance will lead to more positive evaluations of the efficacy of reforms.

H4: Sympathy for the Concertación, positive evaluations of the performance of the Concertación on scandal, and positive perceptions of economic performance will increase the probability of respondents voting for the Concertación.

H4b: Higher perceptions of government corruption alone and in interaction with perceptions of economic performance will increase the probability of respondents' voting for the Concertación.

DATA, METHOD, AND MODELS

The data used to analyze these hypotheses are from surveys conducted by the Centro de Estudios Públicos in December 2002 and June–July 2003.[8] The December 2002 survey features the most questions related to corruption and was conducted immediately after the initial revelations of scandal in fall 2002 and the government's official response to the crisis. The June–July 2003 survey was conducted at the height of the furor over the scandals in 2003 and before a devastating pedophilia scandal in 2003 that significantly damaged the image of the Alianza. Both surveys include questions that allow us to analyze the relationship between perceptions of government performance on the corruption scandals and hypothetical vote choice in legislative elections.

The 2002 poll surveyed 1,505 Chileans and was conducted between December 7 and December 25, 2002, with a margin of error of ± 3 percentage points at the 95 percent confidence level. The 2003 poll surveyed 1,503 Chileans and was conducted between June 28 and July 17, 2005, with a margin of error of ± 3 percentage points at the 95 percent confidence level. In both cases, respondents were interviewed in their homes.

Five regression models were estimated using five different dependent variables measuring the priority that citizens place on corruption, their perception of the amount of corruption in government, the efficacy of reforms, and projected vote choice in legislative elections (in both 2002 and 2003). The data were analyzed using logistic regression analysis in STATA 9. Predicted probabilities were estimated using *Clarify* (see King, Tomz, and Wittenberg 2000), a set of STATA macros available at http://gking.harvard.edu/stats.shtml. The coding of all variables is located in the appendix.

For the priority of corruption, respondents were asked, "Which are the three problems that the government should dedicate the greatest effort to solving?" The variable is coded 1 if the respondent mentions corruption and 0 if they do not. For the perception of the amount of corruption, respondents were asked, "How extensive do you believe bribes and corruption are in Chile?" Responses ranged along a four-point scale on which 1 signifies almost no bureaucrats are involved in bribery and 4 indicates almost all bureaucrats are involved in bribery. For the perception of the efficacy of reforms, respondents were asked, "And, in general, do you believe that the measures proposed by the Government to combat corruption are going to take shape?" For reform, 0 indicates that reform will not take shape, and 1 that reform will take shape. Finally, for vote choice, in both studies respondents were asked, "If the parliamentary elections were next Sunday, for which of the following political parties would you vote?[9] Parties of the Concertación are coded as 1, and parties of the Alianza 0.

The models for priority of corruption and the level of bribes are the same. The independent variables are partisanship—measured with dummy variables for the Concertación, Alianza, and independents—perceptions of retrospective and prospective performance and a factor of respondents' use of information. Unfortunately, the best information variable (Zaller 1992)—citizens' knowledge of political institutions—is unavailable in this data set. Thus, the information variables used are based on the level of respondents' use of information (e.g., frequency of discussing politics with friends). As controls, relevant demographic variables—sex, age, and wealth—were estimated, as well as a dummy variable for Rancagua, because respondents from that state may be more familiar and/or concerned with the corruption allegations, given that the bribery scandal involved vehicle refitting plants in the state.[10] For reform, the model also includes a dummy variable for whether respondents would have liked the UDI's Joaquín Lavín—at the time the frontrunner in the 2005 presidential race—to be the next president, because Lavín supporters furthermore might have more negative attitudes about the corruption reforms than nonsupporters.

In the vote choice models, perceptions of retrospective and prospective performance, partisanship, scores on the bribes and priority of corruption variables and evaluations of the performance of the Concertación and the Alianza with respect to corruption are estimated. The controls are demographic variables, ideology, and Rancagua.

RESULTS AND ANALYSIS OF THE MODELS

Tables 7.1 through 7.5 present the results of the models. For the priority of corruption, only Alianza and sex are significant; importantly, information and evaluations of economic performance have no effect on perceptions of the priority of corruption. This indicates that, in Chile, corruption's priority is a function of partisanship, with opposition supporters prioritizing corruption highly, while government supporters do not.

In terms of bribes, however, partisanship is almost insignificant and information is insignificant, while demographics and economic performance are significant. The lack of a highly significant effect for partisan-

Table 7.1 **Logistic regression results for priority of corruption**

	Logit coefficient	Predicted probability (minimum-maximum)
Retrospective	.0218	.0089
Prospective	−.153	−.017
Information	.0622	.013
Sex	−.414*	−.0211
Age	−.022	−.00613
Education	.076	.033
Wealth	.0023	.013
Independents	−.790	−.013
Alianza	.735***	.044
Concertación	.303	.017
Rancagua	−.009	.004
Number	1407	
Pseudo R^2	.0315	

* < .10. ** < .05. *** < .01.
Source: Data is from Encuesta CEP No. 44, Estudio Nacional de Opinión Pública No. 16—Tercera Serie, December 2002 from the Centro de Estudios Públicos (http://www.cepchile.cl/bannerscep/bdatos_encuestas_cep/base_datos.php). Predicted probabilities were estimated using Clarify in STATA 9. Question used (P1): "¿Cuáles son los tres problemas a los que debería dedicar el mayor esfuerzo en solucionar el Gobierno?"

Table 7.2 **Ordered logistic regression results for bribes**

	Ordered logit coefficient	Predicted probability (minimum-maximum bribes = 4)
Retrospective	−.19***	−.149
Prospective	−.34***	−.141
Sex	.058	.011
Age	−.006**	−.091
Education	−.0741***	−.118
Wealth	.002	.055
Independents	.013	.000
Alianza	−.000	−.001
Concertación	−.303*	−.0609
Information	−.303	.0102
Rancagua	−.138	−.0274
Number	1323	
Pseudo R^2	.0245	

* < .10. ** < .05. *** < .01.
Source: Data is from Encuesta CEP No. 44, Estudio Nacional de Opinión Pública No. 16—Tercera Serie, December 2002 from the Centro de Estudios Públicos (http://www.cepchile.cl/bannerscep/bdatos_encuestas_cep/base_datos.php). Predicted probabilities were estimated using Clarify in STATA 9. Question used (P21): "De acuerdo a las siguientes alternativas, ¿cuán extendida cree used que están en Chile las coimas y la corrupción?"

Table 7.3 **Logistic regression results for reform**

	Logit coefficient	Predicted probability (minimum-maximum)
Retrospective	.3063***	.294
Prospective	.732***	.346
Sex	.016	.003
Age	−.002	−.044
Education	−.135***	−.259
Wealth	−.000	−.017
Independents	.055	.015
Alianza	−.539**	−.132
Concertación	.826***	.201
Information	.101	.086
Lavín	−.33	−.082
Rancagua	.577**	.138
Number	1184	
Pseudo R^2	0.1401	

*< .10.   **< .05.   ***< .01.

Source: Data is from Encuesta CEP No. 44, Estudio Nacional de Opinión Pública No. 16—Tercera Serie, December 2002 from the Centro de Estudios Públicos (http://www.cepchile.cl/bannerscep/bdatos_encuestas_cep/base_datos.php). Predicted probabilities were estimated using Clarify in STATA 9. Question used (P26): "Y, en general, ¿usted cree que las medidad propuestas por el Gobierno para combatir estos hechos se van a concretar?"

Table 7.4 **Logistic regression results for vote choice in legislative elections, 2002**

	Logit coefficient	Predicted probability (minimum-maximum)
Retrospective	.340**	.304
Prospective	.268	.133
Sex	−.129	−.031
Age	.009	.148
Education	.0023	.006
Wealth	.002	.048
Independents	−.017	−.004
Alianza	−1.37***	−.317
Concertación	1.61***	.375
Bribes	−.12	−.089
Priority	−.12	−.036
Concertación evaluation	.219***	.853
Alianza evaluation	−.439***	−.848
Rancagua	.313	.074
Ideology	.276***	−.445
Number	683	
Pseudo R^2	.515	

*< .10.   **< .05   ***< .01.

Source: Data is from Encuesta CEP No. 44, Estudio Nacional de Opinión Pública, December 2002 from the Centro de Estudios Públicos (http://www.cepchile.cl/bannerscep/bdatos_encuestas_cep/base_datos.php). Predicted probabilities were estimated using Clarify in STATA 9. Question used (P11): "Si el próximo domingo hubiera elecciones parlamentarias, ¿por cuál de los siguientes partidos políticos votaría Ud.?"

ship and information may be the most important findings for the bribery variable. In effect, the opposition prioritizes corruption higher, *even though they are no more likely to believe government corruption is widespread*, perhaps reflecting the low level of corruption in Chile. The insignificance of information runs counter to the extant literature linking information to attitudes about scandal and corruption. In effect, citizens may be internalizing both frames from political elites, and they are negating each other.

For the reform variable, economic performance, partisanship, and Ran-

Table 7.5 **Logistic regression results for vote choice in legislative elections, 2003**

	Logit coefficient	Predicted probability (minimum-maximum)
Retrospective	1.414***	.680
Prospective	.510***	.201
Sex	.435*	.084
Age	.008	.006
Education	−.0412	−.1131
Wealth	−.003	−.067
Independents	−.806*	−.176
Alianza	−1.76***	−.375
Concertación	1.11***	.209
Bribes	.732	.435
Priority	.0479	.117
Concertación evaluation	.383***	.422
Alianza evaluation	−.446***	−.478
Rancagua	1.00	.126
Ideology	.647***	.466
Retrospective* bribes	−.379**	
Number	681	
Pseudo R^2	.499	

*< .10.   **< .05.   ***< .01.
Source: Data is from Encuesta CEP No. 45, Estudio Nacional de Opinión Pública, June–July, 2003 from the Centro de Estudios Públicos (http://www.cepchile.cl/bannerscep/bdatos_encuestas_cep/base_datos.php). Predicted probabilities were estimated using *Clarify* in STATA 9. Question used (P11): "Si el próximo domingo hubiera elecciones parlamentarias, ¿por cuál de los siguientes partidos políticos votaría Ud.?"

cagua are significant. Partisanship reflects an expected distrust among the opposition and an expected trust among the governing party about reform. Economic performance suggests that citizens are less likely to view the prospects for reforms favorably if the government had failed them on other counts.

The results of the priority, bribery, and reform variables, then, provide a nuanced picture of attitudes about corruption. Partisanship results in a higher increase in the predicted probability of support for reform than priority of corruption on partisanship, with an increase of 20 percent for parties of the Concertación on the reform variable compared to a 4.4 percent increase for the Alianza on the priority of corruption variable. Priority of corruption and reform attitudes especially are thus powerfully colored by partisanship, even though co-partisans are no more likely to believe that bribery in government is high.

The vote choice models further clarify this picture. In December 2002, just after the first reforms were proposed and the scandals broke, neither bribery nor the prioritization of corruption variables affected projected vote choice. On the other hand, evaluations of the Concertación's and the Alianza's performance on reforms significantly affected vote choice, with stronger perceptions of the Concertación's performance leading to the greater likelihood of the respondent voting for the Concertación. An interaction term with retrospective economic performance and bribery was included but dropped in the final estimation because of colinearity and lack of significance. In the June–July 2003 poll, the same relationships are observed, but the interaction term is now significant, theoretically a result of citizens beginning to relate their perceptions of the economy with the ongoing bribery scandals. The discrepancy in findings between 2002 and 2003 is theoretically a product of the intense news coverage of the scandals in 2003, suggesting, perhaps, an important role for the media in transforming corruption into a politically important issue by linking it to other issues. Further work would investigate whether increased news coverage on corruption compared to cross-national excellence on corruption may explain the result. The results of this chapter regarding vote choice thus provides a more nuanced finding than Peters and Welch (1980) or Blais et al. (2005) because scandal affected vote choice only through citizen evaluations of the government's response to scandal and in interaction with economic performance and was not based on perceptions of the overall level of corruption in government. On the other hand, this finding may be a result of a powerful elite discourse in Chile that relies on international rankings to combat criticism of corruption. The data also analyze national vote rather than individual legislative districts, as is the case with Peters and Welch (1980).

Hence, attitudes about corruption in Chile during the scandals were extremely partisan and had little to do with respondents' beliefs about the actual level of corruption. In addition, attitudes about government corruption and its importance had little direct effect on vote choice and were instead mediated through evaluations of government performance and, in June 2003, after significant media coverage, through retrospective attitudes about government. What these findings mean is that accountability in Chile was heavily colored by partisanship and influenced by economic performance and government performance on corruption, while information had little effect on attitudes, presumably because of the existence of a cross-cutting elite discourse on corruption. In other analyses, information has been found to have even more significant than partisanship (Blais et al. 2005), which suggests that the Chilean case substantially deviated from the norm. However, politicians do have at least a rhetorical interest in reform. The importance of the government performance on scandal variable for citizens' vote choice may constitute enough of an electoral payoff that politicians are forced to initiate some reform, which is another major finding given the reforms that resulted from the scandals. On the other hand, if citizens do not hold politicians accountable for actual levels of the priority of corruption, and evaluations of corruption and reforms are heavily partisan, then it is difficult to believe that politicians need to implement *strong* reforms, because of the amount of time and attention it takes citizens to monitor the likely effectiveness of individual reforms.

RECONSIDERING HOW SCANDALS AFFECT VOTERS

Figure 7.3 illustrates a vote choice model of how government scandals impact vote choice for government. Evaluative conditions—attitudes about government's response to scandal, international discourse, and domestic discourse—are filtered through economic condition and partisanship to explain vote choice. International discourse here also influences domestic discourse and vice versa. Reflecting the contemporary context outlined in the introduction to this volume, this model differs from the Latin America of the past because of the presence of a very prominent international and domestic discourse on corruption. This international discourse clearly labels some countries as decidedly corrupt and others as less so. This international discourse—driven by both international governmental organizations and by international nongovernmental organizations—has a greater impact in many Latin American countries than it has in countries where the global discourse is weaker, such as the United States. In turn, the expansion of a free press in many countries stimulates a more active domestic discourse.

For those studying Latin America, the emergence in the last decade of the evaluative dimension—a real domestic discourse over corruption,

Figure 7.3 **Vote choice model of how corruption scandals impact votes for the government**

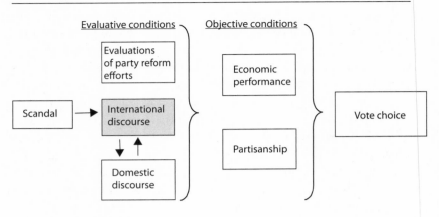

international discussion about corruption, and the ability to evaluate the quality of the government's response to scandal through greater transparency—and its interaction with Latin American partisanship, should become the focus of additional research on the subject of scandal and vote choice in Latin America. The Chilean case makes clear that this dimension is more complicated than simply "more transparency." Instead, international discourse appears to influence domestic discourse and evaluations. For other countries in Latin America, the effect may be opposite to what it has been in Chile—evaluations of government scandals may tilt against the government because of the interplay between domestic and international discourse. Evaluations are influenced by the relative newness of the free press and they are filtered through partisanship that—in many parts of Latin America—is based on clientelistic relationships and personalistic leaders (review chapters 2 and 4 in this volume) or, as in the case with Chile, remembrances of a corrupt and authoritarian past.

Thus, studying the impact of corruption scandals in Latin America is qualitatively different than it is in other regions of the globe. Researchers of Latin America may encounter considerable prediction error if they rely on models tying scandal and vote choice from the United States or Europe. The heightened visibility of an international discourse on corruption; the relative newness of the evaluative dimension in general; and the clientelistic, personalistic, and legacy characteristics of partisanship make the electoral impact of corruption different in Latin America. The presence of an international discourse may inflate or deflate the effect of domestic discourse and reaction to scandal. In turn, clientelism, personalism, and legacy characteristics may considerably raise the bar for scandals to affect vote choice, creating a need for far more aggressive civil society. In future research, analysts will need to model appropriately these dimensions in different Latin American countries in order to capture more fully the political dynamics of corruption scandals and their impact on anticorruption reform efforts.

APPENDIX: KEY FOR THE DECEMBER 2002 AND JUNE–JULY 2003 DATA SETS

Priority of corruption	1 = First mention 0 = No first mention	Bribes	1 = Almost no bureaucrats are involved in bribery 4 = Almost all bureaucrats are involved in bribery
Retrospective	1 = Very bad economic performance 5 = Very good economic performance	Reforms	1 = Reforms will take shape 0 = Reforms will not take shape
Prospective	1 = The economy will not improve 3 = The economy will improve	Sex	1 = Male 2 = Female
Independents	1 = Independents 0 = All others	Education	1 = No studies 9 = Completed university studies
Alianza	1 = Alianza supporter 0 = All others	Wealth	1–14, with higher values equaling more wealth
Concertación	1 = Concertación supporter 0 = All others	Age	1 = 18–24 2 = 25–34 3 = 35–54 4 = 55 and older
Information: Principal component factor of frequency of using:		Rancagua	1 = The state of Rancagua 0 = All other states
Television	1 = Never 2 = Sometimes 3 = Frequently	Concertación evaluation	4–28, higher values mean better performance of the index: Concertación on the scandals 28 means all parties in the Concertación are doing excellent.
Print	1 = Never 2 = Sometimes 3 = Frequently		
Political conversations with family	1 = Never 2 = Sometimes 3 = Frequently	Alianza evaluation index	2–14, higher values mean better performance of the Alianza; 14 means both the RN and the UDI are doing an excellent job.
Political conversations with friends	1 = Never 2 = Sometimes 3 = Frequently	Vote	1 = parties of the Concertación 0 = parties of the Alianza
Lavín	1 = Support for Lavín as the next president of Chile 0 = All others	Ideology	1 = right 9 = left

MATTHEW M. TAYLOR

8   Corruption, Accountability Reforms, and Democracy in Brazil

Over the past decade, the developmental effects of corruption have assumed a central role for academics and policy practitioners at both the local and national level, as well as within multinational institutions such as regional development banks and the World Bank. Corruption is no longer seen as a potentially beneficial instrument of economic and political development: an ample consensus exists that corruption does not grease the wheels of developing economies but rather creates distortions in policy choices, worsens the investment climate, and reduces overall societal well-being (e.g., Kaufmann, Kraay, and Zoido-Lobaton 1999; Lederman, Loayza, and Soares 2005; Mauro 1995; Rose-Ackerman 1999). Social scientists have also noted the pernicious effects of corruption on government and especially its deleterious effects in undermining the basic trust at the core of most conceptions of democracy (e.g., Bailey and Paras 2006; Gambetta 1988; Levi 1998; Warren 2004; see also the discussion by Bailey in chapter 3).

Corruption, as Klitgaard (1988) noted, is the outcome of monopoly plus discretion minus accountability (C=M+D-A). The preva-

I am grateful for constructive feedback received from John Bailey, Chris Blake, David Fleischer, Marcus André Melo, Steve Morris, Tony Pereira, Sérgio Praça, Bruno Speck, Jorge Zaverucha, and the participants in roundtables sponsored by the Goethe Institut, LASA, and the UFPE-Woodrow Wilson Center.

lence of corruption, in other words, is an outcome of the amount of power concentrated in any given political post, plus the discretion given to the postholder, minus the degree of accountability to which a corrupt postholder can expect to respond if corruption is detected. This chapter focuses on the accountability variable and the salience for democracy of the process by which responsibility for allegedly corrupt acts is allocated and accountability is enforced by public institutions, the private sector, and society as a whole.

Brazil offers an important case study of the disconnect between perceptions of corruption and perceptions of accountability: although by most measures it is far from the most corrupt country in Latin America, perceptions of the widespread absence of accountability have contributed to a marked frustration with the broader political system (for a comparison within the region, see the data presented in chapter 2). Most recently, three major scandals have rocked the nation during the Lula government: (1) the *mensalão* scandal, in which the government allegedly held together its legislative alliance by buying off congressmen with monthly payments; (2) the so-called *sanguessuga* (leech) scandal, a scheme—in which one in every eight members of Congress have been implicated—by which ambulances were included in the budget, at inflated prices, in return for kickbacks; and (3) a scandal in the state of Rondônia that has led to the arrests of the head of the state court, several prosecutors, and all but one state assembly member on charges of looting the state treasury.[1]

But Lula's government is not an exception to the rule; in fact, every one of his predecessors during the democratic regime has faced some sort of corruption scandal. Not surprisingly, corruption was one of the biggest themes of the 2006 electoral campaign, and there is no shortage of proposals for reform. Yet despite the growing consensus that something—anything—must be done, past experience suggests that overoptimism about the democracy-enhancing reforms that will emerge from scandals is all too common. One leading scholar, for example, wrote almost a decade and a half ago, referring to yet another congressional budget scandal: "I interpret the recent scandals and the accompanying uproar as the final gasps of traditional politics. First, the elites have been exposed in their perversion of the political process; second, the public is no longer willing to tolerate a state more satisfied with passing laws than with enforcing them honestly" (Da Matta 1993).

Sadly, this appears not to have been the case: despite the continued exposure of high-level corruption of the political process and growing levels of public dissatisfaction with the political system, little has been done to directly confront the problem.[2] A series of highly publicized corruption scandals in the government, and even the impeachment of President Collor in 1992, have generated little response: only a handful of nationally elected officials implicated in the country's perennial political corruption crises have gone to jail since the return to democracy, and of these none have faced prison terms of any consequence.[3] Particularly pernicious is the fact that high-profile corruption continues to be regularly exposed but seldom punished. As Brazilians like to say, most scandals "end up in pizza" (*acabam em pizza*), with investigations of political corruption turning up plenty of evidence of inappropriate and/or corrupt activity, but with few practical repercussions for those involved. What explains this perceived impunity within the political system, and what lessons can be drawn from the Brazilian case about the relationship between accountability and corruption in new democracies?

BRAZIL'S CORRUPTION EQUATION

BUREAUCRATIC, BUT NOT STATE, MONOPOLY

Beginning with the first of the right-hand variables in Klitgaard's equation, democratization has implied a shrinking monopoly over power by federal and state executives since 1985. While the president has extensive agenda-setting and legislative powers, he shares power with a broad range of players across the political system, and public policy decisions are extensively debated in Congress, the media, the courts, and other public venues. Indeed, policy reform has been an agonizing and tortuous process during the post-1985 democratic period, beset by slow legislative procedures, multiple and conflicting interest groups, and a number of potential institutional bottlenecks to policy change (e.g., Ames 2001; Lamounier 1996). While the executive branch has been able to craft majority coalitions that facilitate agenda-setting (Amorim Neto, Cox, and McCubbins 2003) and permit a considerable degree of governability (Figueiredo and Limongi 1999), the executive is far from the only relevant political actor in policy debates.[4] Furthermore, although many government bureaucracies are powers unto themselves, with considerable decision-making authority within specific policy domains, Brazil does not come close to the system-wide monopoly of political power prevalent in authoritarian or personalistic regimes (Klitgaard 1988; Shleifer and Vishny 1993). In other words, top-down monopoly of political power is absent in the broad political system, even though—as in other democracies—some public posts may offer the chance of monopoly rents to midlevel bureaucratic officeholders who control regulatory approvals or other bureaucratic bottlenecks in a specific policy domain.

DECLINING DISCRETION

In terms of the second variable—discretion—the most problematic issues lie in the rules governing spending disbursements and personnel appointments. The executive branch holds a great deal of discretionary power over spending decisions, most notably because it has considerable leeway to shift spending within the budget once it has been approved. Furthermore, the large number of political appointees—twenty thousand in the federal government alone—provides significant opportunities for the discretionary use of executive appointments. This budgetary and staffing discretion has become an especially important problem because it interacts perniciously with the weak political party system: in Brazil's open-list proportional representation system, the independence of candidates from the political parties to which they nominally belong strengthens individual politicians rather than parties and makes it quite possible (even likely) that a congressional representative elected from one party will switch allegiances midway through his or her term.[5] Oftentimes, such discretion in how to carry out one's congressional mandate is accompanied by clear incentives to sway representatives' positions, either licitly or illicitly, as in the *mensalão* scandal that has engulfed the Lula government. Discretion in carrying out political mandates has thus been a clear and pervasive source of opportunities for bargaining at all levels of probity.

Despite these significant problems, however, the dual processes of democratization and economic stabilization have considerably reduced individual politicians' and bureaucrats' discretion over the past two decades by increasing the transparency of government actions to the public and establishing clearer rules on government spending. Until the mid-1990s, hyperinflation, the complex financial arrangements it engendered, and the inflation-driven opacity of public accounts made it extraordinarily difficult to track budget outlays. A number of post-authoritarian reforms have strengthened the rules governing public spending, especially by restricting personnel spending and the indebtedness of state and local governments. Together with currency stabilization, these changes have significantly improved transparency: it is much easier to track public monies when they do not need to be converted daily to comparable amounts, and when the rules governing budgeting are written clearly and in a fashion that commits every governmental institution—from the executive branch to federally owned banks—to a standard set of clear and enforceable rules. While there is still much to be done (and the end goal is not to eliminate discretion entirely but simply to reduce the potential for abuse), the post-authoritarian construction of new institutions of fiscal control has reduced the arbitrary use of public funds (e.g., Nóbrega 2005, 281–309).

NEGLIGIBLE ACCOUNTABILITY?

The final variable in Klitgaard's equation is accountability and the manner by which it is imposed. Taylor and Buranelli (2007) argue that the problem with accountability at the federal level in Brazil is not so much the weakness of Brazilian institutions, but rather the imperfect orthodontia of Brazilian institutions of accountability. That is, even though all the institutional teeth (the individual accountability bureaucracies) exist and are capable of carrying out their mandated duties, the gaps and overlaps between institutions involved in the "web of mechanisms of accountability" (Mainwaring 2003, 30) tend to complicate the process of thwarting corrupt activities and creating accountability in the overall political system. As Speck (2002, 481; translation mine) notes in his comprehensive edited volume on corruption control in Brazil, *Caminhos da transparência*, the "higher number of institutions involved in corruption control certainly does not guarantee a good result . . . the emphasis should be not only on [individual institutions], but also on the concept of cooperation and integration between these various institutions and actors." The congested panoply of potential institutions of accountability, in other words, is no cure-all: these institutions must work smoothly together to share information and resources, if they are to ensure proper oversight, effective investigation, and timely sanction of illegal activities.

Granted, Brazilian accountability institutions are not as strong as might otherwise be desirable: the federal police budget is only 1 percent that of its rough analog, the U.S. Federal Bureau of Investigation; the Federal Prosecutorial Service (the Ministério Público da União) gets by with fewer than 350 prosecutors to carry out its work nationwide; and the Controladoria Geral da União (CGU), a body that is akin to an inspector general within the federal government, was created only in 2001. But by international standards, these institutions are still relatively strong and, despite some serious problems with internal corruption (most markedly in the federal police), their work is carried out in a professional fashion

Figure 8.1   **Stages of the accountability process**

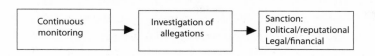

| Continuous monitoring | → | Investigation of allegations | → | Sanction: Political/reputational Legal/financial |

that follows clear rules in a predictable fashion. Furthermore, although they are not my focus here, the work of federal accountability institutions is complemented in the Brazilian case by a range of state-level institutions that are in some cases as strong and potentially important as their federal counterparts.[6]

The more serious issue is that even when they are functioning well, midlevel federal accountability institutions such as the federal police, the Ministério Público, the Tribunal de Contas da União (TCU, an accounting body that audits government accounts), and congressional investigatory committees (known as CPIs), all tend to focus on investigating corruption in a competing fashion; less emphasis is given to preventing corruption during the early stages of the accountability process, through effective and continuous monitoring, or to imposing effective long-term sanctions against corruption in the final stages of the accountability process.

In a study of prominent political corruption cases prosecuted at the federal level during the 1990s, Taylor and Buranelli (2007) found that only rarely had any lasting criminal or civil legal sanctions been imposed; most often the only sanctions imposed in multimillion-dollar corruption scandals were ineffectual condemnations by the TCU to recover lost revenues, or political/reputational sanctions imposed by Congress on the politicians involved. Furthermore, neither the TCU condemnations nor the political sanctions seemed to have had any relevant sanctioning effect. Only 2 to 3 percent of TCU-imposed fines or liens are paid at all (author correspondence with TCU 2004). Impugned legislators are often able to resign their posts before being ejected from office by their colleagues ("*cassados*") and thereby losing their right to run for office at some future date. Furthermore, fewer than one in five congressional investigatory committees actually produce a final report that aggregates and presents all the evidence collected in a manner that could be effectively prosecuted (Figueiredo 2001; O Estado 2005).

The problem, in other words, is that the institutions responsible for imposing accountability all tend to leap to their battle posts when a scandal breaks, but not before, and seldom follow up with great élan afterward. The overall emphasis of the accountability system thus privileges the investigatory stages over continuous monitoring or effective sanctioning that might alter incentive structures and thus deter future corruption (see figure 8.1). In the absence of strong preemptive monitoring, potentially corrupt acts are permitted to continue indefinitely before anyone publicly draws attention to wrongdoing (if they do at all), and all too often corruption is only brought to light as part of bigger and more clearly politically motivated battles. When wrongdoing is found, it tends to be investigated thoroughly but with few rapid, much less effective, legal sanctions. The result is a system with plenty of allegations of corruption, and a good number of clear revelations of corruption, but little effective punishment of corrupt behavior (or, just as important, little chance for the unjustly accused to rapidly clear their names).[7] Even when sanctions are forthcoming, they are extraordinarily slow and often uncertain.

A good example of this phenomenon, drawn from Taylor and Buranelli (2007), emerges from the unusually successful efforts against fraud in the so-called Lalau scandal surrounding construction of a federal labor court during the 1990s. Construction of the regional labor court building in São Paulo, originally budgeted to cost R$60 million, was scheduled to begin in 1992. In March of that year, a committee including Judge Nicolau dos Santos Neto (known by the nickname "Lalau") selected the Incal construction company to build the court. Within the year, the TCU decided that the public bidding had been conducted unfairly and called for a halt to the construction. Nothing further was done at this point, however, and construction began as planned in 1994.

Over the course of construction, R$263 million (roughly US$100 million at the going exchange rate) was transferred from the federal treasury to fund the project, of which only R$70 million was actually spent on the construction. The remainder was siphoned off in a scheme headed by Judge Nicolau, with the alleged participation of a senator, Luiz Estevão, and the president and vice president of Incal, the construction company. In 1998, the Federal Revenue Service opened an investigation into overspending on the building and was soon joined by the Ministério Público and then, in 1999, by a congressional investigatory committee (CPI). Throughout, the media covered the investigations in all their glory, highlighting the extraordinary brazenness of the corruption. The CPI ended in the expulsion ("*cassação*") of Senator Luiz Estevão in June 2000, and in December 2001, the accused were condemned (so far, futilely) by the TCU to return R$169.4 million to the public coffers. Nine years after the TCU first highlighted irregularities in the project, Judge Nicolau was sentenced to eight years in prison. This sentence was later extended to fourteen years, but it was commuted to house arrest because of Nicolau's age and alleged health problems.

As the "Lalau" case illustrates, corruption is often exposed in all its sordid glory in a very public way. But despite a great deal of sunlight, it is seldom effectively punished. Preventive monitoring had very little effect in this case: even when the TCU raised red flags about contracts in the project, nothing was done to put a stop to spending on the courthouse. Congressional investigation led to political sanctions against Senator Estevão, who was forced out of his Senate seat. But the investigations that might lead to effective criminal sanctions went forward in a very haphazard and uncoordinated fashion, with the Ministério Público, the Revenue Service, and the TCU working separately and in competing fashion to investigate the wrongdoing. The sheer scale of the graft—and the resulting media spotlight—may have made Lalau's conviction a foregone conclusion, suggesting that public opprobrium can be a powerful force in the accountability process. But the delays that accompanied the trials of Lalau and Senator Luiz Estevão suggest that the complicated and very loose interaction between institutions of accountability has real consequences for the likelihood that effective sanctions can be imposed on wrongdoers. Particularly troubling is that despite being a rare case of success—that is, a case in which two main culprits was pinpointed *and* punished in a public manner—the sanctions against Lalau and his conspirators were ultimately perceived as quite weak, with house arrest for Lalau and an as-yet-tentative sentence to "semi-reclusion" for Estevão.[8]

In the absence of effective punishments, a politician or civil servant who leans toward corruption may see little benefit in following the rules, further adding to the workload of those attempting to impose some form of accountability and worsening the degree of corruption in snowballing fashion. The notion that the absence of effective sanction may weaken deterrence has been a platitude among criminologists since the eighteenth century: what diminishes crime, it is believed, is not the size of the potential punishment, but the certainty of its application.[9] But how to improve accountability and, in particular, to guarantee the imposition of deterrent sanctions? The next section looks more carefully at the somewhat mixed prospects for change in Brazil's accountability structure.

All countries are plagued by the problem of imposing accountability, especially when the rich and/or powerful are allegedly involved in malfeasance. Furthermore, reform that might improve accountability, especially in the political realm, requires that the status quo be overturned by those who might well be the most harmed by change. In Brazil, this predicament is complicated further by the extraordinary difficulty of carrying out the two macro reforms that might make the most difference in combating corruption: electoral reform and judicial reform.

A number of political scientists have argued that changes in Brazil's party and electoral systems are needed to improve the accountability of politicians to voters. In an emblematic paper, Souza (2004) argued that "party switching remains a prime mechanism for crafting legislative majorities while depriving millions of Brazilians of any meaningful vote. Patronage and pork-barrel politics are still needed to glue all sorts of parties into a governing coalition and to coordinate the ragbag of weak and loosely disciplined parties in Congress." While there is some debate over the extent to which political parties in Congress are truly undisciplined—a growing consensus suggests party leaders have considerable sway over their members in the legislative process; for example, Figueiredo and Limongi (1999)—there is little doubt that legislators, acting either as individuals or parties, are able to trade their vote in exchange for a wide range of pork-denominated currencies to an executive dependent on unstable and shifting coalitions (Geddes and Ribeiro Neto 1992, 643). At the electoral level, meanwhile, without the anchor of stable party identification and in light of open-list proportional representation (by which deputies are elected from among many candidates in the broad geographical district of an entire state), voters have little connection with their representatives or even memory of who they voted for. This means that little direct political accountability is imposed by the public. Broad public outrage is only loosely channeled by the political system, and generally only at moments of great trauma.

Yet despite years of discussion, and the fact that political reform proposals have been repeatedly resurrected in times of scandal, little has been done to change the system. The past decade has brought only marginal changes, such as the implementation of concurrent electoral timetables, tighter rules on small parties, and a rule change permitting the reelection of executives.[10] Broader and deeper reforms to the party system have been slow to emerge. There is no shortage of proposals to reduce the number of parties, tighten the link between downsized and easily identifiable voter districts and their representatives, reform campaign finances, and strengthen the control of party leaders over their congressional representatives. There is also broad support among scholars and journalists for political reforms, especially for changes that would tighten the bonds of electoral accountability between voters and their representatives.[11]

The trouble is that the path to these largely reasonable ends is not at all clear: in fact, it is not evident how self-interested politicians can be goaded into making changes that threaten a status quo that benefits them in the short-term and, indeed, got them where they are. Despite having promised during his campaign to make electoral reform a priority, like his predecessors, once in office Lula invested little political capital to push it forward. Congressional committees addressing political reform have consistently watered down reform to its smallest consensual elements, but even these face an enormous uphill battle against entrenched interests, a busy legislative schedule, and, ironically, the distractions of current corruption scandals. Some of the boldest reforms of the new millennium have come from the electoral courts, but they have been somewhat inconsistent and limited in scope, suggesting that broader reform will have to come via the legislative route.

A second frequent prescription for improving accountability is judicial reform. This makes extraordinarily good sense: although recent reforms, passed after more than a decade of deliberation, have helped at the margins, the judiciary remains a slow and antiquated system that tends to impede any quick or lasting legal sanction of corrupt acts. The judicial process is exasperatingly slow as a result of high caseloads and the glut of cases engendered by the possibility of repeated appeals of lower-court decisions. A typical case that starts at the bottom of the judiciary and works its way through appeal up to the Federal Supreme Court (STF) averages between eight and ten years from start to finish. Sadder still, in most cases, the high court upholds the decision made at the outset (Taylor 2008).

Brazilians demonstrate enormous concern about the state of the courts. Although Brazilian courts are still more trusted than most of their counterparts elsewhere in Latin America, more than three-fifths of Brazilians claim to have little or no confidence in the judiciary. Recent scandals—including the Lalau case—have done nothing to help: the percentage of Brazilians who had "a lot" or "some" confidence in the judiciary fell from 41 percent in 1996 to 32.5 percent in 2002 (Galindo 2003, 32–33). A

2003 poll commissioned by the national bar association (OAB) showed that 86 percent of Brazilians thought judicial reform was urgently needed, and the judiciary inspired less confidence than any other institution in Brazilian society save Congress (Fleischer 2003).

Perhaps as a result, a significant constitutional amendment reforming the judicial system was pushed through Congress in December 2004, after considerable prodding and the expenditure of significant political capital by President Lula. Among other changes, this reform instituted a greater degree of binding precedent in decisions made by the STF and created a National Judicial Council (CNJ) to oversee the court system, two modifications that may help to streamline judicial decisions and prevent the sort of rash corruption by judges evidenced by the Lalau case. But it is also hardly the reform of anyone's dreams. As one STF minister noted, the amendment will "contribute very little to removing the true problem of the Brazilian judiciary, which is the slowness [and] the delays in judicial service" (Velloso 2005; translation mine).

Although some helpful piecemeal procedural changes are under active consideration by Congress, on past evidence, broader judicial reforms that would directly impact the accountability process seem unlikely in the short term. More than forty judicial reform projects have been proposed in Congress since 1988, with only one approved. Strong reactions by the judiciary against perceived challenges from other branches of government have torpedoed many of these proposals. Furthermore, judicial reform has galvanized opposition from a broad, diverse, and powerful set of political players in the legal profession: judges, lawyers, and prosecutors frequently present a unified front against the executive branch on reform, while behind the scenes, each profession lobbies fervently for its particular interests. The result is a stalemate on all but the most narrowly consensual issues, which, together with the scarcity of political capital needed to push Congress forward, suggests deeper institutional reforms of the judiciary are unlikely to occur again in the short term.

In short, both judicial and political reform might contribute significantly to fighting corruption, but they are unlikely and therefore disheartening policy prescriptions for improving Brazil's accountability performance in the near future.

THE GOOD NEWS: MESO AND MICRO REFORM

What, then, is to be done? If both electoral reform and judicial reform are stalemated or moving forward only glacially, and Brazil's tight budgetary situation means that significant new funding for accountability institutions is a low priority, what else can be done to improve the state of accountability in Brazil?

The good news is that small but positive changes are already under way in at least two directions, even if these are seldom the focus of significant media or academic attention. The common thread in both is a focus on internal, "meso," and "micro" level changes in accountability institutions that require little to no broader involvement by congressional representatives, thus sidestepping the enormous collective action problem inherent in most legislative reforms, particularly in those that require the substantial legislative majorities needed to change Brazil's extensive 1988 constitution.

The first change has been increasing cooperation across the web of accountability institutions. Recognizing that joint programs and information sharing are essential, several federal institutions have recently deepened their working relationships. The impetus is the recognition that there is no sense in wasting information obtained in competing investigations by rival agencies, especially if by not sharing corrupt players are enabled to walk scot-free.

Although it remains much smaller and more politically subordinate than is desirable, the 1998 money laundering law created a Council for Control of Financial Activities (COAF) within the Finance Ministry to help control illicit financial transactions. The COAF is an interagency council representing a number of accountability bureaucracies across the federal government, including the federal police, the Central Bank, the social security ministry, and the rough Brazilian equivalent of the U.S. Securities Exchange Commission (CVM, or Conselho de Valores Monetários). This sort of institutionalized if loosely centralized coordination between various bureaucracies may be a helpful way to manage the problem of excessively independent investigations without entirely removing the benefits of competing investigatory processes. For the time being, the COAF has far too small a bureaucratic footprint and is easily susceptible to political manipulation and ad hoc relations with other bureaucracies, but its creation is nonetheless a step in the right direction.

In the recent case of an investigation into large international financial transactions by former São Paulo governor and mayor Paulo Maluf, for example, representatives of the COAF, the Justice Ministry, the São Paulo Ministério Público, and the Federal Ministério Público, after five years of working separately, began sharing information and divvying up responsibilities. As Wannine Lima, the general coordinator of the effort in the Justice Ministry, noted, up until that point, that "while Maluf and his lawyers worked as a team, we moved forward disconnectedly" (*Valor Econômico* 2005; translation mine). Under the new task force model, hierarchy remains a problem, but at least information is shared, there is a single group administering contacts with police and judicial officials abroad, and as a result, stronger legal cases are likely to be brought. In the Maluf case, cooperation helped to streamline information sharing between several competing Brazilian bureaucracies, and perhaps as important, helped make the Brazilian government's efforts more transparent to Jersey Isle and Swiss bank oversight officials who were confused and alarmed by the many requests for information that had come their way from competing Brazilian bureaucracies.[12]

Continued improvements in this vein might include creation of more institutionalized structures for cooperation between bureaucracies. One of the problems with the prevalence and prominence of parliamentary committees of inquiry (CPIs) in Brazil's web of accountability institutions is that these CPIs are by nature temporary, created to investigate a narrowly defined episode, and exist for a limited period only. This clearly makes sense politically—open-ended congressional investigation of government is an invitation to abuse and deadlock—but it means that few long-term institutional links are created. In fact, institutional rivalry also plays a role in the absence of cooperation: in the recent past, for example, members of the Ministério Público Federal have refused to testify before Congress, citing the Ministério's institutional autonomy as a body independent of the executive, judicial, and legislative branches.

Despite such problems, cooperation across accountability institutions is also being extended slowly by the Ministério Público at both the state and federal levels, in part to deal with the fact that the multiple prosecutorial bodies in Brazil mean that competing investigations are more likely than not. The Ministério Público Federal maintains a permanent staff in the TCU, and while that office is largely bureaucratic in nature, mainly tracking the legality of TCU decisions, it could serve as a stepping stone to deeper cooperation. To give another hopeful example, Paulo Lacerda, a former head of the federal police under Lula, pushed for increased cooperation between his bureaucracy and the Ministérios Públicos at both the state and federal level. While these are still not formalized ties—and there are formidable institutional rivalries that stand in the way of the creation of such links—they have been vital to recent efforts to fight corruption within the federal police organization itself. Cross-institutional collaboration also can be applied to Brazilian accountability institutions' relations with their international counterparts, especially as the increasing globalization of financial flows makes it easier for corrupt players in Brazil to conduct their illicit operations abroad, out of ready view of Brazilian prosecutors and law enforcement agents.

The second reason for optimism has been the ongoing internal reform within many of the accountability bureaucracies, which offers productive gains at the margins despite Brazil's tight budget and the difficulty of deeper political or judicial reforms. Such changes can contribute substantially to improving internal practices and incentive structures within bureaucracies so as to improve them gradually over time. The federal police, for example, has undergone a significant internal reform over the past decade that has improved its professional standing without requiring any difficult legislative reforms. While corruption remains a very serious problem—reformist police director Lacerda estimated that 10 percent of his police forces were corrupt and 80 percent tolerated corruption—since 1997 there has been a significant tightening of admission standards for professionals joining the force, juxtaposed with an increased push to eliminate corrupt officials. While some events—such as the 2005 theft of R$2 million from the federal police headquarters in Rio de Janeiro (by most accounts an insiders' job)—suggest things remain far from perfect, internal efforts to improve the esprit de corps and ethical quality of police forces in this reformist vein will provide the most significant gains within the federal police in the short term.

With political will, it may also be possible to improve the incentive structures within individual bureaucracies to improve preventive monitoring and the effective sanctioning of wrongdoing, which are often sacrificed as second priorities to the investigatory stages of the accountability process. Rational calculations influence the way agents within each of the accountability bureaucracies choose to do their jobs: incentives do matter, and oftentimes institutions shape these incentives. It may be possible, therefore, to carry out small tinkering reforms that can improve performance within individual institutions.

Simplifying a bit in the hopes of pointing out some potential areas of improvement, it is possible, for example, to see that loose promotion criteria within the Ministérios Públicos at both the federal and state level tend to create incentives for prosecutors to give greater weight to the investigatory stages of their jobs than to seeking effective punishments in courts. Prosecutors are promoted based on loose criteria of merit and seniority, and because of their hierarchical autonomy from both the executive branch and from each other that often means they are promoted largely on the basis of seniority, unless they stand out for some other reason, such as making a name for themselves via big-media coverage of their investigations.[13] Furthermore, the delays in the judicial system mean that, not infrequently, a prosecutor can spend between one-fifth and one-half of his or her career pursuing a single case to—with some luck—a conviction. Under these conditions, it is only natural that the sanctioning function becomes less interesting to individual prosecutors than investigation, which leads to more immediate public and professional rewards.

By way of further example, both the state and federal Tribunais de Contas are governed by strong hierarchical subordination to the executive branch. Despite formal institutional protections, the Tribunais de Contas tend to be dominated by their politically nominated ministers, who are in turn hypersensitive to the political concerns of those who appointed them. This means that the federal Tribunal de Contas cannot "conclude any audit that runs against the political and economic interests" of its nine ministers (Fleischer 2000, 103–4; translation mine). Furthermore, Tribunal de Contas investigations frequently need to be carried forward to the judiciary by the Ministério Público if they are to have any punitive effect whatsoever. Strengthening the highly capable Tribunais de Contas bureaucracies in relation to their own ministers by making the ministerial function more advisory, increasing the cooperation between the Tribunais de Contas and other accountability institutions, and improving the conditions for promotion from within the Tribunais de Contas to top positions are prescriptions that might all improve the autonomy, and hence the sanctioning power, of the Tribunais.[14]

Finally, some changes external to the accountability institutions themselves nonetheless provide them with significant new clout. Changes in financial regulatory oversight, for example, have been ongoing since the banking crisis at the outset of President Fernando Henrique Cardoso's first term, meaning that it is now easier to track financial flows within Brazil and beyond, as well as for the Federal Revenue service to raise red flags with other accountability institutions about potential scofflaws whose bank holdings far exceed declared income.[15] Changes in public bidding rules have made some public purchasing more transparent (and more such reforms are currently under discussion), and passage of a money laundering bill in the late 1990s was a significant step in improving oversight of potentially illicit transactions.

There is no guarantee, of course, that these meso and micro reforms will lead to more effective sanctions down the road. And it bears repeating that if there were the political will or the financial resources to improve electoral accountability, streamline the judicial process, or broaden the scope of (and the resources available to) the accountability bureaucracy, that would be an infinitely more productive way to proceed toward a healthy combination of both greater sunshine and greater accountability. But in light of the challenges of undertaking institutional reforms in the Brazilian political system, and the failure of past scandals to foment significant reform, it is probably more realistic to aim for smaller, marginal gains that improve the monitoring and sanctioning functions of individual institutions within the constraints of the existing political structure.

FURTHER CHANGES?

It is important to recognize that Brazil is not alone in facing the problem of corruption. Indeed, the World Bank estimates that, worldwide, corruption leads to US$1.5 trillion in losses, or 5 percent of global gross domestic product, each year. And as the campaign finance cases that beset Tom DeLay in the United States, the controversies over European Parliament travel jaunts, and the United Nations oil-for-food scandal illustrate, corruption is a problem even among richer countries and organizations that can devote substantial resources to fighting graft and malfeasance. But this should be a source of innovation rather than discouragement: adapting the lessons and best practices from corruption fighters in other countries may be of great value. Brazil, in other words, does not need to reinvent the wheel. Among the lessons Brazil can adopt from abroad, three that require no macro reforms stand out.

First and perhaps most relevant, the sequencing of corruption-fighting efforts matters. The Mani Puliti ("Clean Hands") campaign in Italy, for example, managed to put criminal investigations ahead of political enquiries. This had the significant advantage of guaranteeing that evidence was collected in a setting that was not driven by parochial electoral calculations, and that politics played a role only once the evidence had been collected. Too often in Brazil that sequence is reversed, with congressional investigations driving public attention to potential malfeasance, competing with existing investigations by the Ministério Público and other bureaucracies, and producing reports whose usefulness in obtaining a conviction in a court of law is extremely limited. As noted earlier, only one in five congressional committees of inquiry (CPIs) in Brazil end up producing a final report. Among those that do produce a report, these are seldom of high enough legal quality to be of much use to prosecutors, and in many cases simply replicate previous investigation by the Ministério Público. During the most recent congressional investigations into the *sanguessuga* scandal, however, the leaders of the CPI helpfully waited until the Ministério Público had fully investigated the case before commencing their own investigation. While the weakness of the congressional investigation meant that, in the end, Congress did little more than delay the Ministério Público's case filings, it is a sequence that seems likely to lead to more effective overall sanctions, since it eliminates political fiddling in the search for evidence.

Second, it is as important to target corruptors in the business community as it is to go after dirty politicians. In the Mani Puliti investigations, for example, Italian judges were able to centralize investigatory powers and mobilize civil society in an effort to obtain support for investigating and punishing powerful members of both the political and the business communities. There are three parties to any corrupt public works program, and only one of them—the public—always loses. Corruption needs to be fought on both the supply and demand ends. Corruption fighting in Brazil focuses almost exclusively on the recipient, and few of the corruptors are ever targeted.[16] Effective punishment of corruptors might also provide other members of the business community a justification for failing to comply with demands from corrupt officials.

Finally, public support matters. The 1988 Brazilian Constitution considerably strengthened the autonomy of the prosecutorial body, the Ministério Público, whose independence and high quality personnel to some extent obviate the need for a body like Hong Kong's Independent Commission against Corruption (ICAC). There are also a number of ways in which whistleblowing is encouraged by various bureaucracies such as the Controladoria Geral da União, at least at the federal level. But there have been few broader efforts to educate the public at large about the pernicious effects of corruption and to enlist public support in fighting it. Instead, the emphasis on investigation and the absence of any perceived sanctions against corrupt acts tends to contribute to apathy. A larger scale effort to educate the public about the economic, social, and political consequences of corruption in all its guises, from petty bribery of traffic cops to political malfeasance, may be needed to build trust, encourage whistleblowing, and introduce integrity mechanisms that are democratic in the truest sense of the word. While changing cultures is a long-term process, it may well be possible to influence tolerance for corruption through education and media awareness programs, especially if these are combined with institutional reforms that increase the likelihood of punishment.

CORRUPTION, ACCOUNTABILITY, AND DEMOCRACY

Brazil's accountability deficit has a number of significant implications for the country's new democracy, both in terms of concrete policy performance and in terms of less easily measured phenomena such as citizens' satisfaction with the political regime. It is well known that political corruption has significant effects on the policy process: corruption undermines the criteria by which policies are chosen; distorts the information needed to design well-functioning policies; weakens the institutions that implement policy; disfigures policy by making it responsive to economic incentives rather than broader conceptions of the public good; and hurts efficiency and efficacy, thereby weakening policy performance (e.g., Bardhan 1997; Della Porta and Vannucci 1997).

But corruption also has significant effects in the political realm. Perceptions of corruption may weaken citizens' trust in institutions and each other (Bailey and Paras 2006; Seligson 2002). As Warren (2004, 328–29) points out, perceived corruption may well make citizens cynical about public speech and participation: "Corruption in this way diminishes the horizons of collective actions and in so doing shrinks the domain of democracy . . . corruption undermines democratic capabilities of association within civil society by generalizing suspicion and eroding trust and reciprocity."

The absence of accountability constitutes a potentially devastating follow-on blow after the impact of corruption itself. Not only are policy objectives and institutions undermined and interpersonal trust weakened by corruption, but both processes are further exacerbated by the ability of corrupt actors to repeat their actions with little fear of detection, and even less of sanction. The effects flow in three waves in Brazil: first, in the exposure of corruption itself, detailed in wave upon wave of revelations arising out of multiple, overlapping, and often competing investigations; second, in the apparent inability to effectively sanction wrongdoers; and, finally, in the overburdening of institutions that might be more profitably employed in the monitoring and sanctioning stages but are consumed by the need to be seen on the front lines of investigation when the latest scandal strikes. Together, these three sequential blows are especially pernicious because they signal the public that even when detected, abuse of public office for private gain has little or no cost; together they weaken faith in the very governmental institutions that are needed to fight corrupt acts, from judges to legislators; and the combination of the three may well influence the cost-benefit calculations of potential wrongdoers in the future, stimulating further acts—both large and small—of corruption at all levels of public life.

The irony is that Brazil, like many of the new democracies of Latin America, is confronting an accountability deficit just as the other two variables in the Klitgaard equation have improved considerably. As a result of the dual economic and political transitions of the past two decades, Brazil faces considerably smaller problems with governmental monopoly and discretion than it has in the past. But the problem is that this progress tends only to spotlight persistent weaknesses in accountability. Accountability, in other words, may not be any worse than it was under the military, and, in fact, corruption may even be far more transparent to the public than it was under the authoritarian regime. Nonetheless, the overwhelming emphasis of the accountability process on the investigatory stage, combined with the vibrancy of the Brazilian press corps, tends to heighten public awareness of governments' ethical shortcomings without any compensating punishments to overcome the popular view that most political corruption will be swept under the carpet.

In the absence of real and lasting sanctions, it is all too easy to paint *all* politicians, judges, and bureaucrats—even those working honestly and sometimes at great personal sacrifice—as corrupt players in an insiders' game, thereby further sapping credibility from Brazil's nascent democratic institutions. It is difficult to say how long this process can continue without seriously straining public faith in Brazil's democratic politics, and whether Brazil's political institutions will channel widespread public discontent into accountability reforms fast enough to outpace strained public faith.

STEPHEN D. MORRIS

9 Corruption and Democracy at the State Level in Mexico

Analysts have long acknowledged the prevalence of political corruption in Mexico. Most associated the corruption of the twentieth
century with Mexico's unique one-party hegemonic, authoritarian
regime. With the PRI monopolizing control of all levels of government, the Mexican president and a powerful state operated virtually
free of political constraints. Mechanisms of horizontal and vertical
accountability were severely limited. Neither the courts, the congress, state and local governments, the bureaucracy, nor elections
did much to check or to balance the power of the federal executive.
Political opposition faced restrictions, the press was muzzled, and
corporatist arrangements tied much of civil society to the official
party in a strict top-down, clientelist fashion. Unchecked, corruption thus offered a system of spoils for members of the political elite
who played by the (informal) rules of the political game; it facilitated an inclusive pattern of co-optation, allowing the regime to buy
off political support or acquiescence; and it even provided the president a mechanism—the anticorruption campaign—to purge political enemies and periodically restore the public's faith in the Mexican Revolution and its political party (Morris 1991).

Yet in recent years Mexico has undergone a slow, gradual, and
yet very real transition to democracy. Though analysts may dis-

agree over the precise start and endpoint of that transition, it is marked by a slow erosion of electoral support for the dominant PRI, losses of key political posts, the concomitant rise in electoral support for opposition parties and their assumption of power at various levels of government—culminating in the presidency in 2000—the growth in the power of the legislature, the courts, state and local governments, and autonomous governmental institutions vis-à-vis the president and the federal government, increasing press freedoms, and the rise in the freedom and activity of civil society (e.g., Camp 2003; Chand 2001; Crandall, Paz, and Roett 2005; Eisenstadt 2004; Lawson 2002; Levy and Bruhn 2001; Mizrahi 2003; Peschard-Sverdrup and Rioff 2005).

Mexico's gradual transition to democracy—which improved the climate for the growth of key mechanisms of horizontal and vertical accountability—offers a distinctive setting to explore the impact of democratization and electoral competition on corruption as well as corruption's impact on voting and the pattern of democratization. This chapter draws primarily on data from three national polls conducted in the 2000s to explore the impact of democratic changes at the state level on both the levels and changes in perceptions and participation in corruption and the impact of corruption on voting. I begin by building a series of hypotheses drawing on prevailing theory linking democracy to corruption. This is followed by a review of the nature of the current approach and how it departs from recent research on corruption.

DEMOCRACY AND CORRUPTION

For years, analysts have held that democracy, electoral competition, and freedom all foster conditions that help reduce the likelihood of corruption. This takes place through a variety of mechanisms. First, elections give voters a means, though crude, to hold public officials accountable and thus the ability to punish with their vote those individuals found to be abusing the public's trust by engaging in corruption. Second, from a rational choice perspective, electoral competition alters the fundamental incentives for those competing for public office. For those on the outside, competition provides incentives to expose the corruption of the incumbents in order to enhance their prospects of winning. Entrenched leaders facing limited competition, by contrast, are better able to buy off voters and manipulate the system (Johnston 2005a, 31). Third, the civil liberties accompanying democracy tend to make government more open and transparent. Such freedoms foster a more independent press and a more active civil society, both of which help expose official wrongdoing and channel demands for accountability, strengthening these important mechanisms of vertical accountability (see Rose-Ackerman 1999).

And yet, despite this rather simple theoretical formula, the relationship linking democracy and corruption is not as clear or sharp as theory suggests, and empirical support is rather weak. For starters, corruption has been common in more mature democratic systems like Italy, Japan, and the United States (see Heidenheimer and Johnston 2002; Della Porta and Vannucci 1997; Johnston 2005a), so democracy does not always succeed in preventing corruption. The "democratic-no corruption" link seems particularly tenuous in the case of Latin America and for new democracies, as demonstrated by the contributions to this volume. Whitehead (2002), for instance, argues against a direct link between democracy and lower levels of corruption, pointing particularly to the rise in electoral corruption that tends to accompany democratization. At least during a transition period, according to Andvig (2006), the time horizons of many actors are foreshortened by uncertainties that can actually facilitate corruption and malfeasance rather than discourage it. Like Whitehead (2002), Weyland (1998) and Manzetti and Blake (1996) all point to an increase in corruption throughout Latin America occurring during the recent transitions to democracy. Constraints on the capacity of elections to promote greater accountability range from the economic conditions of late dependent industrialization and ineffective institutions of representation to weak social capital (Putnam 1993, 2000) and even support for corrupt politicians. Geddes (1994), for example, employs game theory to illustrate the institutional conditions that forge the dilemma helping to foment a form of political corruption in Brazil (see also Geddes and Neto 1992). Though the whole society may benefit from an end to patronage, as she shows, no individual politician or political party has an incentive to unilaterally institute a merit system since it would translate into losing votes. Manuel Alejandro Guerrero (2004), differentiating the democratizing nature of contesting power from the rule of law means of exercising it, similarly shows how the rise of electoral competition, opposition victories, and pluralism in Mexico have not led to greater levels of rule of law and checks and balances, but have instead created an environment in which the opposite has occurred.

Empirical research on the democracy-corruption question is also somewhat ambiguous and has failed to answer the question definitively. Some cross-national studies find support for the theory, suggesting that democracy indeed lowers the levels of corruption. Studies by Ades and DiTella (1997a), Brunetti and Weder (2003), Lederman, Loayza, and Soares (2005), and Montinola and Jackman (2002), for instance, all find an inverse relationship between a nation's level of corruption (measured using Transparency International's Corruption Perceptions Index) and level of democracy (political freedoms and elections usually using Freedom House data). According to analyses by Goldsmith (1999), Paldam (2002), Xin and Rudel (2004), however, the relationship is not particularly robust when controlling for level of development or focusing solely on developing countries. Treisman (2000) similarly fails to confirm any direct link between freedoms and corruption and instead finds that the number of consecutive years a country has enjoyed democracy correlates with less corruption. This suggests that the relationship may in fact be curvilinear, with corruption increasing during the initial years of democracy but diminishing as democracy matures, deepens, or consolidates. Thacker's research in this volume lends further support for the notion that democracy's effect on corruption takes time. Of course as Latin American reality makes clear, there is no reason to expect democracy to deepen or consolidate a priori.

Studies by Beer (2003) and Cleary and Stokes (2006) on Mexican states also highlight the impact of political competition and democracy. In her analysis of Mexican entities, Beer (2003, 21) finds evidence "that increasing electoral competition strengthens representative institutions in ways that decentralize power away from the national executive and improve the separation of powers and therefore has significant consequences for accountability and the rule of law." As political competition increases, it alters incentives and opportunities for politicians and party leaders, forging more autonomous legislatures, participatory methods to select candidates, and demands for greater local control over resources. It is precisely through this mechanism, Beer contends, that the states have led the way in Mexico's democratic transition. Unfortunately, Beer does not include measures or indicators of corruption in her analysis, leaving open the question as to whether such structural and institutional changes translate into a lessening of corruption. From a slightly different angle, Cleary and Stokes (2006) highlight the development of a culture of skepticism in Mexico. Analyzing just four states, they find that the more democratic the state, the higher the level of institutional trust and respect for the rule of law and the lower the levels of trust in politicians and reliance on clientelism and personal favors. Though one might expect greater

respect for rule of law and institutional trust to have an impact on perceived and/or real levels of corruption, the authors find no relationship.
Unlike Beer's study, Cleary and Stokes do include data on perceptions of
corruption and again, contrary to expectation—given the higher levels of
trust in institutions in the more democratic states—they found no relationship to perceived levels of corruption. In other words, they uncovered
no difference among the four states studied between the more democratic
and less democratic states in terms of perceptions of whether politicians
are corrupt.

The relationship linking democracy and corruption can be approached
from various directions, to be sure. Heretofore discussion has centered
mainly on how democracy impacts on the likelihood of corruption. Turning the causal arrow around, however, raises questions about the impact
of corruption on political participation, particularly voting, on feelings of
legitimacy or popular satisfaction with democracy. While research shows
that the perception of corruption tends to erode support for institutions,
politicians, and regime legitimacy (Seligson 2006), its impact on voting
is not entirely clear. In their study on Mexican public opinion, McCann
and Dominguez (1998) found that individual opinions on corruption do
not translate into a vote for the opposition, but rather to not voting. That
finding, however, relates to the period of PRI hegemony and may have
been a consequence of the perceived inefficacy of the voter during the
time rather than on corruption per se. Where competition is intense and
the opposition actually has a chance of winning—where, as Przeworski
(1991, 10) notes, the outcome is truly unknown—voters' perceptions of
corruption might translate into a vote against the incumbent party and in
favor of the opposition that has a chance of winning. This impact would
be more likely of course if and when the voter considers corruption a salient issue. The relationship may therefore be partially endogenous since
the perception of corruption tends to be more pronounced among individuals who identify with the opposition parties (Davis, Camp, and Coleman 2004; Canache and Allison 2005).

For current purposes, these essential components of democratic theory suggest the following hypotheses:

- Mexican states with higher levels of democracy, greater electoral
  competition, and alternation in power will exhibit lower levels
  of corruption; states where the PRI has maintained its hegemony
  will exhibit higher levels of corruption.

- States with higher levels of democracy, greater electoral competition, and alternation in power will show greater reductions in the levels of corruption over time; states where the PRI has maintained its hegemony will show limited reductions in the level of corruption over time.

- States with initially higher levels of corruption or perceptions that corruption has increased are more likely to produce a greater vote for the opposition than the party in power at the state level and are more likely to turn the incumbents out of office.

CURRENT APPROACH

The current study departs from the existing literature in three ways. The first difference relates to the unit of analysis. In most empirical studies on corruption the nation-state serves as the unit of analysis. Such cross-national studies have rendered important insights into the causes and consequences of corruption. In this study, by contrast, the focus is on the subnational unit of the state or federal entity: Mexico's thirty-one states and the Federal District. This approach helps maintain key national factors constant and facilitates a more detailed analysis of the causes and consequences of corruption. The few empirical studies on corruption focusing on the subnational unit all come from the United States. Work by Alt and Lassen (2003), Hill (2003), Johnston (1983), Meier and Holbrook (1992), and Schlesinger and Meier (2002), for instance, all offer cross-sectional analyses to explain variations in the levels of corruption across U.S. states. These studies highlight a range of factors some also found to be influential at the national level.

The current approach also differs from recent studies in its treatment of the dependent variable. Despite the boom in recent years in empirical research on the causes and consequences of corruption, there has been very little focus on changes in corruption.[1] Just as in the not-too-distant past when few analysts tackled corruption empirically because of the absence of data, there remains a lack of reliable data measuring changes in corruption over time.[2] Though Transparency International (TI) compiles and publishes its widely used Corruption Perceptions Index (CPI) annually, potentially allowing a means to track corruption over time, the data carries a methodological warning about using the index for such longitudinal purposes. This methodological shortcoming is particularly troubling because it hampers our ability to gauge the effectiveness of anticorruption initiatives or understand the political, economic, or cultural conditions that influence change. Cross-sectional studies may hint at the impact of certain crucial variables that influence changes in the levels of corruption, but drawing dynamic conclusions from cross-sectional analyses is always a second-best approach.

Third, most empirical studies of corruption have used popular or expert perceptions of corruption to measure corruption—usually TI's CPI. Among others, Seligson (2002, 2006) questions this approach, providing a convincing argument for the use of measures looking more at individual participation or experience in corruption as opposed to simple perceptions. As most authors acknowledge, popular or even elite perceptions of corruption, though perhaps related to one's involvement in corrupt exchanges, is not the same as actual participation in corrupt acts, and the two can behave quite independently (see Del Castillo 2003; Johnston 2000; Mocan 2004; Morris 2008; Weber Abramo 2007). While in a strict sense scholarly attention to corruption really refers to a form of behavior such that participation in corruption should be considered the most valued measure of the phenomenon, perceptions of corruption are nonetheless important in terms of their impact on regime legitimacy, trust in the political system and leaders, the potential to mobilize the citizenry to fight corruption, corruption's impact, and perhaps even political participation. Indeed, politics is often a game of perception. Disaggregating the two is therefore critical in clarifying the causes, the consequences, and the dynamics of corruption. Analysis here targets both measures of participation in corruption as well as perceptions of corruption.

One way of empirically exploring corruption in Mexico and to explore the impact of democracy is to examine the levels of corruption and variations among federal entities (thirty-one states plus the Federal District [DF]). Measures of popular perceptions of corruption and actual participation in corrupt exchanges for this study are taken from the massive 2001, 2003, and 2005 *Encuestas Nacionales de Corrupción y Buen Gobierno* (ENCBG) conducted by Transparencia Mexicana.[3]

This chapter examines three distinct aspects or dimensions of corruption: participation, perception, and change. Measures of actual levels of corruption center on individual participation in corrupt exchanges. Each of the three polls calculates an Index of Corruption and Good Government (ICBG) for each national entity based on the respondents' direct experiences with corruption. This index gauges participation based on a composite measure of the number of occasions within a specified time period that an individual paid a bribe (*mordida*) to obtain thirty-eight different types of public services from the three levels of government for the 2001 and 2003 polls and thirty-five services for the 2005 survey. It is calculated on a 0 to 100 scale using the following formula:

$$\text{ICBG} = \frac{\text{number of times a service was acquired using corruption}}{\text{number of times the same service was used}} \times 100$$

In contrast to participation, perception of corruption refers to the perception that corruption exists in the country. Equally subjective as questions about direct experience, perception is much more ambiguous and may encompass one's own experiences, those of others, and general views on politics and politicians. Perception may even incorporate characteristics wholly unrelated to corruption. Though hardly an ideal measure, perception of corruption is the most commonly used measure, as noted earlier. To gauge popular perception, I use the percentage of respondents in each poll who consider "all" politicians corrupt.

Finally, two approaches are taken to measure change in corruption within the state. To gauge change in actual corruption or participation, I calculated the percent change in the ICBG from 2001 to 2003 and from 2001 to 2005 for each state. To measure the change in perceptions of corruption, however, I rely on a much more direct question that asks respondents whether corruption over the past year within the entity has increased, remained the same, or decreased. For this study, I use the percentage of respondents expressing the view that corruption has decreased. This measure of change is better for a couple of reasons. First, this measure refers to change itself rather than a comparison of two data sets. Second, the measure gauges change specifically within the entity rather than at the federal level—there is actually a separate question for change at the national level—and thus more closely fits the type of corruption included in the ICBG and coincides more with our unit of analysis.

Table 9.1 lays out the measures of participation, perceptions, and change in corruption by federal entity. A brief comparison of the data shows a wide variation among the states based on participation and perception. Nationally, corruption fell ever so slightly during the period. Participation rates clearly fell from 2001 to 2003, but by 2005 they had almost returned to their 2001 level. Over the 2001 to 2005 period, actual corruption fell in twelve states and increased in twenty. Popular perceptions of corrupt politicians are quite high throughout the country, as shown. These also fell slightly on average from 2001 to 2003, falling in nineteen states and increasing in twelve states. Unfortunately, the 2005 measure is not entirely comparable, making it impossible to track changes through 2005 using this variable.[4] In terms of perceptions of change in the levels of corruption during the prior year, the data show a clear decline in the optimistic assessments of change. Whereas an average of 24.6 percent of respondents believed corruption was trending downward in 2001, that percentage had fallen to just 17.7 percent by 2005. Because data for participation levels (ICBG) for 2001 and 2003 are heavily skewed (2.237 for 2001 and 1.367 for 2003), logs of both measures were calculated (thereby reducing the skewness to <1 [.713 and .303 for the two years respectively]) for the subsequent analysis.

Table 9.2 presents the simple correlation matrix for the dependent variables. A number of observations should be noted. First, the matrix reveals a relatively strong correlation across the three time periods for both participation rates and perceptions respectively. This indicates that entities with higher levels of corruption in 2001 continued to suffer high levels of corruption in 2003 and 2005 for both participation and perceptions. Assuming that change in corruption—participation and perceptions—is slow and gradual, this finding tends to bolster the reliability of the measures themselves. Second, the table shows a positive correlation linking participation and perception. Though deciphering cause and effect here is difficult,[5] the correlation suggests that entities with high levels of participation in corruption also supported a high percentage of respondents believing that politicians are corrupt. Even so, the coefficient shows that the two—participation and perception—are not identical. Third, in looking at the issue of change the matrix reveals a somewhat mixed pattern. Some evidence suggests that the initial level of corruption does tend to influence subsequent changes in that measure. As one might expect, states with higher levels of corruption in 2001 tended to enjoy the sharpest reductions in corruption over the subsequent 2001 to 2005 period, but not over the intermediate period from 2001 to 2003, though the direction of change is consistent. Yet, such a reduction in participation levels did not seem to impact popular perceptions of politicians or vice versa. By contrast, there does seem to be a weak though consistent positive correlation linking change in participation rates with perceptions of corrupt politicians. That is, states where more of the population felt that all politicians are corrupt in 2001 and 2003 were slightly more likely to see corruption increasing or remaining the same. More important, perhaps, there seems to be virtually no relationship linking participation rates or changes in participation levels and percep-

Table 9.1   **Participation, perceptions, and change in corruption, 2001–2005 (by federal entity)**

	Participation index[1]			% change		Perceptions[2]			Decrease prior year[3]		
	2001	2003	2005	2001– 2003	2001– 2005	2001	2003	2005	2001	2003	2005
Aguascalientes	4.5	3.9	6.2	−.13	.38	75.8	80.2	87.2	26.1	19.7	18.7
Baja California	5.7	6.0	6.9	.05	.21	76.6	73.5	89.8	25.0	22.5	11.3
Baja California Sur	3.9	2.3	4.8	−.41	.23	70.9	63.0	83.8	28.1	17.4	12.0
Campeche	7.3	5.7	7.8	−.22	.07	80.2	74.3	82.4	24.1	19.5	25.5
Coahuila	5.0	4.4	6.5	−.12	.30	93.4	80.0	93.4	17.9	28.0	21.0
Colima	3.0	3.8	7.0	.27	1.33	75.9	73.9	91.1	31.5	27.0	27.6
Chiapas	6.8	4.0	2.8	−.41	−.59	61.4	70.1	72.3	23.6	12.3	13.5
Chihuahua	5.5	5.7	7.4	.04	.35	78.7	81.6	92.6	27.4	16.9	17.3
Distrito Federal	22.6	13.2	19.8	−.42	−.12	85.9	79.5	90.2	15.2	23.8	10.1
Durango	8.9	12.6	11.1	.42	.25	83.8	87.1	86.2	20.1	11.6	18.4
Guanajuato	6.0	8.9	5.2	.48	−.13	84.7	81.4	86.6	22.3	30.3	19.2
Guerrero	13.4	12.0	11.1	−.10	−.17	81.4	77.3	95.1	20.8	22.4	15.9
Hidalgo	6.7	3.9	11.4	−.42	.70	79.0	87.6	90.8	21.3	18.2	18.9
Jalisco	11.6	6.5	7.2	−.44	−.38	75.8	75.5	89.7	29.0	17.1	21.2
Mexico	17.0	12.7	13.3	−.25	−.22	82.1	85.3	89.1	22.2	20.4	16.0
Michoacán	10.3	4.8	10.8	−.53	.05	80.4	81.1	85.3	24.0	19.2	15.6
Morelos	7.7	8.3	11.0	.08	.43	83.2	80.4	91.0	24.4	21.8	13.3
Nayarit	6.4	5.8	5.7	−.09	−.11	77.4	75.5	84.5	38.1	24.5	22.8
Nuevo León	7.1	9.9	9.3	.39	.31	82.0	75.1	89.2	29.0	12.5	15.7
Oaxaca	7.4	6.8	8.1	−.08	.09	77.6	76.2	93.2	21.1	11.5	19.0
Puebla	12.1	18.0	10.9	.49	−.10	83.2	75.2	93.2	23.0	26.6	19.8
Querétaro	8.1	6.3	2.0	−.22	−.75	74.9	68.1	88.9	34.2	27.2	28.0
Quintana Roo	6.1	3.7	9.4	−.39	.54	78.9	81.7	90.9	25.4	18.0	11.2
San Luis Potosí	5.7	10.2	6.6	.79	.16	76.9	73.3	87.0	25.7	19.3	14.6
Sinaloa	7.8	5.5	6.6	−.29	−.15	78.7	79.6	88.7	18.2	17.2	8.8
Sonora	5.5	4.5	5.2	−.18	−.05	77.5	77.4	86.6	29.2	19.6	27.3
Tabasco	8.5	6.9	13.6	−.19	.60	86.9	84.3	87.9	18.6	14.6	14.2
Tamaulipas	6.3	5.1	6.8	−.19	.08	80.2	78.2	87.4	28.0	19.2	16.2
Tlaxcala	6.6	7.8	10.0	.18	.52	83.3	83.5	90.5	21.9	31.0	15.6
Veracruz	7.9	6.4	10.8	−.19	.37	73.0	76.2	94.5	27.4	20.3	24.0
Yucatán	6.8	4.8	6.7	−.29	−.01	78.2	78.5	85.1	15.7	21.8	21.9
Zacatecas	6.2	5.6	5.3	−.10	−.15	73.6	78.1	88.5	27.6	21.5	12.7
NATIONAL	10.6	8.5	10.1	−.078	.125	78.9	77.8	88.4	24.6	20.4	17.7

1. Index is based on respondents having paid a bribe to obtain thirty-eight public services.
2. Percentage of respondents agreeing with the statement "los políticos son corruptos." For 2005, includes responses of total agreement and partial agreement.
3. Percentage of respondents answering "less" when asked, "En comparisión a hace un año, ¿actualmente la corrupción en la entidad es mayor, igual o menor?"

Table 9.2 **Bivariate correlations of participation and perceptions of corruption and change, 2001 and 2003**

	Participation (ICBG)					Perception		Decrease over prior year	
	2001	2003	2005	2001–2003	2001–2005	2001	2003	2001	2003
Participation 2003	.71***								
Participation 2005	.68***	.54***							
Change 2001–2003	–.21	N/A	N/A						
Change 2001–2005	–.49***	N/A	N/A	.23					
Perception 2001	.30**	.46***	.55***	.26*	.25*				
Perception 2003	.28*	.28*	.55***	.03	.32**	.59***			
Decrease 2001	–.40**	–.27*	–.52***	.09	–.04	–.46**	–.48**		
Decrease 2003	–.06	.12	–.06	.02	.02	.32**	–.02	.08	
Decrease 2005	–.22	–.10	–.32**	.09	.02	–.03	–.15	.42***	.28*

*= < .10   **= < .05   ***= < .01

tions of a decrease in corruption over the prior year. The perception that corruption is decreasing seems to be linked somewhat to initial participation levels and perceptions of corruption, but not to change in participation levels over the period.

Analysis begins by exploring the impact of various measures of democracy and competitiveness on the levels of corruption—both participation and perception. This is followed by an examination of the impact of democracy on changes in both dimensions of corruption. Before flipping the causal arrow around to briefly explore the impact of corruption on voting patterns at the state level, I examine, as an alternative approach, the impact of a series of institutional variables on corruption and change.

THE IMPACT OF DEMOCRACY ON CORRUPTION
IN THE MEXICAN STATES

Three measures of democracy and democratic competitiveness are employed here. The first is the comparative index of local democracy developed by Hernández (2000). This index measures democracy for 1989–99 based on PRI vote in local elections, the vote for the opposition, and human rights abuses in the state as recorded by the national commission on human rights. Unfortunately, the measure does not include the Federal District since it did not elect its local officials until 2000. The measure thus has an $n = 31$. Two additional measures of democracy and competitiveness are used encompassing all thirty-two entities: the vote for the PRI in the 2000 election for the Chamber of Deputies and the political party in power at the gubernatorial level. Following the approach of Hernández (2000) and others, support for the PRI is considered a proxy measure of the lack of democratic competitiveness and democratic change within the state. Political party in power, in turn, measures alternation in power, a key feature in the literature on democratic transitions. In Mexico, the opposition only began to wrest control of the states in 1989. Since then, the PRI has lost almost half of the nation's thirty-two entities to the National Action Party (PAN) and the Democratic Revolutionary Party (PRD).

Looking first at the comparative index of democracy, the data suggest that democracy may have some effect in lowering the levels of corruption and lowering popular perceptions about corrupt politicians. Despite the direction of the bivariate coefficients, both scatterplots shown in figure 9.1 suggest a curvilinear relationship, wherein states at lower and higher levels of democracy tend to have lower levels of corruption (participation and perception), while states at a more intermediate democratic level tend to exhibit slightly higher levels of corruption. Note also that the inverse relationship linking the level of democracy to actual levels of corruption in 2001 ($r = -.36^*$) remains robust when controlling for state gross domestic product per capita. This finding is consistent with much of the literature in suggesting that democratization may at first lead to an increase in corruption, but that with time democracy can play a role in diminishing corruption. Using the vote for the PRI in 2000 to measure the level of democracy in the state in the subsequent analysis, however, reveals that the vote for the PRI is only weakly related to overall levels of corruption or perceptions of corruption. Though falling short of statistical significance, the linear correlation actually shows that states with a higher PRI vote tend to have slightly lower levels of corruption.

Using political party in power at the gubernatorial level as a measure of alternation in power facilitates a comparison of the mean levels of corruption by state. Table 9.3 presents the averages for the three major political parties, which again fall short of statistical significance due in large part to the low n—note that in five of the six observations, the seventeen PRI-controlled states on average exhibit higher levels of corruption, measured as both participation and perception, than the states controlled by the PAN or the PRD. Only in 2001 did the PRD have a higher average level of corruption due to the exceedingly high levels registered in the

Figure 9.1   **Scatterplots of corruption and comparative index of local democracy**

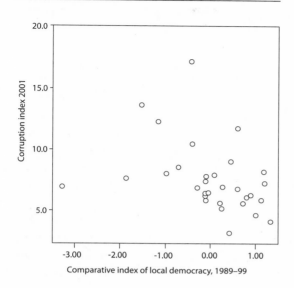

Comparative index of local democracy, 1989–99

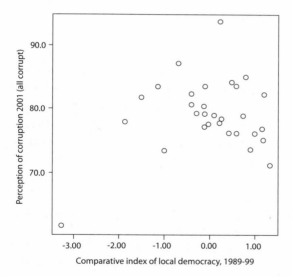

Comparative index of local democracy, 1989-99

Table 9.3 Means of corruption by party in power at state level

Party of governor	ICBG 2001	ICBG 2003	ICBG 2005	Perception 2001	Perception 2003
PAN (*n*=9)					
Mean	7.100	6.711	6.689	78.733	76.467
Standard deviation	2.0037	1.9554	2.5281	3.6184	4.1896
PRD (*n*=6)					
Mean	9.400	6.283	8.917	75.917	75.883
Standard deviation	6.7844	3.8442	6.1743	9.1165	7.7801
PRI (*n*=17)					
Mean	7.888	7.524	9.035	80.435	79.365
Standard deviation	3.4342	4.0990	2.5870	4.6644	4.5914
Total					
Mean	7.950	7.063	8.353	79.109	77.897
Standard deviation	3.8943	3.5089	3.5175	5.5669	5.2662

Federal District (note the high standard deviation for the PRD). Interestingly, PAN states enjoyed the lowest average on measures of participation in corruption, but the PRD-controlled states registered the lowest average for respondents considering politicians to be corrupt. This supports the notion that real results in lowering corruption may not necessarily translate into public perceptions about politicians and vice versa.

Turning our attention to the various measures of change in corruption—change in the participation levels and perceived change over the prior year—two sets of multiple regression equations were run: one including the index for democracy (and thus excluding the Federal District), the other dropping this variable so as to include all thirty-two cases. Both analyses controlled for initial levels of corruption and state level of development using gross domestic product per capita. The index of democracy had no impact, so table 9.4 presents the results only from the second analysis. Here again, in four of the five equations the initial level of democracy—measured here by the vote for the PRI and PRI control of the state executive—had no impact on subsequent changes in actual levels of corruption or perceptions of change. Solely in the model analyzing change in the participation rate from 2001 to 2005 did gubernatorial control of the state significantly influence change as hypothesized. PRI-controlled states registered the lowest rates of change in actual corruption, or, stated differently, non-PRI administrations were more successful at lowering corruption than were PRI-held states. If taken as a proxy measure of democratization, this supports the notion that states with higher levels of local democracy as indicated by alternation in power did tend to enjoy greater reductions in actual levels of corruption over the period, but that this did not necessarily translate into the perception of change among the public.

Table 9.5 provides a slightly closer look at this, breaking down average changes by party in power at the state level. From 2001 to 2003, on average all parties enjoyed a slight reduction in levels of corruption, led by the PRD-controlled states. For the entire period from 2001 to 2005, however, PAN and PRD states maintained this downward trend, but PRI-held states showed an average increase in corruption. In terms of public perceptions of change, the downward trend in positive assessments of change for all three parties is quite clear. Moreover, the three periods consistently show PAN-governed states to have the highest percentage of respondents expressing the view that corruption had fallen in the prior year. On average, though, less than 4 percent of respondents were more likely to believe that corruption was trending downward in PAN-held states versus PRI-controlled states in any of the three years. This suggests that the party in power had only a limited effect per se on real or perceived changes in corruption.

One variable that might impact on the perceptions of change in corruption relates to the stage of the gubernatorial term. In Mexico, state elections are staggered so that a survey taken in 2001 or 2005 might be

Table 9.4   **Multiple regression of change in corruption**

	Change in participation		Decrease in corruption		
	2001–2003	2001–2005	2001	2003	2005
Constant	.300	1.332**	22.360*	27.292***	13.812**
	(.600)	(.620)	(8.459)	(8.370)	(6.688)
PRI vote 2000/03	−.344	−1.792	3.472	−16.740	11.566
	(1.149)	(1.186)	(17.214)	(17.034)	(13.352)
Non–PRI governor (dummy)	−0.99	−.361**	2.197	1.177	−.664
	(.133)	(.138)	(2.084)	(2.062)	(2.245)
GDP/pc	−3.3E−006	6.53E−006	−1.3E−005	−5.7E−005	−1.8E−005
	(.000)	(.000)	(.000)	(.000)	(.000)
ICBG 2001	−.019	−.054***			
	(.017)	(.017)			
(Adjusted) R^2	−.066	.256	−.062	−.025	−.040
F	.518	3.663	.401	.747	.601
Significance	.723	.017	.753	.533	.620

Coefficients are unstandardized. Robust standard error in parentheses.
*** = < .001.   ** = < .01.   * = < .05.

Table 9.5 Means of change in corruption by party in power at state level

Party of governor	Change in ICBG 2001–2003	Change in ICBG 2001–2005	Decrease in entity in prior year 2001	Decrease in entity in prior year 2003	Decrease in entity in prior year 2005
PAN (n=9)					
Mean	−.0194	−.0070	27.089	21.933	19.122
Standard deviation	.30625	.38847	6.5606	5.2681	5.1400
PRD (n=6)					
Mean	−.2811	−.0105	23.400	20.867	13.250
Standard deviation	.26987	.37491	4.6823	6.3226	2.1399
PRI (n=17)					
Mean	−.0376	.2435	23.641	19.429	18.571
Standard deviation	.33386	.39355	4.1116	4.7119	5.2950
Total					
Mean	−.0781	.1254	24.566	20.403	17.728
Standard deviation	.32150	.39732	5.0940	5.1293	5.1829

Table 9.6 Means of decrease in corruption by year of gubernatorial term

Year of gubernatorial term	Decrease in corruption year prior 2001	2003	2005
1	22.2 (6)		17.0 (10)
2	24.8 (7)	21.2 (3)	23.1 (6)
3	24.1 (10)	20.0 (6)	
4	29.0 (6)	21.3 (7)	16.3 (3)
5		19.5 (10)	15.2 (6)
6	21.6 (3)	20.8 (6)	16.8 (7)

during the initial, middle, or final period of a governor's six-year term. I have argued previously in relation to the federal government that corruption (and perceptions) are patterned on the presidential *sexenio*, with greater enthusiasm for fighting corruption marking the early years of a term and greater disillusionment and even an increase in corruption marking the waning years—the famous *año de Hidalgo* (Morris 1991). To test this, I examine the mean level of change in perceptions of corruption during the prior year based on the year of the governor's term. As shown in table 9.6, for 2001 and 2003, the most positive assessments of change took place not during the initial years of the administration, as expected, but rather during the fourth year of the term, while in 2005, the best assessments marked the second year of the governor's term. Even so, the data do tend to reveal a tendency for fewer individuals to believe corruption is on the decline during the latter years of the governor's term. This trend could also be discerned from the data overall at the national level. As the term of President Vicente Fox wore on, fewer and fewer, when asked, expressed the view that corruption had fallen the year before, from 24.6 percent in 2001 to just 17.7 percent by 2005.

THE ROLE OF INSTITUTIONAL FACTORS

As many analysts of democracy are quick to point out, elections alone may not do much to reduce corruption. Elections are a very crude tool of accountability, and as Guerrero (2004) suggests, progress in the electoral realm may have little direct impact on the rule of law or governance. Instead, institutions are critical to effective governance. Can more of the variation in levels of corruption and change by states be explained by institutional differences? As an alternative approach, I explore here the impact of three measures of rule of law and bureaucratic efficiency. The first is an index of honesty and efficiency in public infrastructure constructed by Del Castillo et al. (2005). This index measures state leakage by comparing the amount spent on infrastructure to the stock of infrastructure in the state over a period of time. The second measure is the index of state budgetary information presented by Pardinas (2004). This is a measure of the laws and availability of information regarding the use of state's resources. This is an important variable given the emphasis in the current anticorruption campaign on transparency. A final indicator focuses on the efficiency of the state judicial system based on the average rate of indictments by state in 2000, as presented in Zepeda (2004). Of course, it is hypothesized that greater bureaucratic efficiency, transparency, and an effective judicial system, by providing the tools to effectively combat corruption, will correlate with declining levels of corruption in the state.[6]

As shown in the first three columns of table 9.7, however, these institutional variables were largely unrelated to changes in actual levels of corruption over the 2001–2005 period. Whereas measures of budgetary transparency and the judiciary similarly had virtually no impact on corruption as measured by participation or perception levels, honesty and efficiency in state infrastructure turned out to be a rather robust predictor of the level of participation in corruption using the ICBG 2005, but not in the expected direction. Contrary to expectation, the higher the honesty and efficiency within the state, the higher the level of corruption (as mea-

Table 9.7 **Multiple regression of corruption and change along institutional variables**

	Change in corruption 2001–2005			Level of corruption 2005	Perception 2003
	1	2	3		
Constant	.424*	.478*	.299	8.041***	77.729***
	(.223)	(.236)	(.266)	(2.288)	(4.206)
Index of honesty	.070			2.096***	.848
	(.100)			(.645)	(1.186)
Budgetary transparency		−.004		.022	.056
		(.004)		(.028)	(.051)
Judicial efficiency			.002	−.087	−.049
			(.008)	(.063)	(.115)
State GDP/pc	4.53E	9.10E	1.00E	−9.5E	.000
	(.000)	(.000)	(.000)	(.000)	(.000)
Initial levels of corruption	−.054**	−.038*	−.044**		
	(.022)	(.019)	(.019)		
(Adjusted) R^2	.126	.099		.312	-.038
F	2.314	2.489	2.134	4.511	.716
Significance	.098	.081	.118	.006	.588

Coefficients are unstandardized. Robust standard error in parentheses.
*** = < .001.   ** = < .01.   * = < .05.

sured by actual participation in corrupt activity). Honesty and efficiency also had a similar though less significant impact on perception of corruption in 2003. It is not entirely clear why this might be the case. Beyond the methodological challenges of measuring leakage and potential problems in the approach employed by Del Castillo et al. (2005), one could speculate based on this finding that bureaucratic corruption may in some way facilitate the efficient use of resources at the state level. Clearly this measure and its relationship to participation in corruption warrants more careful analysis.

CORRUPTION AND VOTING

As alluded to earlier, corruption not only impacts democracy but also shapes opinions of politicians, institutions, and democracy and may influence voting and thus the pattern of democratization. What impact do the levels of corruption and perceptions of corruption have on voting patterns at the state level? This question is crucial in the overall analysis since part of the mechanisms linking democracy to a reduction in corruption include the notion that voters respond to past performance of political leaders and reward or punish officials and parties with their vote. If corruption—either real or imagined—has little impact on voting, then its use as a measure of vertical accountability is much diminished.

To explore the impact of corruption—both participation and perception—on voting at the state level, I begin by looking at the impact on abstentionism. The scatterplots in figure 9.2 show the relationship between abstentionism in the state during the 2003 federal midterm election and the levels of corruption in 2001 and perceptions of corruption in 2003. As the graphs make clear, however, neither the level of real nor perceived corruption has a direct linear impact on rates of abstentionism. To explore this issue further, I hypothesize that in states where corruption is higher there will be a greater decline in the vote for the PRI and a lesser likelihood to return the incumbent political party in the state to power. The graphs presented in figure 9.3, however, show no direct relationship linking initial levels of corruption and the subsequent change in the vote for the PRI over the 2000–2003 period. Similarly, a simple comparison of means among the states that voted out the incumbent party in the subsequent gubernatorial election ($n=5$) and those that returned the governor's party to office ($n=22$) shows virtually no relationship to the initial levels of corruption or to changes in the real or perceived corruption. Though the five states where incumbents were turned out of office at the state level registered slightly higher levels of corruption and limited reductions in corruption, the differences were minimal and the results varied across the time periods. For example, whereas an average of 80.2 percent of respondents in the five states in 2001 that subsequently voted the incumbents out of office considered all politicians corrupt, an average of 79.4 percent of respondents in the twenty-two states that subsequently returned to office the party in power held this view.

Cognizant of the ecological fallacy here and the danger of using aggregate data to draw inferences about individual behavior like voting, it is important to step briefly outside of the subnational context of this chapter to incorporate individual-level analysis of these questions. Clearly the best way to gauge the impact of corruption on voting is through individual-level data. Unfortunately, the ENCBG surveys do not include questions regarding voting. The 2004 Latin American Public Opinion Project (LAPOP) poll on Mexico from Vanderbilt University, however, does provide such data.[7] Using respondents' retrospective account of having voted or not and their vote in the 2003 Chamber of Deputies election for the

Figure 9.2   **Scatterplots of corruption and abstentionism**

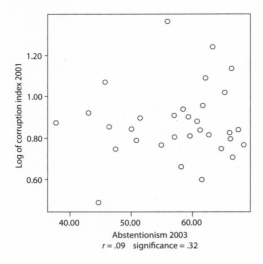

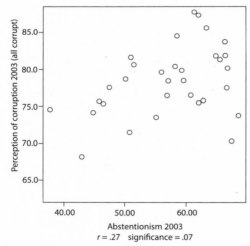

Figure 9.3 **Scatterplots of corruption and change in PRI vote, 2000–2003**

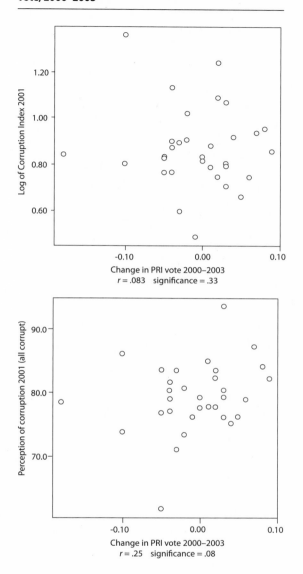

Table 9.8   Corruption and voting at the individual level

Retrospective voting in 2003 by perception of corruption (*n* = 1345)

	Level of corruption among politicians			
	Muy generalizada	Algo generalizada	Poco generalizada	Nada generalizada
Voted	67.2	71.5	70.6	80.8
Abstained	32.8	28.5	29.4	19.2

Retrospective vote by party in 2003 by perception of corruption (*n* = 809)

	Level of corruption among politicians			
Vote in 2003 election	Muy generalizada	Algo generalizada	Poco generalizada	Nada generalizada
PAN	41.5	38.3	40.2	27.8
PRI	36.3	37.7	45.9	55.6
PRD	13.5	20.4	9.8	11.1

Retrospective voting in 2003 by experience in corruption (*n* = 1497)

	Experience/participation in corruption		
	No experience	Some	More experience
Voted	72.3	66.8	72.2
Abstained	27.7	33.1	27.8

Retrospective vote by party in 2003 by experience in corruption (*n* = 908)

	Experience/participation in corruption		
Vote in 2003 election	No experience	Some	More experience
PAN	40.4	37.9	37.4
PRI	38.0	38.2	38.2
PRD	16.9	17.1	17.9

three major parties as the dependent variables, table 9.8 explores the impact of the individual's perception of and participation in corruption on voting. Perception of corruption is measured by the individual's response to the question: "Taking into account your experience, corruption among politicians is *muy generalizada, algo generalizada, poco generalizada,* or *nada generalizada.*" The composite measure of participation in corruption draws on a series of questions asking the respondent whether s/he has paid a bribe, witnessed the payment of a bribe, or been requested to pay a bribe over the prior year in distinct contexts (police, municipality, bureaucracy). As shown through simple cross-tabulations, the perception of corruption may indeed influence the decision to vote and the vote itself. Respondents considering corruption among politicians more pronounced were more likely to abstain than those considering corruption less generalized and more likely to vote for the PAN. This is consistent with the earlier findings of McCann and Dominguez (1998). Moreover, while those considering corruption less generalized were more likely to vote, they were slightly more likely to cast their vote for the PRI. Experience or participation in corruption, by contrast, seemed to have no impact on the decision to vote. This again indicates the distinct nature of perception versus participation as alluded to earlier. Those with limited experience with corruption, however, were slightly more likely to cast their vote for the PAN. Such findings, though suggestive, contrast the state-level findings.

SEPARATING PERCEIVED CORRUPTION FROM CORRUPT BEHAVIOR

Examining the impact of democratization and democratic competition in Mexico, this analysis finds some limited support linking democracy to lower levels of corruption and success at combating corruption. Evidence suggests that a curvilinear relationship may exist, with initial democratization increasing the real and perceived levels of corruption before having some impact on lowering these two dimensions of corruption. The defeat of the PRI at the state level and the rise of opposition-controlled state executives did seem to play a role in lowering the overall levels of corruption and perception, but the impact seemed to diminish somewhat over time.

What the evidence presented here rules out is even more critical. Though weakly related to each other, perceptions of corruption tend to respond to different determinants and to behave somewhat independently from actual levels of participation in corruption. This suggests that the two should be treated separately unless evidence in a particular setting indicates otherwise. In addition, though measures of change in corruption seem to relate somewhat to initial levels of corruption—with change more likely where corruption is high to begin with—change seems to respond to factors distinct from those that determine the levels of real or perceived corruption. Explaining the level of corruption, in short, may provide only limited insights into what works to combat corruption. The overriding conclusion, however, is that a series of measures of democracy and democratic competitiveness was able to explain very little of the overall variation of the rates of participation in corruption, perceived corruption, or change in corruption at the subnational level in Mexico. This finding bolsters the view that while democracy may play some role in shaping the patterns of corruption and change in a positive direction in the short term, the impact of democracy on corruption may be less than expected in the medium run.

Such results, in turn, point in three directions for further analysis. First, it is important to explore the subnational unit in greater detail through case studies to uncover what works and what does not work in combating corruption. Second, we should disaggregate actual participation in corruption from perceptions, recognizing that both are critical in a political sense and worthy of study. Third, future research needs to work harder to uncover how and under what conditions advances in democracy "cross the great divide" to have an impact on governance, the strengthening of institutions, and the reduction of corruption.

CHARLES H. BLAKE AND STEPHEN D. MORRIS

Conclusion Scholarly Avenues and Policy Directions for the Twenty-first Century

Corruption and impunity remain prevalent in Latin America despite democratization and recent anticorruption reforms. In turn, the resilience of corruption is buoyed by the perception (and the reality) of enduring impunity: relatively few government officials face serious sanctions. This combination of robust corruption and continuing impunity has corrosive implications for those striving to extend the scope of democratic rule and to build a more just society.

The resilience of corruption highlights the desire to devise better solutions to the corruption problem, which, in turn, points to the need for better analytical tools to enhance our understanding of this thorny issue. In this chapter we reflect on the contributions that the studies presented here make to each of the three major areas of corruption research: institutional dynamics, cultural factors, and anticorruption efforts. We also consider the implications of these findings for surmounting the political challenges that characterize the contemporary landscape in Latin America.

THE STUDY OF POLITICAL CORRUPTION REVISITED

Despite a perhaps naive or romantic optimism accompanying democratization in Latin America, evidence suggests that corruption and impunity continue largely unabated throughout much of the region. Scandals continue to mark the contemporary news scene and perceptions of corrupt politicians, and corrupt institutions remain strikingly and stubbornly high. But as Thacker shows, "democracy's beneficial effects on the quality of government appear to be time-dependent and best captured over the long term." To reduce corruption, democracy needs time to develop and strengthen key institutions of accountability and the supporting political attitudes and culture.

Is Latin America currently on the right track to accomplish such feats? It is perhaps too early to tell, but the institutional reforms and political trends described by several of the authors in this volume may lower the incidence of corruption with time. From this perspective, the anticorruption glass in the region might be described as one-quarter full rather than three-quarters empty. Give the region more time, in other words, and corruption will recede as patterns of democratic governance deepen. Alternatively, others in Latin America—including many of its politicians— might claim that this region is different in ways that entrench corruption. From this more pessimistic perspective, the distinctive cultural, structural, and political foundations of these countries destine them to exhibit high levels of political corruption.

Does democratization in Latin America augur a more optimistic or pessimistic future for corruption-fighting? Is democratic governance, in other words, progressing in such a way as to reduce eventually the region's historically high levels of corruption? If so, this would be consistent with the cross-regional and regional findings by Thacker and the national case study of Chile by Brinegar. Or, by contrast, are both new and deeply embedded old forms of corruption arresting democratization in ways that inhibit the emergence of the forms of horizontal and vertical accountability needed to make corruption less frequent? This short-circuiting of democratic accountability mechanisms was discussed conceptually in this volume by Rehren and examined empirically in a cross-regional study by Manzetti and Wilson. The essays in this volume weigh in on these and other questions—highlighting the institutional and cultural underpinnings of corruption in the region, the "uniqueness" of Latin America, and the impact of recent and future reforms.

INSTITUTIONAL INFLUENCES ON CORRUPTION

Strom Thacker's study situates the Latin American experience within the contemporary debate over the role of economic and political institutions as influences on corruption. Market-oriented economic policies stimulate a reduction in corruption by limiting the discretionary control that government might otherwise have over economic resources. Democracy, over time, constitutes a second set of institutions that can limit corruption via the emergence of greater transparency and separation of powers that enhance horizontal accountability. Democracy also reduces the probability of corruption over time by nurturing the emergence of a more vibrant media and a voting public that can exercise vertical accountability at the ballot box. These economic and political institutions are also invigorated by economic prosperity. Economic wealth combats corruption by changing the calculus of government officials. In middle-income and lower-income settings, public-sector employees often earn little but presume that corrupt practices can yield a higher wage that often exceeds their earning prospects in the private sector. In contrast, public officials get paid better in affluent settings and they also enjoy the possibility of even higher wages in several private-sector career paths.

One can find politicians and ordinary citizens alike in different countries in Latin America who will proclaim that institutional reforms may work elsewhere, but that they cannot reduce corruption in their country because *their* country is different. Simply put, is Latin America an island to itself or not? Thacker convincingly demonstrates through empirical analysis that the major economic and political influences on corruption around the world are similarly important in Latin America. Greater trade openness, democracy, and greater affluence all constitute factors associated with lower levels of corruption in Latin America and beyond. In particular, Thacker confirms some recent research by him and other scholars that shows that democratic institutions tend not to reduce corruption immediately, but rather over substantial periods of time.

Rehren and Bailey conceptualize the complex interactions between democratic governance and corruption in ways that inform the design of the middle-range studies that comprise the remainder of this volume. In different ways, these two analyses help us to understand why democracy's constraining effect on corruption takes time to emerge throughout the world and continues to struggle in the Latin America of the early twenty-first century. Rehren focuses on the impact that clientelist politics and neopopulism have on the linkages between democracy and corruption. Amid weak horizontal accountability among governing institutions in new democracies, electoral competition often focuses on the distribution of targeted resources that are either obtained by illegal means, distributed illegally, or both. This helps explain why, despite elections, the corruption associated with clientelism has continued to characterize the region.

Bailey's examination of these issues disaggregates the ties between democracy and corruption still further. Bailey highlights the possibility that the prevalence of corruption in a given country may be systemic or may be concentrated in particular agencies or in particular levels of government. In particular, he illustrates how the frequent failings in certain institutions (auditing agencies, service-providing agencies, law enforcement, and the judiciary) contribute both individually and collectively to the resilience of corruption. In Latin America, the weakness of such key institutions, particularly the weak rule of law, goes a long way in creating the conditions so conducive to corruption. Without effective reforms in these critical areas, anticorruption measures are often short-lived and of little effect.

Morris explores these themes by studying intranational variation in the prevalence of corruption across Mexican states. His analysis at the subnational level lends some support to the theory that Thacker examined cross-nationally: that it takes time for democratic institutions to influence the level of corruption. The recent emergence of democratic elections and alternation in power did not consistently constrain people's participation in corruption nor was it associated robustly with changes in the perceived level of corruption over the short term. Beyond these findings, Morris's study highlights some differences between the dynamics of corrupt behavior and the level of perceived corruption. This serves as a cautionary tale reminding us that perceived corruption should not be viewed as an interchangeable proxy for corruption itself. Each is important in its own right.

CULTURAL AND ATTITUDINAL INFLUENCES ON CORRUPTION

Manzetti and Wilson examine the interaction of clientelist scenarios, corruption, and government support that Rehren and Bailey raised by studying the individual attitudes of citizens in and beyond Latin America. On its face, a democratic election is an institution of vertical accountability: voters have the chance to remove leaders whom they believe have engaged in corrupt behavior. Manzetti and Wilson calculated predicted probabilities that illustrate how ineffective institutions mediate the relationship between perceived corruption and government support. Where stronger institutions exist, citizens who perceive corrupt activity are unlikely to support the government. Conversely, where weak institutions permit more frequent use of clientelist exchanges, the link between corruption and government support weakens markedly. As they point out, "countries with the weakest democratic institutions are likely to continue to support the status quo, even if there is considerable corruption." This finding helps further explain the lack of democratic progress in many Latin American countries and the weak tendency (to date) for democracy to undermine corrupt activities.

Another important factor framing the opportunities for corrupt activity is the public's tolerance for corruption, particularly when faced with weak political institutions. Blake focuses on the issue of tolerance of corruption, analyzing the influence of another institution examined by Bailey—the role of law enforcement. Via a cross-regional study of individual attitudes toward bribe-taking, Blake demonstrates that public confidence in the police tends to have a significant and negative impact on the tolerance of corruption. When people lack confidence in the police, they are more likely to tolerate bribe-taking. However, Blake also finds that this cross-regional relationship between police confidence and the tolerance of corruption does not hold in Latin America. Instead, income and life satisfaction are more powerful influences on tolerance in Latin America than they are elsewhere in the world. This finding dovetails with the dynamic revealed by Manzetti and Wilson: the poor and the discontented are more likely to tolerate corruption when faced with weak state institutions than those more fortunate. While Manzetti and Wilson focus on the capacity for clientelism's impact on corruption attitudes, Blake complements that study by showing that the most vulnerable members of Latin American society tend to be more tolerant of corruption.

The distortion of democratic institutions highlighted by Manzetti and Wilson and Blake is partly driven by the region's deep-seated poverty and inequality. Manzetti and Wilson show that (coupled with weak institutions of representation) poverty feeds clientelism and the corruption that so often accompanies it. Blake similarly finds the poor are particularly tolerant toward corruption when facing a corrupt police. In both cases, corruption and clientelism can be seen as a type of survival strategy for the poor that has the effect of rewarding the status quo and preventing the strengthening of democratic institutions. This highlights the need to reduce poverty and inequality if democratic and institutional anticorruption reforms are to bear fruit. This point is underscored further in the study by López-Cálix, Seligson, and Alcázar. Their examination of a Peruvian subsidized milk program identified the difficult subsistence choices faced by many poor families in Peru and beyond. Impoverished families could let the intended recipients (poor children) drink the milk to protect their long-term physical and mental development. Or, alternatively, they could choose to divert the milk to adults to assist their efforts to earn crucial wages from day to day in the present. The reduction of poverty and of income inequality can work in tandem with institutional changes to reduce the share of the population that finds itself in dire economic straits that can foment both tolerance of corruption and corrupt behavior itself.

Brinegar shifts this volume's consideration of attitudes toward corruption from the cross-national examination of individuals to a series of studies within a shared national context. He examines Chileans' perceptions regarding corruption's importance and prevalence, the evaluation of anticorruption reform efforts, and the potential link between perceived corruption and vote choice. By working within a shared Chilean context, Brinegar can isolate the role that partisanship plays as a filter in the formation of public attitudes. Supporters of the governing coalition in the early twenty-first century were less influenced by corruption scandals, while opponents of the Concertación coalition were more likely to perceive corruption as prevalent, problematic, and a potential rationale for their choices on Election Day.

The role of partisan filters highlights the interplay between the nature of the party system, democratic governance, and corruption. When one party dominates the political system (and has many loyal adherents), it will be more difficult to build a political coalition that wants to limit corruption. In addition, it is harder for elections to emerge as a vehicle for vertical accountability. If most citizens identify with the governing party (or, at a minimum, see its reelection as almost inevitable), attitudinal filters make it less likely that corruption concerns could produce an electoral surge against the incumbent party.

In contrast, the Chilean scandals of the early twenty-first century emerged on the heels of a narrow electoral victory for the Concertación coalition both in the presidential election and in the lower house of the legislature. Both the governing Concertación coalition and the opposition Alliance coalition were operating in a context of perceived and real electoral competitiveness. In this context, leaders of both sides observed a volatile electoral situation in which corruption issues could conceivably sway enough voters to affect the outcome of the next national elections. Accordingly, the Concertación leaders were more motivated to respond quickly to the scandals with a series of executive branch actions as polls indicated declining support among swing voters and the scandals played out during 2002. These November 2002 reforms by the Lagos government, in turn, motivated the Alliance legislators to pursue anticorruption legislation in an effort not to "lose" this corruption issue in the 2004 local elections and 2005 national elections. In a competitive electoral context, this engendered an embrace of these initiatives by the Concertatión's legislative bloc and by Lagos himself.

The contemporary Chilean experience testifies to the delicate linkages between democratic governance, attitude formation, and the political dynamics of corruption. When several conditions (reduced clientelism, declining poverty, and a competitive electoral situation) are largely in place, public attitudes, electoral dynamics, and legislative politics can promote more robust efforts to combat corruption. In turn, in scenarios dominated by the clientelist dynamics revealed by Rehren, Bailey, Manzetti and Wilson, and Blake, public attitudes are less likely to evolve in a manner that would motivate governments to combat corruption.

ANTICORRUPTION REFORM EFFORTS

Perhaps what most distinguishes the current period in Latin America is not a high level of corruption per se, but rather the high level of corruption in the face of significant anticorruption reforms in the late twentieth and early twenty-first centuries. Questions center not only on what works and what does not, but also on identifying what course(s) of action should be taken. While many of the essays in this volume show that democratization and current reform initiatives generally have failed to reduce corruption very effectively thus far, the studies by López-Cálix, Seligson, and Alcázar and by Taylor examine the impact or likely impact of several specific reform measures.

Anticorruption advocates have frequently called for decentralization as a remedy for corruption, for instance. By bringing government closer to the people, corruption is said to become easier to identify and to sanction. Some reform advocates take this logic one step further by advocating the delegation of program administration to nongovernmental organizations that are believed to be less prone to corruption than governments. López-Cálix, Seligson, and Alcázar put these claims to the test by analyzing the results of an innovative auditing procedure designed to identify the leakage of public funds at each level of government—from the national level on down to the individual recipients—in the Peruvian Vaso de Leche program. Their analysis finds no support for the decentralization approach. To the contrary, program funds were diverted mainly at the local level of government and among the private citizens empowered to ensure that milk got to the children who were the intended beneficiaries.

Taking a broader approach, Taylor's study of anticorruption reforms in Brazil examines the interplay among democratic institutions, socialized patterns of behavior, and the prospects for future reform. Echoing a fundamental point raised earlier, Taylor notes that the "over-optimism about the democracy-enhancing implications of the recurring patterns of scandals is all-too-common." He demonstrates that the proliferation of anticorruption initiatives need not reduce corruption markedly as long as agencies continue to work in relative isolation and in an oft-overlapping fashion. Taylor shows that Brazilian anticorruption efforts have focused on the investigation of allegations. In turn, the pursuit of ongoing monitoring and the effort to sanction those found to have engaged in corruption both lag behind. "The overall emphasis of the accountability system thus privileges the investigatory stages over continuous monitoring or effective sanctioning that might alter incentive structures and thus deter future corruption." He also details political obstacles to the adoption of a new electoral system that might reduce the prevalence of clientelist politics. Despite these problems and obstacles to reform, Taylor identifies some success stories in informal cooperation across disparate anticorruption bodies and improved auditing.

THE ROAD AHEAD

The last decade of the twentieth century and the first decade of this century have witnessed more scholarly and governmental attention to corruption than ever before. In this volume we have attempted to build on this recent wave of research by carrying out a series of middle-range studies on issues that received insufficient attention amid the rush to make use of aggregate measures of corruption developed by Transparency International and by the World Bank. In this closing section we highlight some lessons that we hope can inform scholars and policymakers.

THE FUTURE OF RESEARCH ON CORRUPTION

Cross-national, aggregate-level studies of perceived corruption can, will, and should continue. To date, such studies have provided a wealth of knowledge regarding the causes and consequences of corruption. We need to know if the major causal trends highlighted ably by Thacker in this volume extend into the future. In addition, there is always the possibility that additional influences on the aggregate level of perceived corruption can be identified. Still further, the aggregate level of perceived corruption can have an impact on other issues.

At the same time, we hope that this collection of essays demonstrates the utility of work in the middle range on the politics of corruption. Rehren and Bailey improve upon most existing discussions of corruption and democracy by detailing how specific aspects and nuances of democracy in Latin America can shape the patterns of corruption and how they can affect governability. Both Rehren and Bailey remain open to the possibility that corruption dynamics vary within countries—across subnational units, across individuals, and across governmental agencies.

The other studies in this volume carry forward this dual agenda of disaggregating both the concept of corruption and the unit of analysis at which it is studied. The research by Morris and by López-Cálix, Seligson, and Alcázar develops approaches to measuring the presence of corrupt behavior rather than depending on perception alone. As Morris indicates, the dynamics of corruption itself need not be equivalent to the dynamics of perceived corruption. The two phenomena at issue—perception and behavior—differ, and each is important in its own right. These two studies also highlight subnational variation in corruption levels. In turn, the contributions from Manzetti and Wilson, Blake, and Brinegar focus primarily on individual citizens and on questions that have received insufficient attention to date. Finally, Taylor's case study highlights some factors that make interagency cooperation and institutional reform difficult.

Conducting these middle-range studies requires considerable fieldwork. Whether one utilizes survey research, formal auditing, archival research, elite interviewing, or some combination of these techniques, the middle-range approach requires careful research design and intensive data collection. Research costs increase still further when the study contemplates subnational variation. Frankly, cost factors play an important role in steering most existing research to the national level. These costs notwithstanding, we hope that the insights developed via this eclectic approach improve our understanding of corruption dynamics in ways that improve the prospects for combating corruption in Latin America and beyond.

The resilience of corruption—and of impunity, corruption's "evil twin"—is a source of frustration for anticorruption activists inside and outside of Latin America. It can also disenchant citizens who have seen more high-profile corruption scandals discussed in the news media than ever before. If corruption undermines support for democracy or hollows out democracy, it can conceivably prevent the maturity of democracy needed to curb corruption. Nonetheless, we believe that this volume has provided some grounds for hope. Thacker demonstrates that the broad set of economic and political influences on the level of perceived corruption operates in Latin America just as it does elsewhere. Similarly, Manzetti and Wilson test a theory of clientelist influences on governmental support in which Latin American countries exhibit dynamics observed in other countries. In turn, while Blake identifies some regional distinctiveness in the dynamics of tolerance toward corruption, his study finds that Latin Americans exhibit less tolerance of corruption than their low level of confidence in the police would predict. In short, the cross-regional studies in this volume demonstrate that Latin America does not seem to be culturally doomed to suffer high levels of corruption. The dynamics of corruption are largely similar to those observed elsewhere and, to the extent that Latin America is different, citizens are less tolerant of corruption than their life circumstances would predict.

Within those broad trends, several studies in this volume testify to the potential for intranational distinctiveness related to corruption. While more transparent accounting, freedom of information laws, and greater horizontal and vertical accountability constitute a useful set of principles, the precise path to progress is likely to differ both across and within countries. The clientelism that inhibits vertical accountability (and which is empowered by weak horizontal accountability) varies in its prevalence across and within Latin American countries—a point raised by Rehren and then reinforced by Bailey, Manzetti, and Wilson, and Brinegar, Taylor, and Morris.

Similarly, building a political coalition designed to support the enactment and implementation of anticorruption reform is tricky work. The reform agenda and its political dynamics vary in accord with the context. Life circumstances (Blake and Manzetti and Wilson), partisan filters (Brinegar and Morris), bureaucratic politics (Taylor), legislative politics (Brinegar and Taylor), and the dynamics of scandal politics (Brinegar and Taylor) all affect the prospects for reform.

Perhaps the most politically charged yet powerful recommendation that could be drawn from our research is the need to measure corrupt behavior and not merely its perception. Morris demonstrates different causal dynamics (and measurement outcomes) in a longitudinal examination of perceived corruption and corrupt behavior in Mexico. Taylor highlights insufficient routine monitoring as a major need in Brazilian anticorruption efforts. In turn, López-Cálix, Seligson, and Alcázar demonstrate the usefulness of a comprehensive approach to program auditing. Rather than simply tracking funding at the initial and final disbursements, their multilevel approach shows great promise as a tool that could be defended politically not just as an anticorruption effort but also as part of a thorough effort to assess program effectiveness.

We are not naive enough to believe that the mere recommendation of more widespread accounting will stir governments to enact these programs. Detailed intranational auditing is costly. It also potentially threatens government officials and private officials engaged in corrupt activities. It is a challenge to mobilize public pressure on behalf of auditing improvement when many citizens in Latin America (and elsewhere) are struggling to live day to day. Combating corruption—particularly in the countries or subnational regions where it is more prevalent—is hard.

Despite the difficulties identified in this volume and in other previous research, it can safely be said that progress can be made. If poverty and inequality decline, the prospects for robust democratic governance—and for corruption control—will improve considerably. Public support for reform also can be cultivated by emphasizing savings that should exceed the costs of more extended monitoring. Research on corruption dynamics can be incorporated into campaigns that emphasize both the feasibility and the desirability of reform. There is a long road ahead in these linked efforts to understand and to combat corruption. We hope that this volume has advanced us a little farther down that road. Moreover, we remain convinced that it is indeed a road worth traveling.

NOTES

CHAPTER 1   **DEMOCRACY, ECONOMIC POLICY, AND POLITICAL
CORRUPTION IN COMPARATIVE PERSPECTIVE**

1. See Gerring and Thacker (2004) for a recent review of the literature.

2. Note that this is a purposefully broad definition of political corruption, a term that some might interpret more narrowly as corruption within the electoral or legislative spheres. But corruption within the government more generally, including the bureaucracy, is certainly a political phenomenon, as it involves public officials who have either been elected themselves or have been appointed by elected politicians. For these reasons, I prefer the term "political corruption," which encompasses both the narrow concept of electoral or legislative corruption as well as what others may call "bureaucratic" or "administrative" corruption. This broad definition of political corruption is also consistent with the empirical measures used in this chapter (see Gerring and Thacker 2005).

3. Other, more intermediate-level institutions such as federalism/unitarism and presidentialism/parliamentarism also influence corruption (see Gerring and Thacker 2004). But there is insufficient variation in these institutional arrangements in Latin America to get empirical leverage on them in a regional context.

4. This segment of the chapter draws upon Gerring, Thacker, and Alfaro (2006).

5. For example, see Alt and Lassen (2008) for a treatment of the role of elected (as opposed to appointed) judges in reducing corruption.

6. Democracy is not a necessary condition for the presence of a strong civil society. But it is likely that, all else being equal, civil society networks will be stronger in a democratic system than a nondemocratic one.

7. Institutional decay can occur under democratic rule, too, as the cases of Venezuela and Peru have demonstrated in recent years. The present argument is probabilistic: old democracies are more likely than new democracies and authoritarian regimes to have strong institutions.

8. For an excellent summary and intellectual history of neoliberalism, see Colclough (1991).

9. This section draws upon Gerring and Thacker (2005).

10. The privatization process, for example, has been fraught with abuse in many countries. See also La Palombara (1994, 340); Snyder (1999); Tanzi (1998, 563).

11. The classic Stigler-Peltzman theory of regulation, in which utility-maximizing

interest groups offer political support to regulators in exchange for favorable treatment, is apropos here. See Stigler (1971) and Peltzman (1976).

12. The World Bank calculates this indicator every other year, beginning in 1996. The present study covers the four observations from 1996 through 2002. This indicator is available for two additional observation years (2004 and 2006), but insufficient coverage of some of the control variables precludes an analysis of those data points.

13. The World Bank indicator and Transparency International's more well-known Corruption Perceptions Index are very highly correlated ($r = 0.92$). Because of the World Bank index's greater coverage, I focus here on that measure. For discussion of the relative merits of cross-national corruption polls, see Elliott (1997); Gerring and Thacker (2004); Heywood (1997); Jain (1998); Johnston (2000); and Robinson (1998).

14. This index is a poll of polls. The polls (of businesspeople, country residents, and experts) ask respondents to rate the general level of corruption among public officials, the effectiveness of anticorruption initiatives, the frequency of additional payments necessary to "get things done," and corruption as an obstacle to foreign investment and domestic business enterprise (for further details, see Kaufmann, Kraay, and Mastruzzi 2003). Recent scholarship has explored the relationship and the differences between the perception of corruption and actual corruption (see Morris's contribution to this volume for one example). One might question whether perceptions of corruption as judged by survey responses accurately reflect an empirical reality (actual, existing corruption). It could be that perceptions measure precisely that—perceptions—and nothing more. There is no question that corruption is to some extent, here and everywhere, a matter of perception. Yet, at the same time, it is likely that perceptions of corruption have some substantial basis in reality. Olken (2007) has shown, for example, that while perceptions of corruption do typically contain valid information about levels of corruption, that information is often incomplete. At the same time, perceptions themselves can matter; if foreign investors believe a country to be corrupt, that belief itself may alter their investment patterns (Treisman 2007). In this sense, the perception of corruption may be at least as important as its reality. In employing the World Bank perception-based measure of political corruption, this chapter does not claim to provide definitive tests of the actual practice of corruption. Rather, it explores factors that influence the level of perceived political corruption in Latin America and elsewhere, a factor that likely correlates reasonably well with actual levels of corruption and that is also important in its own right. Finally, there is the question of whether or not perception-based measures are biased systematically in one direction or another in terms of the factors analyzed here. If they simply under- or overestimate the level of actual corruption across the board (in democratic and authoritarian countries, and in open and closed economies), we have less reason for concern here. In this case, impressions of corruption may be systematically higher in more open societies, as democratic regimes and open economies typically allow better and more varied access to information for citizens. Watchdog groups and media scrutiny, for example, should be more robust in open societies than closed (see above). Such factors may artificially increase the perception—as compared to the reality—of corruption in open societies. If this is true, it should bias results against the hypotheses under consideration here, thus providing a more difficult test than a "true" measure of actual corruption might.

15. To correct for Polity2's exclusion of micro-states, an exclusion that might bias the sample, democracy scores for these excluded cases were imputed using other democracy indices that are conceptually and empirically close to the Polity2 measure: (1) the Freedom House Political Rights indicator; (2) Ken Bollen's Liberal Democracy variable (Bollen 1993), (3) Tatu Vanhanen's Competition variable (Vanhanen 1990), (4) Arthur Banks's Legislative Effectiveness variable, and (5) Banks's Party Legitimacy variable (Banks 1994). These measures of democracy, which correlate strongly with the Polity2 measure, take into account the degree to which citizens can participate freely in the political process, the extent of suffrage, the competitiveness of national-level elections, the degree of party competitiveness, and the degree to which the legislature affects public policy.

16. Because the historical component of this index weighs heavily on our understanding of the concept and because the Polity data set ignores nonsovereign states in its coding procedures, the Polity2 coding was supplemented with new coding of several nation-states that were previously part of contiguous empires. The procedure is as follows. For each year that a nation-state belonged to a contiguous imperial power it receives the same Polity2 score as its imperial ruler; for example, Estonia receives the same score as the Soviet Union from 1941 through 1990. This procedure applies only to nation-states contiguous with the empire to which they previously belonged, under the assumption that contiguous colonies are likely to be governed in the same manner as the imperial power itself, a dynamic less likely to be true for overseas colonies. This recoding affects the following countries: Albania (1900–1912, Ottoman Empire), Andorra (1900–present, France), Armenia (1900–1990, Russia/USSR), Azerbaijan (Russia/USSR, 1900–1990), Belarus (Russia/USSR, 1900–1990), Bosnia-Herzegovina (1908–1917, Austria-Hungary; Yugoslavia 1929–1991), Croatia (1900–1917, Austria-Hungary; Yugoslavia 1929–1991), Czech Republic (1900–1917, Austria-Hungary), Slovakia (1900–1917, Austria-Hungary), Estonia (1900–1916 and 1941–1990, Russia/USSR), Finland (1900–1916, Russia), Georgia (1900–1990, Russia/USSR), Iraq (1900–1917, Ottoman Empire), Israel (1900–1917, Ottoman Empire), Kazakhstan (1900–1990, Russia/USSR), Kyrgyzstan (1900–1990, Russia/USSR), Latvia (1900–1917 and 1941–1990, Russia/USSR), Lithuania (1900–1917 and 1941–1990, Russia/USSR), Macedonia (1922–1990, Yugoslavia), Moldova (1900–1945, Romania; 1946–1990, USSR), Mongolia (1900–1920, China), Bangladesh (1947–1971, Pakistan), Slovenia (1900–1917, Austria-Hungary; Yugoslavia 1929–1991), Syria (1900–1917, Ottoman Empire), Tajikistan (Russia/USSR, 1900–1990), Turkmenistan (1900–1990, Russia/USSR), Ukraine (1900–1917 and 1920–1990, Russia/USSR), Uzbekistan (1900–1990, Russia/USSR), and East Timor (1976–1999, Indonesia).

17. Kaufmann et al. standardize scores within each observation year to facilitate cross-national comparison and interpretation. This means, however, that the same score may have different meanings in different years.

18. It is possible that a collinear relationship between democracy level and stock washes out the potential effects of the level variable. The correlation between democracy level and democracy stock is 0.63, a notable but not likely crippling level of collinearity.

19. I retain the imports variable rather than the import duties variable due to its better data coverage.

20. For the results of these tests, contact the author.

21. The analysis of Latin American cases excludes nonsignificant control vari-

ables in order to maximize the degrees of freedom with so few available cases. Including all of the original control variables generates a very similar coefficient for the democracy stock variable and a p-value of 0.08.

22. To simplify matters, I focus here only on imports. A model of only Latin American cases with a full set of controls yields a similar coefficient for imports but a lower level of statistical significance, likely due at least in part to the loss of degrees of freedom.

CHAPTER 2 THE CRISIS OF THE DEMOCRATIC STATE

1. According to Freedom House (2003) the countries classified as "free" in the region have increased from thirteen to twenty-three in the last thirty years; those classified as "partially free" have increased from nine to ten; and two have remained as "not free."

2. This section is based on Rehren (2002).

3. For a discussion on the definition of corruption, see Gardiner (2002).

4. See the seminal article by Scott (1969), as well as Hutchcroft (1997) and the articles on Italy, Spain, Brazil, Mexico, and Venezuela in Little and Posada-Carbó (1996).

5. It has been reported that between 15 and 30 percent of the gross amount of public works contracted in Brazil was charged as bribes to finance the expenses of President Collor de Mello. On Brazil, see Geddes and Ribeiro Neto (1992) and Fleischer (1997). In the case of Peru, Vladimir Montesinos, national security advisor to President Fujimori, was charged with the irregular and unaccounted use of funds from the presidency to pay off legislators, judges, and entrepreneurs and with taping the clandestine meetings. For an in-depth description of corrupt practices in the Fujimori government, see Ego Aguirre (2001). Other early scandals, mainly in Central America and the Caribbean are covered in Maingot (1994).

6. Extending the period to 2005 for the transparency perception index makes no changes in the apparently nonexisting relationship.

7. For other countries, see Alvarez (1995), Fleischer (1997), and McCann and Domínguez (1998).

8. For early cases of corruption under the Concertación governments, see Rehren (1999, 2002).

9. See Boría O. (1995) and on party systems Dix (1992), Mainwaring and Scully (1995), and Davis et al. (2004).

10. According to Freedom House (1994–2002), the press freedom index has fluctuated between 35 and 39 between 1994 and 2002 for the whole region. The 0–100 scale considers countries scoring between 0 and 30 to have a free press.

CHAPTER 3 CORRUPTION AND DEMOCRATIC GOVERNABILITY

1. The discussion of democratic governability is drawn from a broader discussion about public security (taken as a problem complex that includes crime, violence, corruption, and impunity) in relation with regime and state in Latin America. See Bailey (2004).

2. O'Donnell (2004a, 15–20) emphasizes the need to differentiate between democratic regime and democratic state.

3. Dahl (1971, 3) includes "institutions for making government policies depend on votes and other expressions of preference" as a requirement for democracy. Presumably, he implies two things here: (1) there are institutions that make and implement policies, and (2) these institutions are accountable to a democratic regime that, in turn, is accountable to an electorate. Bresser Pereira and Nakano (1998, 36 n. 20) make another useful distinction: "Governability—the effective power to govern—does not assure governance, the quality and effectiveness of government action." As will become clear, I am more interested in the capacity of the state to voluntarily persuade or impose its versions of law than I am in assessing quality or effectiveness of policy in a larger sense.

4. Putnam (1993, 8–9) emphasizes the need to move beyond regime dynamics (e.g., parties, elections, policy deliberation) to emphasize institutional performance in implementation. "Institutions are devices for achieving *purposes*, not just for achieving *agreement*. We want governments to *do* things, not just *decide* things—to educate children, pay pensioners, stop crime, create jobs, hold down prices, encourage family values, and so on."

5. Heidenheimer and Johnston (2002, 3–14) discuss public office, market, public interest, and public opinion as the main approaches to defining corruption. Warren (2004) offers a good example of a broader conception of corruption, one that involves abuse of a position of trust for private gain and to the detriment of the shared interest. His approach encompasses corrupt exchanges in the private realm as well.

6. For example, Heidenheimer's (1970) notions of "black, gray and white" corruption.

7. World Bank terminology differentiates between administrative corruption—"private payments to public officials to distort the prescribed implementation of official rules and policies"—and state capture—"shaping the formation of the basic rules of the game (that is, laws, rules, decrees, and regulations) through illicit and non-transparent private payments to public officials" (quoted in Bhargava and Bolongaita 2004, 24). Thompson (1993) provides a valuable discussion of what he calls "mediated corruption," or the types of corruption that actors engage in to gain influence in the political process through borderline or unethical acts that may not benefit the actors' personal finances but which strengthen their position.

8. The imagery and language are drawn from systems analysis (e.g., Easton 1965) and structure-functionalism (Almond and Powell 1996, 26–30). The output side is arguably less politically sensitive and more amenable to policy intervention. Warren (2004) offers a more complex classification of arenas.

9. Recall Robert Dahl's influential list of requisites for polyarchy (Dahl 1971, chap. 1).

10. My approach is vulnerable to the criticism of reviving a politics-administration dichotomy that has proven to be misleading. Even so, one can make rough—but useful—distinctions between inputs, rule making, and rule application/adjudication.

11. Antolova (2003) analyzes this point usefully.

12. Conversations about corruption among our Africanist colleagues focus on failed states and near-anarchic violence in which ruling elites deliberately undermine legal systems and public bureaucracies in order to reinforce their own power and wealth. See, for example, Reno (2000) and Bayart et al. (1999).

13. Dahl (1971, chap. 1) sets out the most frequently cited requisites of polyarchy.

In an interesting exercise of ranking the gravity of corrupt acts, Karklins (2005, 25) includes "undermining elections and political competition" and "corruption in and of the media" among the most serious (Level III) forms of corruption.

14. By way of anecdote, Da Silva (2000, 188–89) describes the complex relationships between the Brazilian media and government. The "price" of a journalist may be in terms of money, information, or praise, and a politician needs to be careful about what to offer. "Outside Sao Paulo and Rio, it is still the rule rather than the exception that journalists work for both a newspaper and as public servants in government, although as long as they write positive things, or at least not negative things, about their government bosses, they need not show up at the office." A Mexican friend once commented on journalists who blackmail politicians and government officials to *not* publish information.

15. Gallup Argentina (1999, 47–48), for example, finds vote buying in primary elections of *Justicialismo* and *La Alianza*.

16. As one of my students in a seminar at the Universidad Católica in Córdoba, Argentina, put it in 2004: "This analysis of principal-agent-client is interesting, but what do you do when the principal is the most corrupt point in the triangle?"

17. This is quite a sweeping generalization. The Chilean *Carabineros* were an important exception in the six countries covered in Bailey and Dammert (2006).

18. The creation of special anticorruption agencies in many Latin American countries is a reminder that the judicial system is seen as inadequate to deal with corruption.

19. "¿En qué medida cree usted que la corrupción afecta diferentes esferas de la vida en este país?"

20. Peters and Welch (2002) and Johnston (2002) provide useful discussions of gradients of "seriousness" of corruption in the U.S. case. Their findings are roughly in line with Seligson's.

21. Enrique Bravo suggested this possibility.

22. Seligson (2001, 26) reports that "over 70% of our respondents believed that corruption was common or very common. This finding contradicts the information provided by respondents regarding direct and indirect experience with corruption and suggests that Colombians as a general rule believe that the levels of corruption that escape the public eye are very underreported." Bailey and Paras (2006) find a similar disparity in the Mexican case.

23. I have no data from Latin America at hand to support the hypothesis. Eric M. Uslaner finds that high-level corruption has greater negative effects on trust than "ordinary corruption." He did a 2003 survey of Romanians that distinguished between high- and low-level corruption. "Low-level corruption focuses on the extra 'gift' payment people make to doctors, banks, the police and teachers. High-level corruption involves bribery and corruption by politicians, business executives and the courts. We found that low-level corruption did not lead to lower levels of trust. Most people do not see these payments as making others 'rich,' and often see such 'gifts' as making a bureaucratic system more efficient. In contrast, we found that high-level corruption affected perceptions of growing inequality, the evaluations of the performance of the government improving the quality of life, and trust both in other people and in government. Having to pay off city officials and especially officers of the court, together with the beliefs that most politicians and business people were corrupt, led people to believe that the system was stacked against them, that

government could not be trusted, and that even ordinary people were not trustworthy. There are different types of corruption, and citizens in post-communist countries clearly distinguish among them" (TI 2005, 263–64).

24. Central America in the past decade would seem to be an interesting testing ground, especially since it includes the recent experience of Costa Rica, one of the few arguably consolidated democracies, where several past presidents have been accused of grand corruption.

CHAPTER 4 WHY DO CORRUPT GOVERNMENTS MAINTAIN PUBLIC SUPPORT?

1. In a kleptocracy, bribes are just one means of acquiring wealth. More overt forms of corruption are stealing government funds and expropriating property for personal aggrandizement rather than for distribution. Presidents Mohamed Suharto of Indonesia, Ferdinand Marcos of the Philippines, Sani Abacha of Nigeria, and Mobutu Sésé Seko of Zaire are a few notable examples of leaders who pursued this type of grand corruption.

2. Following this rationale, majoritarian electoral systems produce incentives for the "personal vote" similar to open-list proportional representation and non-transferable vote systems.

3. The original Portuguese slogan was "Rouba, mas faz." For an analysis of Adhemar de Barros's clientelist politics, see Mauricio Puls, "Ex Prefeito ocupou vazio politico deixado por Adhemar de Barros," Folha de São Paulo, September 17, 2005. As for Edwards, a few years after winning his last gubernatorial election he was convicted in U.S. Federal Court on multiple counts of corrupt activities.

4. This strategy is further facilitated if countries have little oversight and a weak capacity to detect and punish corrupt behavior and if citizens have scarce information about politicians' behavior (Adserá, Boix, and Payne 2003; Burgess and Besley 2002).

5. The most extreme form of corruption, kleptocracy, would not be a winning electoral strategy, since such regimes do not widely distribute spoils.

6. Of course, these statements are all probabilistic. There are no institutional arrangements that prevent patronage networks from forming altogether. However, these institutions provide the likely opportunity structure politicians encounter. So, the nature of democratic institutions makes it more or less likely that a politician will be rewarded for the development and maintenance of clientelistic networks.

7. Perception of corruption (our key independent variable) was not asked in more recent waves of the World Values Study. While the World Values Study samples more than seventy countries, not all questions are asked in all countries. In only fourteen countries were all questions used in our analysis asked.

8. The results from an ordered logit procedure that keeps all four response categories do not differ substantially from the logit analysis. The analysis is available from the authors.

9. See Lucio Brom (2004) for an analysis of the differences in perceptions of acts as corrupt in Argentina.

10. Additional sociodemographic variables such as age and income were not asked in all countries in the sample. In a smaller sample of countries where age, income, and education levels were recorded, only education was significant. Therefore, we retain this variable in the full model without the other sociodemographic variables in order provide a larger number of countries in the analysis.

11. The marginal effects of the independent variables are calculated using the delta method with the *predictnl* command in STATA 8.2.

12. All predicted probabilities reported in this analysis were estimated with *Clarify*, a statistical program implemented in the Stata statistical package. *Clarify* uses a stochastic simulation technique to simulate parameters such as the predicted probabilities following statistical estimation. For more information about *Clarify*, see King, Tomz, and Wittenberg (2000) and Tomz, Wittenberg, and King (2003).

13. In addition to the analysis presented in table 4.1, we test the robustness of the findings by eliminating the two cases with one-party dominant systems (Taiwan and Mexico) to determine if citizens' level of support is a function of political alternatives available to them. The results of this analysis are available from the authors. There are no significant differences in the coefficients or in the substantive conclusions drawn from analyses.

CHAPTER 5 PUBLIC ATTITUDES TOWARD CORRUPTION

1. On corruption's implications for legitimacy, see Seligson (2002). Regarding the negative effect of corruption on economic growth, see Mauro (1995).

2. Translation by author.

3. Regarding the dynamics of perceived corruption and its implications in Latin America, see Canache and Allison (2005). For additional research on the implications of perceived corruption in Latin America, see Seligson (2002) and Davis, et al. (2004).

4. I want to thank the participants in the research workshop series sponsored by the Department of Political Science at James Madison University for their helpful comments on an initial rough draft of this study. In particular, I thank Margaret Williams for her assistance with two portions of the data analysis for this project. In turn, I also benefited greatly from the suggestions made by Roberto de Michele of the Inter-American Development Bank in his comments at the 2006 LASA Congress.

5. Although fewer citizens interact with the court system, a similar argument can be made regarding the judiciary. In conducting this research, I have also examined the relationship between confidence in the judiciary and tolerance of corruption. Unfortunately, respondents in many countries in the data under analysis were not asked to express an opinion regarding the judicial system—making it difficult to compare the data on this issue with the data regarding confidence in the police. As a result, confidence in the judiciary has been omitted from this study.

6. Case studies of contemporary corruption dynamics in Latin America include Brown and Cloke (2005); Di Tella and Savefoff (2001); Fleischer (1997); Flynn (1993); Geddes and Ribeiro Neto (1992); Maingot (1994); Manzetti and Blake (1996); Morris (1991, 1999, 2003, 2005); Rehren (1997); Rosenn and Downes (1998); Saba and Manzetti (1997); Shelly (2001); Sives (1993); Tulchin and Espach (2000); Weyland (1998); and Whitehead (1989, 2002). Case studies from a broader cross-regional perspective include Heidenheimer, et al. (1989); Heidenheimer and Johnston (2002, 2005); Little and Posada-Carbó (1996); and Williams (2000).

7. Five of the largest cross-national quantitative studies of corruption dynamics are Goldsmith (1999); Sandholtz and Koetzle (2000); Treisman (2000); Gerring and Thacker (2004); and Blake and Martin (2006).

8. From this point forward, this data set will be referred to by the abbreviation WVS.

9. Regarding the results for the full data set (which includes the nondemocratic contexts excluded from this analysis), contact the author for details. The 64 countries examined in this chapter are: Albania, Argentina, Armenia, Australia, Austria, Azerbaijan, Bangladesh, Belgium, Brazil, Bulgaria, Canada, Chile, Colombia, Croatia, Czech Republic, Denmark, Dominican Republic, El Salvador, Estonia, Finland, France, Georgia, Germany, Greece, Hungary, Iceland, India, Indonesia, Ireland, Italy, Japan, Jordan, Latvia, Lithuania, Luxembourg, Macedonia, Malta, Mexico, Moldova, Netherlands, New Zealand, Nigeria, Peru, Philippines, Poland, Romania, Russia, Slovakia, Slovenia, South Africa, South Korea, Spain, Sweden, Switzerland, Taiwan, Tanzania, Turkey, Uganda, Ukraine, United Kingdom, United States, Uruguay, Venezuela, and Zimbabwe.

10. In 57 of the 64 countries under analysis, 90 to 99 percent of the distribution expressed a response of 1 to 5 on this 10-point scale. In Azerbaijan, Hungary, Moldova, Philippines, Slovakia, and Uganda, the percentage in the lower half of the scale ranged from 81.8 to 89.5 percent. Brazil is the lone outlier in this regard: only 68.3 percent of the population gave responses from 1–5 while 15.6 percent of the population expressed the view that taking a bribe was always justifiable. Brazil is the only country in the data set in which more than 6.5 percent of the population expresses the view that bribe-taking is always justifiable; in only five other countries did that figure exceed 3 percent. Systematic consideration of why Brazil is such an outlier in this regard lies beyond the scope of the study in this chapter. For the specific, country-by-country distributions of responses to variable F117 in the WVS, contact the author.

11. Logistic regression is used in this analysis to identify the factors associated with some tolerance versus zero tolerance of bribe-taking. Robust standard errors are calculated to adjust for clustering on the countries represented within these cross-national data using Variable S003 in the WVS. The data are weighted using Variable S017 in the WVS to adjust for differences in sample size across sixty-four countries.

To measure citizens' confidence in the police, Variable E074 was transformed into a dummy variable. Respondents with confidence "most" or "much" of the time are coded 1, while those with "little" or "no" confidence are coded 0. Variable X047 in the WVS measures income in all countries on a 10-point scale from lowest to highest. Variable A170 in the WVS measures life satisfaction on a 10-point scale from lowest to highest. University-level education is a dummy variable constructed out of Variable X025 in the WVS; all respondents with some university schooling or a university degree are coded 1, while all other respondents are coded 0. Female gender is a dummy variable based on Variable X001 in the WVS, in which women are coded 1 and men are coded 0. Age is the respondent's age in years based on Variable X003 in the WVS. Interpersonal trust is a dummy variable in which those with high trust are coded 1, while others are coded 0; variable A165 in the WVS asks respondents to choose between two statements: "most people can be trusted" or "you can't be too careful."

1. This argument is reviewed in Campbell (2003), but see also other key studies (Litvack, Ahmad, and Bird 1998; Rodden, Eskeland, and Litvack 2003).

2. Volatility is calculated as the standard deviation of the annual percentage changes in the transfer amounts.

3. For the pilot the following rule was established: three Vaso de Leche committees if there were fewer than thirty committees total, four if the number of committees were between thirty and seventy, and five if there were more than seventy committees.

4. When the pilot was carried out, the project had not yet formally included surveys at the level of household beneficiaries. A tentative instrument was tested on households to evaluate the importance and viability of including beneficiaries. Therefore, the pilot survey was shorter than and different from the survey applied to beneficiaries during the final fieldwork.

5. $FGT_2 = \frac{1}{N}\sum_{i=1}^{Q}\left(\frac{PL - EXPpc_i}{PL}\right)^2$ where PL = poverty line, EXPpc = per capita household expenditures, Q = number of poor, and N = population.

6. PPS is a method used in sample selection whereby the probability that a given element enters the sample is proportional to some quantity (in our particular case, the district's total population).

7. Leakages found at this stage were also quite small. In Lima, it appears to have amounted to 3.03 percent of the totals transfer, whereas in the rest of Peru it amounted to 0.63 percent. We were able to document a number of worst-case offenders. We found one municipality in Lima in which this leak was 18 percent of the transfers and another where it was 15 percent. In the rest of Peru, we found four municipalities out of seventy-six surveyed in which the leakage at this stage was over 10 percent, with one reaching 15.5 percent. Thus, although the national averages are low, these isolated cases in which the leakage at this point exceeds 10 percent of the total transfer amount are serious. Without taking into consideration any of the leakages at subsequent transfer stages, the beneficiaries—mainly children up to age six—already are receiving less than 90 cents on the dollar. About one-tenth of all municipalities surveyed were found to have leaks higher than 5 percent. In addition to this, one would have to consider the possibility of overpricing reflected in two facts: the high price variability found amongst districts for purchasing similar products, and the premium paid when comparing those prices to leading retail supermarket prices, even when adjusting them for quality and transportation costs. For instance, (1) the price of generic Enriquecido Lácteo, a milk substitute, distributed in thirty-two out of one hundred districts visited, varies from NS/.1–15 per kilogram; (2) and the price of cans of milk are in some cases outside Lima twice the price as in a Lima supermarket!

8. It is important to note that this leakage was computed at the committee level with 320 observations. Many committees had a zero leakage, and therefore their average is lower than that of the worst offenders.

9. This complication appears because the committee representatives do not follow the criteria established by the program regulation. Instead, they make decisions at their discretion as to how to proceed regarding the distribution of the product.

In most cases, the committee representatives have been democratically elected and mostly rely on the approval of the population of their communities. So, our methodology originally contemplated the comparison of per-direct beneficiary rations at the household level with the total per-direct beneficiary rations at the committee level, but this was complicated due to the fact that multiple products get distributed to beneficiaries and the only way to aggregate them was to use a common measurable indicator. To complicate matters further, in the cases of distribution of "prepared" products, there was no way to gauge whether the servings-per-container directive was followed and therefore there was no way to measure the amount of raw product a household was actually receiving, so we eliminated from the sample the cases in which the product was not distributed in raw form.

CHAPTER 7 EVALUATING CITIZEN ATTITUDES ABOUT CORRUPTION IN CHILE

1. In 2001, the Concertación won 51.7 percent of the House of Deputies compared to 47.5 percent for the Alianza, while in 1997 the Concertación won 57.5 percent compared to 38.3 percent for the Alianza (data retrieved from the Political Database of the Americas http://www.georgetown.edu/pdba/Elecdata/Chile/chile.html).

2. Campaign Finance reform became Law No. 19.884 and was published in the official diary on August 5, 2003. The Professionalization of the Civil Service reform became Law No. 19.882 and was published in the official diary June 23, 2003.

3. A wide variety of Spanish and English language press accounts were consulted. Among them were the following: "Chile Politics: Corruption Crackdown at the Top," *Economist Intelligence Unit: Country ViewsWire*, November 15, 2002; "Chile Politics: Corruption Cases Taint Government," *Economist Intelligence Unit: Country ViewsWire*, January 15, 2003; "Losing Its Shine: Corruption in Chile," April 5, 2003; "Chile Politics: Corruption Probes Widen," *Economist Intelligence Unit: Country ViewsWire*, May 6, 2003; "Juez Aránguiz inhabilita por seis años a diputados Pareto, Jiménez y Lagos," *El Mercurio*, December 16, 2003; "Paying the Price," *Latin America Monitor: Southern Cone Monitor 20* (2003); "Corruption Allegations Emerge," *Latin America Monitor: Southern Cone Monitor 20* (2003); "Cross-Party Corruption Initiative," *Latin America Monitor: Southern Cone Monitor 20* (2003); "Diputado Eduardo Díaz renuncia a la Unión Demócrata Independiente; diputado Eduardo Díaz renuncia a la UDI: 'no estoy dispuesto a avalar actos de corrupción,'" *El Mercurio*, October 22, 2004; "Renovación Nacional recoge denuncias de corrupción de funcionarios," *El Mercurio*, January 10, 2005.

4. "Chile Politics: Corruption Crackdown at the Top," *Economist Intelligence Unit: Country ViewsWire*, November 15, 2002.

5. "Chile Politics: Corruption Cases Taint Government," *Economist Intelligence Unit: Country ViewsWire*, January 15, 2003.

6. Law No. 19.653 (probidad administrativa aplicable de los órganos de la administración del Estado) provides the right to access information except under certain conditions, which have led to criticisms of the law from, among other organizations, Human Rights Watch (Human Rights Watch 2001). The law was entered in the official diary on December 14, 1999.

7. See Zaller (1992) on the importance of information and predispositions for public opinion analyses.

8. Available online at http://www.cepchile/cl/bannerscep/bdatos_encuestas _cep/base_datos.php.

9. All translations of questions by the author.

10. See Canache and Allison (2005); also see Swamy and Knack (2001) on gender.

CHAPTER 8 CORRUPTION, ACCOUNTABILITY REFORMS, AND DEMOCRACY IN BRAZIL

1. For a discussion of the role that corruption has played in the Workers' Party (PT) government, see Goldfrank and Wampler (2006).

2. Important improvements took place in Congress as a result of past scandals, such as a series of changes in the budget process after the 1994 budget scandals, but the point is that these have had little effect on the sanctioning process.

3. Collor was absolved of any criminal wrongdoing by the STF in 1994, meaning that even though he faced political sanctions—including an eight-year ban on political participation—he faced no more serious legal repercussions. Collor's campaign manager, P. C. Farias, went to jail briefly and then was murdered under murky circumstances.

4. Similarly, at the state level, although the concentration of power varies widely from state to state, the multiple and overlapping institutions of the federalist system largely prevent the accumulation of monopoly power by executives.

5. Court decisions in 2006–7 determined that party loyalty should be more strictly controlled in future, although it is possible that these rulings will be overruled by Congress.

6. See, for example, Sadek (2000) for a useful analysis of various state-level institutions.

7. This problem is also widespread at the state and municipal levels: accountability institutions tend to focus on investigating cases of corruption, to the detriment of the monitoring and punishment stages. While the newly created Controladoria Geral da União (CGU) has instituted a very promising program that randomly audits the accounting and contracting practices of fifty to sixty municipal governments nationwide each year, this is still a somewhat embryonic effort in light of the more than 5,000 municipalities in Brazil. Meanwhile, although they are an innovative step in the right direction, the CGU's reports on these municipalities have had little punitive effect to date, as they must be sent to the Attorney General (*Advogacia Geral da União*) or *Ministério Público* for prosecution.

8. This common sentiment was perhaps best expressed by two prosecutors, who wrote in an editorial that: "More abstract dangers such as the loss of elected office, the loss of public jobs, or reports by congressional committees, by themselves, do not intimidate these wrongdoers. . . For the corrupt, there is only one possible solution: jail." (Porto and Carneiro 2005; translation mine).

9. Former Brazilian Justice Minister Márcio Thomaz Bastos never tired, for example, of citing Beccaria's admonition that it is not the length of the punishment, but its certainty, that dissuades wrongdoing.

10. Reelection is a somewhat controversial reform in this regard, and many question whether executives have more incentives to act corruptly when they are able to run for reelection. Suffice it to note that the implications of reelection for corruption are poorly understood and worthy of further study.

11. For a comprehensive discussion of reform proposals for various institutions at the center of Brazilian politics, see, for example, Avritzer and Anastasia 2006.

12. On a pessimistic note, it is worth noting that the case against Maluf has run into significant obstacles, and not only is he no longer in jail, but he received the most votes of any candidate in São Paulo state when he ran for Congress in the 2006 elections. By being elected to Congress, Maluf is now able to benefit from privileged standing in the Supreme Federal Tribunal.

13. On the independence of prosecutors and the loose criteria for promotion, see Kerche (1999, 2003).

14. Only two of the nine TCU ministers today come from within the TCU's ranks; the rest are political appointees.

15. Congress's recent refusal to reject the CPMF tax on financial movements may be a step in the opposite direction, as this tax was a useful instrument that enabled revenue collectors to directly compare tax returns with the volume of an individual's transactions.

16. A survey by Transparency Brazil, for example, found that greater oversight and punishment (86 percent) and the punishment of corruptors (62 percent) were businesspersons' leading prescriptions for fighting corruption (Lambsdorff et al. 2002).

CHAPTER 9 CORRUPTION AND DEMOCRACY AT THE STATE LEVEL IN MEXICO

1. Spector, Johnston, and Dininio (2005) offer an exception to this trend. In a brief yet informative analysis, they examine a number of countries in an effort to determine what types of anticorruption efforts seem to produce the best results.

2. Juarez González (2004) offers one example. In a short yet informative study, he tracks public perceptions in Mexico over time, showing how spikes in the importance of corruption as a political issue occur during periods when corruption scandals dominate the news.

3. The 2001 survey of households was conducted during June and July, approximately seven months after Fox was sworn in as the nation's first non-PRI president in seventy-plus years. The survey thus came on the heels of the unveiling of the president's high-profile anticorruption program. It is based on a probabilistic sample and includes 13,790 interviews nationwide with between 388 to 506 interviews per national entity (Transparencia Mexicana 2001). The *Encuesta Nacional de Corrupción y Buen Gobierno 2003* was also based on a probabilistic sample of 14,019 households with 388 to 514 interviews per national entity. It was conducted in June and July of 2003, midway through the Fox *sexenio* and following the implementation of the Fox anticorruption campaign in early 2001 and the passage of critical legislation like the Access to Information law in 2002. Finally, the 2005 survey included a sample of 15,123 households with between 397 and 569 per entity. The surveys were carried out between November 2005 and February 2006. The 2005 measured just thirty-five services, eliminating seven from the earlier studies and adding four. With that exception, the three surveys contained basically the same questions and data.

4. Whereas the 2001 and 2003 surveys recorded the values "agree," "disagree," and "neither," the more refined 2005 survey included response categories of "total" agreement and disagreement and "some" agreement and disagreement. The data

shown in table 9.1 reflects the combination of respondents expressing "some" or "total" agreement.

5. Inductive reasoning would suggest that one's direct experience fashions broader perceptions about the political system. Deductive reasoning, however, would contend that broader perceptions of the operation of the system influence one's decision to participate in corruption. Despite widespread recognition that perception of corruption is not the same as real corruption, few studies explore in detail the relationship between the two dimensions (see Morris 2008 and Weber Abramo 2007). They reveal, however, a rather weak though positive relationship.

6. In one study looking at state-level institutions, Juarez (2005) uses ICBG for 2001 and 2003 as dependent variables and finds an inverse correlation linking corruption and the level and nature of statutory punishment for bribery within the state. States where the level of punishment found "on the books" for bribery is more severe tend to exhibit lower levels of corruption.

7. The 2004 Latin American Public Opinion Project poll on Mexico was conducted by Jorge Buendía and Alejandro Moreno. The sample design included 130 randomly selected sampling sites. Individual respondents were chosen by quota based on age and gender to create a representative sample of the adult population. The survey has a margin of error is +/-2.5 percent with a confidence interval of 95 percent. See Buendía and Moreno (2004, 13–18, 75–77) for technical details of the survey design. They also provide a copy of the questionnaire (79). Technical information can also be acquired at http://sitemason.vanderbilt.edu/files/i6Byz6/Technical Information of The Political Culture of Democracy in Mexico 2004.pdf, and the questionnaire can be found at http://sitemason.vanderbilt.edu/files/k63iiQ/Mexico CAMS questionnaire 2004.pdf.

REFERENCES

Ades, Alberto, and Rafael Di Tella. 1994. Competition and corruption. Working paper, Oxford Institute of Economics and Statistics, Oxford, UK.

———. 1997a. The new economics of corruption: A survey and some new results. *Political Studies* 45 (3): 465–515.

———. 1997b. The causes and consequences of corruption: A review of recent empirical contributions. *Institute of Development Studies Bulletin* 27:6–12.

———. 1997c. National champions and corruption: Some unpleasant interventionist arithmetic. *Economic Journal* (July) 197: 1023–42.

———. 1999. Rents, competition and corruption. *American Economic Review* 89: 982–93.

Adserá, Alicia, Charles Boix, and Mark Payne. 2003. Are you being served? Political accountability and quality of government. *Journal of Law, Economics and Organization* 19 (2): 445–90.

Aguirre, Manuel Dammert Ego. 2001. *Fujimori-Montesinos: El estado Mafioso.* Lima: Ediciones El Virrey.

Akhter, Syed H. 2004. Is globalization what it's cracked up to be? Economic freedom, corruption, and human development. *Journal of World Business* 39: 283–95.

Alesina, Alberto, Arnaud Devleeschauwer, William Easterly, Sergio Kurlat, and Romain Wacziarg. 2002. *Fractionalization.* Harvard University, Department of Economics.

Ali, Abdiweli M., and Hodan Said Isse. 2003. Determinants of economic corruption: A cross-national comparison. *Cato Journal* 22 (3): 449–66.

Allende, Isabel.2003. *My invented country: A nostalgic journey through Chile.* Trans. Margaret Sayers Peden. New York: HarperCollins.

Almond, Gabriel A., and G. Bingham Powell Jr., eds. 1996. *Comparative politics today: A world view.* New York: HarperCollins Press.

Alt, James E., and David Dreyer Lassen. 2003. The political economy of institutions and corruption in American states. *Journal of Theoretical Politics* 15 (3): 341–66.

———. 2008. The role of checks and balances in curbing corruption: Evidence from American state governments. *Economics and Politics* 20 (1): 33–61.

Alvarez, Angel Eduardo. 1995. El dinero en las campañas y la corrupción política en Venezuela. *Contribuciones* 12 (4): 69–103.

Ames, Barry. 1995a. Electoral rules, constituency pressures, and pork barrel: Bases of voting in the Brazilian congress. *Journal of Politics* 57 (2): 324–43.

———. 1995b. Electoral strategy under open-list proportional representation. *American Journal of Political Science* 39 (2): 406–33.

———. 2001. *The deadlock of democracy in Brazil.* Ann Arbor: University of Michigan Press.

Amorim Neto, Octavio, Gary W. Cox, and Mathew D. McCubbins. 2003. Agenda power in Brazil's Camara dos deputados, 1989–98. *World Politics* 55:550–78.

Anderson, Christopher J., and Yuliya V. Tverdova. 2003. Corruption, political allegiances, and attitudes toward government in contemporary democracies. *American Political Science Review* 47 (1): 91–109.

Andvig, Jens C. 1996. International corruption—is it on the increase? *NUPI Working Paper*, no. 567.

———. 2006. Corruption and fast change. *World Development* 34 (2): 328–40.

Andvig, Jens C., and Karl Ove Moene. 1990. How corruption may corrupt. *Journal of Economic Behavior and Organization* 13:63–76.

Antolova, Lucia. 2003. Typology of corruption. Unpublished paper, December 16.

Armony, Ariel. 2004. *The dubious link: Civic engagement and democratization.* Palo Alto: Stanford University Press.

Avritzer, Leonardo, and Fátima Anastasia, eds. 2006. *Reforma política no Brasil.* Belo Horizonte: UFMG/PNUD.

Bailey, John. 2004. Public security and democratic governability: Theorizing about crime, violence, corruption, state and regime. Paper presented at the annual meeting of the Midwest Political Science Association, April 15–18, Chicago.

Bailey, John, and Lucía Dammert. 2006. *Public security and police reform in the Americas.* Pittsburgh: University of Pittsburgh Press.

Bailey, John, and Roy Godson. 2001. Introduction. In *Organized crime and democratic governability: Mexico and the U.S.-Mexican borderlands*, ed. Bailey and Godson, 1–29. Pittsburgh: University of Pittsburgh Press.

Bailey, John, and Pablo Paras. 2006. Perceptions and attitudes about corruption and democracy in Mexico. *Mexican Studies/Estudios Mexicanos* 22 (1): 57–82.

Bailey, John, and Arturo Valenzuela. 1997. The shape of the future. *Journal of Democracy* 8:43–57.

Banks, Arthur S. 1994. Cross-national time-series data archive. Center for Social Analysis, State University of New York at Binghamton.

Bardhan, Pranab. 1997. Corruption and development: A review of issues. *Journal of Economic Literature* 35:1320–46.

———. 2006. The economist's approach to the problem of corruption. *World Development* 34 (2): 341–48.

Bayart, Jean-Francois, Stephen Ellis, and Beatrice Hibou. 1999. From kleptocracy to the felonious state. In *The criminalization of the state in Africa*, ed. Bayart, Ellis, and Hibou, 1–31. Bloomington: Indiana University Press.

Bayley, David. 1985. *Patterns of policing: A comparative international analysis.* New Brunswick, NJ: Rutgers University Press.

Beck, Adrian, and Ruth Lee. 2002. Attitudes to corruption amongst Russian police officers and trainees. *Crime, Law and Social Change* 38 (4): 357–72.

Beer, Caroline. 2003. *Electoral competition and institutional change in Mexico.* Notre Dame: University of Notre Dame Press.

Bermúdez, Norberto, and Juan Gasparini. 2001. *La Prueba: Sobornos en el Senado de la nación por la reforma laboral quiénes y cómo completaron.* Buenos Aires: Ediciones B. Argentina, S.A.

Beroes, Agustín. 2002. *La corrupción en tiempo de Chávez.* Caracas. http:// es.geocities.com/malversacion.

Bhagwati, Jagdish N. 1982. Directly unproductive, profit-seeking (DUP) activities. *Journal of Political Economy* 90:988–1002.

Bhargava, Vinay, and Emil Bolongaita. 2004. *Challenging corruption in Asia: Case studies and a framework for action.* Washington, DC: World Bank.

Blais, André, Joanna Everitt, Patrick Fournier, Elisabeth Gidengil, and Neil Nevitte. 2005. The political psychology of voters' reactions to a corruption scandal. Paper presented at the meeting of the American Political Science Association, August 31–September 3, Washington, DC.

Blake, Charles, and Christopher Martin. 2006. The dynamics of political corruption: Reexamining the influence of democracy. *Democratization* 13 (1): 1–13.

Bohara, Alok K., Neil J. Mitchell, and Carl F. Mittendorf. 2004. Compound democracy and the control of corruption: A cross-country investigation. *Policy Studies Journal* 32 (4): 481–99.

Bollen, Kenneth A. 1993. Liberal democracy: Validity and method factors in cross-national measures. *American Journal of Political Science* 37:1207–30.

Boone, Catherine, and Jake Batsell. 2001. Politics and AIDS in Africa: Research agendas in political science and international relations. *Africa Today* 48 (2): 1–32.

Boría O., Alberto. 1995. Corrupción y justicia en América Latina. *Contribuciones* 12 (October–December): 163–80.

Boswell, Nancy Zucker. 1996. Combating corruption: Focus on Latin America. *Southwestern Journal of Law and Trade in the Americas* (Spring): 179–93.

Bratton, Michael, and Nicolas van de Walle. 1994. Neopatrimonial regimes and political transitions in Africa. *World Politics* 46:453–89.

Bresser Pereira, Luis Carlos, and Yoshiaki Nokano. 1998. The missing social contract: Governability and reform in Latin America. In *What kind of democracy? What kind of market? Latin America in the age of neoliberalism,* ed. Philip D. Oxhorn and Graciela Ducatenzeiler, 21–41. University Park: Penn State Press.

Brinegar, Adam. 2003. Political reformers and anti-corruption preferences in Latin America. Paper presented at the meeting of the American Political Science Association, August 28–31, in Philadelphia.

Brom, Lucio. 2004. Avances para un catálogo lego de situaciones corruptas. Paper presented at the meeting of the Latin American Studies Association, October 6–8, in Las Vegas.

Brown, Ed, and Jonathan Cloke. 2004. Neoliberal reform, governance and corruption in the South: Assessing the international anti-corruption crusade. *Antipode* 36 (2): 272–94.

———. 2005. Neoliberal reform, governance and corruption in Central America: Exploring the Nicaraguan case. *Political Geography* 24:601–30.

Brunetti, Aymo, and Beatrice Weder. 2003. A free press is bad news for corruption. *Journal of Public Economics* 87 (7–8): 1801–24.

Brusco, Valeria, Marcelo Nazareno, and Susan C. Stokes. 2004. Vote buying in Argentina. *Latin American Research Review* 39 (2): 66–88.

Buendía, Jorge, and Alejandro Moreno. 2004. The political culture of democracy in Mexico, 2004: Mexico in times of electoral competition. Nashville: Latin American Public Opinion Project, Vanderbilt University.

Bueno de Mesquita, Bruce, Alastair Smith, Randolph M. Siverson, and James D. Morrow. 2003. *The logic of political survival*. Cambridge: MIT Press.

Burgess, Robin, and Timothy Besley. 2002. The political economy of government responsiveness: Theory and evidence from India. *Quarterly Journal of Economics* 117 (4): 1415–51.

Burkholder, Mark A., and Lyman L. Johnson. 1994. *Colonial Latin America*. 2nd ed. New York: Oxford University Press.

Caiden, Gerald E., O. P. Dwivedi, and Joseph G. Jabbra. 2001. *Where corruption lives*. Bloomfield, CT: Kumarian Press.

Cain, Bruce, John Free, and Fiorina Morris. 1987. *The personal vote: Constituency service and electoral independence*. Cambridge: Harvard University Press.

Calvo, Ernesto, and Maria Victoria Murillo. 2004. Who delivers? Partisan clients in the Argentine electoral market. *American Journal of Political Science* 48 (4): 742–57.

Camp, Roderic Ai. 2001. Democracy through Latin American lenses: An appraisal. In *Citizen views of democracy in Latin America*, ed. Roderic Ai Camp, 5–23. Pittsburgh: University of Pittsburgh Press.

———. 2003. *Politics in Mexico: The democratic transformation*. 4th ed. New York: Oxford University Press.

Campbell, Tim. 2003. *The quiet revolution: Decentralization and the rise of political participation in Latin American cities*. Pitt Latin American Series. Pittsburgh: University of Pittsburgh Press.

Canache, Damarys, and Michael Allison. 2003. Corrupted perceptions: The effect of corruption on political support in Latin American democracies. Paper presented at the meeting of the Latin American Studies Association, March 27–29, in Dallas.

———. 2005. Perceptions of political corruption in Latin American democracies. *Latin American Politics and Society* 47 (3): 91–111.

Carey, John M., and Matthew Soberg Shugart. 1995. Incentives to cultivate a personal vote: A rank ordering or electoral formulas. *Electoral Studies* 14 (4): 417–39.

Carothers, Thomas. 1998. The rule of law revival. *Foreign Affairs* 77:95–106.

———. 1999. *Aiding democracy abroad: The learning curve*. Washington, DC: Carnegie Endowment for International Peace.

Centro de Estudios Públicos. 2002. *Estudio Nacional de Opinión Pública* 42 (December–January).

Chand, Vikram K. 2001. *Mexico's political awakening*. Notre Dame: University of Notre Dame Press.

Chile politics: Corruption crackdown at the top. 2002. *Economist*, Country Views Wire, November 15.

Chile politics: Corruption cases taint government. 2003. *Economist*, Country Views Wire, January 15.

Chile politics: Corruption probes widen. 2003. *Economist*, Country Views Wire, May 6.

Chowdhury, Shyamal. 2004. The effect of democracy and press freedom on corruption: An empirical test. *Economics Letters* 85:93–101.

Clapham, Christopher. 1982. Clientelism and the state. In *Private patronage and public power*, ed. Christopher Clapham, 1–35. London: Frances Pinter.

Cleary, Matthew R., and Susan C. Stokes. 2006. *Democracy and the culture of skepticism: Political trust in Argentina and Mexico*. New York: Russell Sage Foundation.

Clutterbuck, Richard. 1995. Peru: Cocaine, terrorism and corruption. *International Relations* 12 (5): 77–92.

Coady, David, Margaret Grosh, and John Hoddinot. 2004. Targeting of transfers in developing countries: Review of lessons and experience. *World Bank Research Observer* 19 (1): 61–85.

Colazingari, Silvia, and Susan Rose-Ackerman. 1998. Corruption in a paternalistic democracy: Lessons from Italy for Latin America. *Political Science Quarterly* 113 (3): 447–70.

Colclough, Christopher. 1991. Structuralism versus neo-liberalism: An Introduction. In *States or markets? Neoliberalism and the development policy debate*, ed. Christopher Colclough and James Manor, 1–25. Oxford: Clarendon Press.

Collier, Ruth Berins, and David Collier. 1991. *Shaping the political arena: Critical junctures, the labor movement, and regime dynamics in Latin America*. Princeton: Princeton University Press.

Cordova, Ana Beatriz. 2003. Analyzing poverty in El Salvador: A research using probit model, quantile regression and bootstrap econometric technique. Nashville: Vanderbilt University.

Cornelius, Wayne. 2002. Mobilized voting in the 2000 elections: The changing efficacy of vote-buying and coercion in Mexican electoral politics. TS. University of California, San Diego, Center for U.S.-Mexican Studies, La Jolla.

Coronel, Gustavo. 1996. Curbing corruption in Venezuela. *Journal of Democracy* 7 (3): 157–65.

Correa, Hector. 1985. A comparative studies of bureaucratic corruption in Latin America and the USA. *Socio-Economic Planning Science* 19 (1): 63–79.

Corruption allegations emerge. 2003. *Southern Cone Monitor* 20 (1): 5–7.

The corruption notebooks. 2004. Washington, DC: Center for Public Integrity.

Crandall, Russell, Guadalupe Paz, and Riodran Roett, eds. 2005. *Mexico's democracy at work: Political and economic dynamics*. Boulder: Lynne Rienner.

Crime in uniform: Corruption and impunity in Latin America. 1997. Transnational Institute and Accion Andina. Bolivia: CEDIB. http://www.tni.org/drugs/folder3/contents.htm.

Cross-party corruption initiative. 2003. *Southern Cone Monitor* 20 (3): 5–7.

Dahl, Robert. 1971. *Polyarchy: Participation and opposition*. New Haven: Yale University Press.

Dalton, Russell. 1996. *Citizen politics: Public opinion and political parties in advanced industrial democracies*. 3rd ed. New York: Chatham House.

Da Matta, Roberto. 1993. Is Brazil hopelessly corrupt? *New York Times*, December 13. Reprinted in Robert M. Levine and John J. Crocitti, *The Brazil reader: History, culture, politics*. Durham: Duke University Press, 1999.

Davis, Charles L., Roderic Ai Camp, and Kenneth M. Coleman. 2004. The influence of party systems on citizens' perceptions of corruption and electoral response in Latin America. *Comparative Political Studies* 37 (6): 677–703.

Del Castillo, Arturo. 2003. *Medición de la corrupción: Un indicador de la rendición de cuentas*. México, D.F.: Auditoría Superior de la Federación.

Del Castillo, Arturo, Manuel Alejandro Guerrero, Eduardo Rodríguez-Oreggia, and Eduardo R. Ampudia. 2005. *Índice de honestidad y eficiencia en la generación de Infraestructura: Análisis acumulado en la generación de infraestructura pública en los últimos 30 años*. Mexico: CEI Consulting and Research.

Della Porta, Donatella. 2000. Social capital, beliefs in government and political corruption. In *Disaffected democracies: What's troubling the trilateral countries?* ed. Susan J. Pharr and Robert D. Putnam, 202–30. Princeton: Princeton University Press.

———. 1999. *Corrupt exchanges, actors, resources and mechanisms of political corruption*. New York: Aldine de Gruyter.

Della Porta, Donatella, and Alberto Vannucci. 1997. The "perverse effects" of political corruption. *Political Studies* 45 (3): 516–38.

De Speville, B. 1997. *Hong Kong: Policy initiatives against corruption*. Paris: OECD Development Center.

Dhillon, Amrita, and Leonard Wantchekon. 2003. Policy commitment through intermediaries: A theory of electoral clientelism. New York: New York University.

Diamond, Larry. 1999. *Developing democracy: Toward consolidation*. Baltimore: Johns Hopkins University Press.

Diamond, Larry, and Leonardo Morlino, eds. 2005. *Assessing the quality of democracy*. Baltimore: Johns Hopkins University Press.

Di Franceisco, Wayne, and Zvi Gitelman. 1989. Soviet political culture and modes of covert influence. In *Political corruption: A handbook*, ed. Heidenheimer, Johnston, and LeVine, 467–88.

Di Tella, Raphael, and William D. Savefoff. 2001. *Diagnosis corruption: Fraud in Latin America's public hospitals*. Washington, DC: Inter-American Development Bank.

Di Tella, Raphael, and Ernesto Schargrodsky. 2003. The role of wages and auditing during a crackdown on corruption in the city of Buenos Aires. *Journal of Law and Economics* 46:269–92.

Dix, Robert H. 1992. Democratization and the institutionalization of Latin American political parties. *Comparative Political Studies* 24:488–511.

Djankov, Simeon, Rafael La Porta, Florencio Lopez de Silanes, and Andrei Shleifer. 2002. The regulation of entry. *Quarterly Journal of Economics* 117:1–37.

Doig, Alan, and Robin Theobald, eds. 2000. *Corruption and democratization*. London: Frank Cass.

Dollar, D., Raymond Fishman, and Roberta Gatti. 1999. Are women really the "fairer" sex? Corruption and women in government. *Policy Research Report on Gender and Development*. Working Paper Series, No. 4. Washington, DC: World Bank.

Domingo, Pilar, and Rachel Sieder, eds. 2001. *Rule of law in Latin America: The international promotion of judicial reform*. London: Institute of Latin American Studies.

Duncan, Nick, and Indranil Dutta. 2006. Guest editors' introduction. *World Development* 34 (2): 324–27.

Easterly, William, and Ross Levine. 1997. Africa's growth tragedy: Politics and ethnic divisions. *Quarterly Journal of Economics* 112:1203–50.

Easton, David. 1965. *A systems analysis of political life*. New York: John Wiley & Sons.

Eisenstadt, Samuel N., and Rene Lemarchand, eds. 1981. *Political clientelism, patronage and development.* Newbury Park: Sage.

Eisenstadt, Todd A. 2004. *Courting democracy in Mexico: Party strategies and electoral institutions.* New York: Cambridge University Press.

Elliott, Kimberly Ann, ed. 1997. *Corruption and the global economy.* Washington, DC: Institute for International Economics.

Emerson, Patrick M. 2006. Corruption, competition and democracy. *Journal of Development Economics* 81:193–212.

Estévez, Federico, Beatriz Magaloni, and Alberto Díaz-Cayeros. 2002. A portfolio diversification model of policy choice. Paper presented at the conference Clientelism in Latin America: Theoretical and comparative perspectives, May 21–22, Stanford University, Palo Alto, CA.

European Values Study Group and World Values Survey Association. 2005. European and World Values Surveys Integrated Data File, 1999–2002, Release I [Computer file]. 2nd ICPSR version. Cologne, Germany: Zentralarchiv fur Empirische Sozialforschung (ZA); Tilburg, Netherlands: Tilburg University; Amsterdam, Netherlands: Netherlands Institute for Scientific Information Services (NIWI); Madrid, Spain: Analisis Sociologicos Economicos y Politicos (ASEP) and JD Systems (JDS); Ann Arbor, MI: Inter-university Consortium for Political and Social Research [producers], 2004. Cologne, Germany: Zentralarchiv fur Empirische Sozialforschung (ZA); Madrid, Spain: Analisis Sociologicos Economicos y Politicos (ASEP) and JD Systems (JDS); Ann Arbor, MI: Inter-university Consortium for Political and Social Research [distributors].

Ewell, Judith. 1977. The extradition of Marcos Pérez Jiménez, 1959–63: Practical precedent for enforcement of administrative honesty? *Journal of Latin American Studies* 9 (2): 291–313.

Fabbri, José Miguel. 2002. Corruption in Bolivia: Reforming the judiciary system. CIPE.org Feature Service, March 13.

Faundes, Juan Jorge. 2002. Periodimso de investigación en Sudamerica: Obstáculos y propuestas. Capitulo chileno de Transparencia Internacional, Corporación FORJA. http://www.geocites.com/Athens/Forum/2829/Cinep1/LibroPerInvestigativo.pdf.

Figueiredo, Argelina Cheibub. 2001. Instições e política no controle do executivo. *Dados—revista de ciencias sociais* 44 (4): 689–727.

Figueiredo, Argelina Cheibub, and Fernando Limongi. 1999. *Executivo e legislativo na nova ordem constitucional.* Rio de Janeiro: Editora FGV.

Fiorina, Morris, and Roger Noll. 1978. Voters, bureaucrats and legislators: A rational choice perspective on the growth of bureaucracy. *Journal of Public Economics* 9 (2): 239–54.

Fleischer, David. 1995. Attempts at corruption control in Brazil: Congressional investigations and strengthening internal control. Paper presented at the meeting of the Latin American Studies Association, September 28–30, in Washington, DC.

———. 1997. Political corruption in Brazil: The delicate connection with campaign finance. *Crime, Law and Social Change* 25:297–321.

———. 2000. Além de collorgate: Perspectivas de consolidação democrática no Brasil via reformas políticas. In *Corrupção e reforma política no brasil: O im-*

pacto do impeachment de Collor, ed. Keith Rosenn and Richard Downes, 81–110. Rio de Janeiro: FGV.

———. 2002. *Corruption in Brazil: Defining, measuring and reducing*. Washington, DC: Center for Strategic and International Studies (CSIS).

———. 2003. *Brazil Focus: Weekly Report*. Brasilia. November 14.

Flynn, Peter. 1993. Collor, corruption and crisis: Time for reflection. *Journal of Latin American Studies* 25 (2): 351–71.

———. 2005. Brazil and Lula, 2005: Crisis, corruption and change in political perspective. *Third World Quarterly* 26 (8): 1221–67.

Foweraker, Joe, and Roman Krznaric. 2002. The uneven performance of third wave democracies: Electoral politics and the imperfect rule of law in Latin America. *Latin American Politics and Society* 44 (3): 29–61.

Fox, Jonathan. 1994. The difficult transition from clientelism to citizenship: Lessons from Mexico. *World Politics* 46 (2): 151–84.

Fraser, Barbara. 2003. Minor corruption just part of life in Peru. *NotiSur* (April 4).

Freedom House. 1994–2002. *Annual survey of press freedom, 1994–2002*. Washington, DC: Freedom House.

———. 2001. Spreadsheet with Freedom in the World data for 1972–2000. Retrieved March 4, 2002 from http://www.freedomhouse.org/research/freeworld/FHSCORES.xls.

———. 2003. *Freedom in the world 2003*. Washington, DC: Freedom House.

Friedrich, C. J. 1966. Political pathology. *Political Quarterly* 37 (1): 70–85.

Galarza, Napoleón Saltos. 1999. *Etica y corrupción: Estudio de casos*. Quito, Ecuador: Artes Gráficas Silva.

Galindo, Pedro. 2003. *Reporte sobre el estado de la justicia en las Américas, 2002–3*. Santiago: Centro de Estudios de Justicia de las Américas, CEJA.

Gambetta, Diego. 1988. *Trust: Making and breaking cooperative relations*. Oxford: Basil Blackwell.

Ganuza, Juan-Jose, and Esther Hauk. 2004. Economic integration and corruption. *International Journal of Industrial Organization* 22:1463–84.

Gardiner, John. 2002. Defining corruption. In *Political corruption: Concepts and contexts*, ed. Heidenheimer and Johnston, 25–40.

Gatti, Roberta. 2003. Individual attitudes toward corruption: Do social effects matter? World Bank Policy Research Working Paper 3122, World Bank, Washington, DC.

Geddes, Barbara. 1994. *The politician's dilemma: Building state capacity in Latin America*. Berkeley: University of California Press.

Geddes, Barbara, and Artur Ribeiro Neto. 1992. Institutional sources of corruption in Brazil. *Third World Quarterly* 13 (4): 641–61.

———. 1999. Institutional sources of corruption in Brazil. In *Corruption and political reform in Brazil*, eds. Keith Rosenn and Richard Downes, 21–48.

Gerring, John, and Strom C. Thacker. 2004. Political institutions and corruption: The role of unitarism and parliamentarism. *British Journal of Political Science* 34:295–330.

———. 2005. Do neoliberal policies deter political corruption? *International Organizations* 59:233–54.

Gerring, John, Strom C. Thacker, and Rodrigo Alfaro. 2006. Democracy and human development. Unpublished manuscript, Boston University.

Gibson, Charles. 1966. *Spain in America*. New York: Harper and Row.

Gibson, Edward. 1997. The populist road to market reform: Policy and electoral coalitions in Mexico and Argentina. *World Politics* 49:339–70.

Goldfrank, Benjamin, and Brian Wampler. 2006. From good government to politics as usual: The rise and possible demise of the workers' party. Paper presented at the Conference of Brazilian Studies in Northern California, November 11, St. Mary's College, Moraga, CA.

Goldsmith, Arthur A. 1999. Slapping the grasping hand: Correlates of political corruption in emerging markets. *American Journal of Economics and Sociology* 58 (4): 865–83.

Goodman, Timothy. 1994. Political corruption: The payoff diminishes. *American Enterprise* 5 (9): 19–27.

Graeff, P., and G. Mehlkop. 2003. The impact of economic freedom on corruption: Different patterns for rich and poor countries. *European Journal of Political Economy* 19 (3): 605–21.

Graham, Carol, and Sandip Sukhtankar. 2004. Does economic crisis reduce support for markets and democracy in Latin America? Some evidence from surveys of public opinion and well being. *Journal of Latin American Studies* 36 (2): 349–77.

Grosse, Robert E. 2001. *Drugs and money: Laundering Latin America's cocaine dollars*. Westport, CT: Praeger.

Groves, Roderick T. 1967. Administrative reform and the politics of reform: The case of Venezuela. *Public Administration Review* 27:436–45.

Guerrero, Manuel Alejandro. 2004. *México: La Paradoja de la democracia*. México, DF: Universidad Iberoamericana and CEI Consulting and Research.

Guerrero, Manuel Alejandro, and Arturo del Castillo. 2003. Percepciones y representaciones de corrupción en la ciudad de México: ¿Predisposición al acto corrupto? Paper presented at the meeting of the Escuela Iberoamerican de Gobierno y Política Pública, Centro de Investigación y Docencia Económica (CIDE), August 25–26, México, DF.

Gupta, Akhil. 1995. Blurred boundaries: The discourse of corruption, the culture of politics, and the imagined state. *American Ethnologist* 22 (2): 375–402.

Haggard, Stephan. 1991. Inflation and stabilization. In *Politics and policy making in developing countries: Perspectives on the new political economy*, ed. Gerald M. Meier, 233–49. San Francisco: ICS Press.

Hall, David. 1999. Privatization, multinationals, and corruption. *Development in Practice* 9 (5): 539–56.

Hardin, Russell. 1999. *Liberalism, constitutionalism, and democracy*. Oxford: Oxford University Press.

Heidenheimer, Arnold J., ed. 1970. *Political corruption: Readings in comparative analysis*. New Brunswick: Transaction Books.

———. 1989. Perspectives on the perception of corruption. In *Political corruption: A handbook*, ed. Heidenheimer, Johnston, and LeVine, 149–63.

———. 2001. Disjunctions between corruption and democracy? A qualitative exploration. Paper presented at the meeting of the American Political Science Association, August 30–September 2, San Francisco.

———. 2002a. Parties, campaign finance and political corruption: Tracing long-term comparative dynamics. In *Political corruption: Concepts and contexts*, ed. Heidenheimer and Johnston, 761–76.

————. 2002b. Perspectives on the perception of corruption. In *Political corruption: Concepts and contexts*, ed. Heidenheimer and Johnston, 141–54.

Heidenheimer, Arnold J., Michael Johnston, and Victor T. LeVine, eds. 1989. *Political corruption: A handbook*. New Brunswick: Transaction Publishers.

Heidenheimer, Arnold J., and Michael Johnston, eds. 2002. *Political corruption: Concepts and contexts*. New Brunswick: Transaction Publishers.

Hellman, Joel S. 1998. Winners take all: The politics of partial reform in post communist transitions. *World Politics* 50:203–34.

Hernández Valdez, Alfonso. 2000. Las causas estructurales de la democracia local en México, 1989–1998. *Política y Gobierno* 7 (1): 101–44.

Heywood, Paul, ed. 1997. Political corruption. *Political Studies* (Special Issues) 45.

Hill, Kim Quaile. 2003. Democratization and corruption. *American Politics Research* 31 (6): 613–32.

Hinton, Mercedes S. 2006. *The State on the streets: Police and politics in Argentina and Brazil*. Boulder: Lynne Rienner.

Hite, Katherine, and Paola Cesarini, eds. 2004. *Authoritarian legacies and democracy in Latin America and southern Europe*. Notre Dame: University of Notre Dame Press.

Hopkin, Jonathan. 1997. Political parties, political corruption, and the economic theory of democracy. *Crime, Law and Social Change* 27 (3–4): 255–74.

Hopkins, Jack W. 1969. Comparative observations on Peruvian bureaucracy. *Journal of Comparative Administration* 1:301–20.

————. 1974. Contemporary research on public administration and bureaucracies in Latin America. *Latin American Research Review* 9:109–39.

Horowitz, Joel. 2005. Corruption, crime and punishment: Recent scholarship on Latin America. *Latin American Research Review* 40 (1): 268–77.

Humphreys, Macartan. 2004. Natural resources, conflict, and conflict resolution: Uncovering the mechanisms. *Journal of Conflict Resolution* 49(4): 508–37.

Huntington, Samuel P. 1968. *Political order in changing societies*. New Haven: Yale University Press.

Husted, Bryan W. 1999. Wealth, culture, and corruption. *Journal of International Business Studies* 30 (2): 339–60.

————. 2002. Culture and international anti-corruption agreements in Latin America. *Journal of Business Ethics* 37:413–22.

Hutchcroft, Paul D. 1997. The politics of privilege: Assessing the impact of rents, corruption, and clientelism on third world development. *Political Studies* 45:639–58.

Inglehart, Ronald. 1981. Post-materialism in an environment of insecurity. *American Political Science Review* 75 (4): 880–900.

————. 1990. *Culture shift in advanced industrial society*. Princeton: Princeton University Press.

————. 1997. *Modernization and postmodernization: Cultural, economic, and political change in 43 societies*. Princeton: Princeton University Press.

Inglehart, Ronald, et al. 2000. World values surveys and European values surveys, 1981–1984, 1990–1993, and 1995–1997 [Computer file], 2000. ICPSR version. Ann Arbor: Institute for Social Research [producer], 2000. Ann Arbor: Inter-university Consortium for Political and Social Research [distributor].

Inglehart, Ronald, and Christian Welzel. 2005. *Modernization, cultural change, and democracy: The human development sequence.* Cambridge: Cambridge University Press.

Jain, Arvind K., ed. 1998. *Economics of corruption.* Boston: Kluwer.

Johnston, Michael. 1983. Corruption and political culture in America: An empirical perspective. *Publius* 13:19–39.

———. 1996. The search for definitions: The vitality of politics and the issue of corruption. *International Social Science Journal* 149:321–35.

———. 1999. Corruption and democracy: Threats to development, opportunities for reform. http://people.colgate.edu/mjohnston/MJ%20papers.htm. Published in revised form as Corruption et democratie: Menaces pour le developpement, possibilities de reforme, *Revue Tiers Monde* (Paris) 161 (January–March 2000): 117–42.

———. 2000. The new corruption rankings: Implication for analysis and reform. Paper presented at the meeting of the International Political Science Association, August 2, Quebec City, Canada.

———. 2002a. Party systems, competition, and political checks against corruption. In *Political corruption: Concepts and contexts,* eds. Heidenheimer and Johnston, 777–94.

———. 2002b. Right and wrong in American politics: Popular conceptions of corruption. In *Political corruption: Concepts and contexts,* ed. Heidenheimer and Johnston, 173–94.

———. 2005a. *Syndromes of corruption: Wealth, power and democracy.* Cambridge: Cambridge University Press.

———, ed. 2005b. *Civil society and corruption: Mobilizing for reform.* Lanham: University Press of America.

Johnston, Michael, and Sahr Kpundeh. 2005. Building social action coalitions for reform. In *Civil society and corruption,* ed. Johnston, 149–68.

Juárez, Vladimir. 2005. ¿A mayores penas, menos corrupción? *Recta Ratio* 2 (3): 123–40.

Juárez González, Leticia. 2004. ¿Tenemos remedio en asuntos de corrupción e impunidad? *Nexos* (June): 22–27.

Karklins, Rasma. 2005. *The system made me do it: Corruption in post-communist societies.* New York: M. E. Sharpe.

Kaufmann, Daniel. 1997. Corruption, the facts. *Foreign Policy* 107:11–31.

———. 2005. 10 myths about governance and corruption. *Finance and Development* 42 (3): 41–43.

Kaufmann, Daniel, and Shang Jin Wei. 1999. Does "grease money" speed up the wheels of commerce? National Bureau of Economic Research Working Paper no. 7093. Washington, DC.

Kaufmann, Daniel, Aart Kraay, and Massimo Mastruzzi. 2002. Governance matters II: Updated indicators for 2000/01. Policy Research Working Paper 2772. The World Bank Development Research Group and World Bank Institute Governance, Regulation and Finance Division. Washington, DC: World Bank.

———. 2003. Governance matters III: Governance indicators for 1996–2003. World Bank Policy Research Working Paper no. 3106. Washington, DC: World Bank.

Kaufmann, Daniel, Aart Kraay, and Pablo Zoido-Lobaton. 1999. Governance matters. World Bank Policy Research Working Paper 2196. Washington, DC: World Bank.

Keefer, Philip. 2005. Democratization and credibility: Why are young democracies badly governed? Policy Research Working Paper, No. 3594 (May). Washington, DC: World Bank.

Kerche, Fábio. 1999. O Ministério público e a constituinte de 1987/88. In *O Sistema de justiça*, ed. Maria Teresa Sadek, 61–77. São Paulo: Editora Sumaré.

———. 2003. O Ministério público no Brasil. Ph.D. diss., University of São Paulo.

King, Gary, Michael Tomz, and Jason Wittenberg. 2000. Making the most of statistical analyses: Improving interpretation and presentation. *American Journal of Political Science* 44 (2): 347–61.

Kite, Eric, and Margaret Sarles. 2006. Survey research sheds light on Latin Americans' experience with corruption. In *Global Corruption Report 2005*, 350–53. Transparency International. London: Pluto Press.

Kitschelt, Herbert. 2000. Linkages between citizens and politicians in democratic polities. *Comparative Political Studies* 33 (6/7): 845–79.

Kitschelt, Herbert, Zdenka Mansfeldova, and Radoslaw Markowski. 1999. *Post-communist party systems competition, representation, and inter-party cooperation*. Cambridge: Cambridge University Press.

Klitgaard, Robert. 1988. *Controlling corruption*. Berkeley: University of California Press.

Knack, Stephen, and Omar Azfar. 2000. Are larger countries really more corrupt? World Bank Policy Research Working Paper No. 2470 (November). Washington, DC: World Bank.

Knack, Stephen, and Philip Keefer. 1995. Institutions and economic performance: Cross-country tests using alternative institutional measures. *Economics and Politics* 7:207–27.

Knight, Alan. 1998. Populism and neo-populism in Latin America, especially Mexico. *Journal of Latin American Studies* 30:223–48.

Kpundeh, Sahr. 1995. *Politics and corruption in Africa: A case study of Sierra Leone*. London: Lanham.

Kraay, Aart, and Caroline Van Rijckeghem. 1995. Employment and wages in the public sector: A cross-country study. Working Paper 95/70. Washington: International Monetary Fund.

Kramer, John M. 1989. Political corruption in the U.S.S.R. In *Political corruption: A handbook*, ed. Heidenheimer, Johnston, and LeVine, 449–65.

Krueger, Anne O. 1974. The political economy of the rent-seeking society. *American Economic Review* 64 (3): 291–303.

———. 1993. *Political economy of policy reform in developing countries*. Cambridge: MIT Press.

Lagos, Marta. 1997. Latin America's smiling mask. *Journal of Democracy* 8 (3): 125–38.

———. 2001a. Perceptions of corruption in Latin America. In *Global corruption report 2001*, 313. Transparency International. London: Pluto Press.

———. 2001b. Between stability and crisis in Latin America. *Journal of Democracy* 12 (1): 136–45.

———. 2003. Public opinion of corruption in Latin America. *Global corruption report 2002*, 282–84. Transparency International. London: Pluto Press.

Lambsdorff, Johann Graf. 1999. Corruption in empirical research: A review. Transparency International Working Paper, November.

Lambsdorff, Johann Graf, Wilton de Olíveira Bussab, Salo Vinocur Coslovsky, and

Henrique Ostronoff. 2002. *Fraude e corrupção no Brasil: A perspectiva do setor srivado*. São Paulo: Transparência Brasil e Kroll.

Lamounier, Bolívar. 1996. Brazil: The hyperactive paralysis syndrome. In *Constructing democratic governance: South America in the 1990s*, ed. Jorge I. Domínguez and Abraham F. Lowenthal. Baltimore: Johns Hopkins University Press.

Lancaster, Thomas D., and Gabriela R. Montinola. 2001. Comparative political corruption: Issues of operationalization and measurement. *Studies in Comparative International Development* 36 (3): 3–28.

La Palombara, Joseph. 1994. Structural and institutional aspects of corruption. *Social Research* 61 (2): 325–50.

La Porta, Rafael, Florencio Lopez-de-Silanes, Andrei Shleifer, and Robert W. Vishny. 1997. Trust in large organizations. *American Economic Review* 87 (2): 333–38.

———. 1999. The quality of government. *Journal of Economics, Law and Organization* 15 (1): 222–79.

Lawson, Chappell H. 2002. *Building the fourth estate: Democratization and the rise of a free press in Mexico*. Berkeley: University of California Press.

Lawyers Committee for Human Rights. 2000. Building on quicksand: The collapse of the World Bank's judicial reform project in Peru. New York: Lawyers Committee for Human Rights.

Lederman, Daniel, Norman V. Loayza, and Rodrigo R. Soares. 2005. Accountability and corruption: Political institutions matter. *Economics and Politics* 17 (1): 1–35.

Leff, Nathaniel. 1964. Economic development through bureaucratic corruption. *American Behavioral Scientist* 8 (3): 8–14.

Leftwich, Adrian. 1995. Bringing politics back in: Towards a model of the developmental state. *Journal of Development Studies* 31 (3): 400–435.

Leite, Carlos, and Jens Weidmann. 1999. Does mother nature corrupt? Natural resources, corruption and economic growth. International Monetary Fund Working Paper, 99/85, July.

Lemarchand, René. 1972. Political clientelism and ethnicity in tropical Africa: Competing solidarities in nation-building. *American Political Science Review* 66 (1): 68–90.

———. 1981. Comparative political clientelism: Structure, process and optic. In *Political clientelism, patronage and development*, ed. S. N. Eisenstadt and René Lemarchand, 7–32. Beverly Hills: Sage Publications.

Levi, Margaret. 1998. A state of trust. In *Trust and governance*, ed. Valerie Braithwaite and Margaret Levi, 77–101. New York: Russell Sage Foundation.

Levitsky, Steven. 1998. Institutionalization and Peronism: The concept, the case, and the case for unpacking the concept. *Party Politics* 4 (1): 77–92.

———. 2003. The labor politics to machine politics: The transformation of party-union linkages in Argentine Peronism, 1983–1999. *Latin American Research Review* 38 (3): 3–36.

Levy, Daniel C., and Kathleen Bruhn. 2001. *Mexico: The struggle for democratic development*. Berkeley: University of California Press.

Lewis, Peter, and Howard Stein. 1997. Shifting fortunes: The political economy of financial liberalization in Nigeria. *World Development* 25:5–22.

Linz, Juan J., and Alfred Stepan. 1996. *Problems of democratic transition and con-*

solidation: Southern Europe, South America, and post-communist Europe. Baltimore: Johns Hopkins University Press.

Linz, Juan J., and Arturo Valenzuela, eds. 1994. *The failure of presidential democracy: The case of Latin America.* Baltimore: Johns Hopkins University Press.

Lipset, Semour Martin, and Gabriel Salman Lenz. 2000. Corruption, culture and markets. In *Culture matters: How values shape human progress,* ed. Samuel P. Huntington and Lawrence Harrison, 112–24. New York: Basic Books.

Little, Walter, and Antonio Herrera. 1996. Political corruption in Venezuela. In *Political corruption in Europe and Latin America,* ed. Little and Posada-Carbó, 267–85.

Little, Walter, and Eduardo Posada-Carbó, eds. 1996. *Political corruption in Europe and Latin America.* London: Institute of Latin American Studies. New York: Macmillan Press.

Litvack, Jennie I., Junaid Ahmad, and Richard Miller Bird. 1998. Rethinking decentralization in developing countries. Washington, DC: World Bank.

Liu, Alan P. L. 1989. The politics of corruption in the People's Republic of China. In *Political corruption: A handbook,* ed. Heidenheimer, Johnston, and LeVine, 489–512.

Lizzeri, Alessandro, and Nicola Persico. 2001. The provision of public goods under alternative electoral incentives. *American Economic Review* 91 (1): 225–39.

Lomnitz, Larissa A. 1994. *Redes sociales, cultura y poder: Ensayos de antropología latinoamericana.* Mexico: FLACSO.

López-Cálix, José R., and Alberto Melo. 2004. *Peru: Restoring fiscal discipline for poverty reduction.* Washington, DC: World Bank.

Lopez-Carlos, Augusto, Michael E. Porter, and Klaua Schwab, eds. 2005. *Global competitiveness report, 2005–2006.* New York: Palgrave Macmillan.

López Presa, José Octavio, ed. 1998. *Corrupción y cambio.* Mexico: Fondo de Cultura Económica.

Lu, Xiaobo. 2000. Booty socialism, bureau-preneurs, and the state in transition: Organizational corruption in China. *Comparative Politics* 32 (3): 273–96.

Luttmer, Erzo. 2001. Group loyalty and taste for redistribution. *Journal of Political Economy* 109 (3): 500–528.

MacKinnon, James. 2002. Bootstrap inference in econometrics. Paper presented at the Presidential Address, Canadian Economics Association, May 30–June 2, Calgary, Alberta.

Mahoney, James. 2002. *The legacies of liberalism: Path dependence and political regimes in Central America.* Baltimore: Johns Hopkins University Press.

Maier, Karl. 2000. *This house has fallen: Nigeria in crisis.* Boulder: Westview Press.

Maingot, Anthony. 1994. Confronting corruption in the hemisphere: A sociological perspective. *Journal of Interamerican Studies and World Affairs* 36 (3): 49–74.

Mainwaring, Scott. 2003. Introduction: Democratic accountability in Latin America. In *Democratic accountability in Latin America,* ed. Scott Mainwaring and Christopher Welna, 3–33. New York: Oxford University Press.

Mainwaring, Scott, and Timothy Scully. 1995. Introduction: Party systems in Latin America. In *Building democratic institutions: Party systems in Latin America,* ed. Mainwaring and Scully, 1–36. Palo Alto: Stanford University Press.

Mainwaring, Scott, and Matthew Soberg Shugart, eds. 1997. *Presidentialism and democracy in Latin America.* Cambridge: Cambridge University Press.

Mainwaring, Scott, and Christopher Welna, eds. 2003. *Democratic accountability in Latin America*. New York: Oxford University Press.

Malesky, Edmund. 2001. Enduring clientelism in Vietnam. Paper presented at the conference Citizen-Politician Linkages in Democratic Politics, March 30–April 1, Duke University, Durham, NC.

Manfroni, Carlos A., and Richard S. Werksman. 1997. *La convención interamericana contra la corrupción: Anotada y comentada*. Buenos Aires: Abeledo-Perrot.

Manzetti, Luigi. 1994. Economic reform and corruption in Latin America. *North South Issues* 3 (1): 1–6.

———. 1999. *Privatization South American style*. New York: Oxford University Press.

———. 2000. Market reforms without transparency. In *Combating corruption in Latin America*, ed. Joseph S. Tulchin and Ralph H. Espach, 130–72. Washington, DC: Woodrow Wilson International Center for Scholars.

Manzetti, Luigi, and Charles Blake. 1996. Market reforms and corruption in Latin America. *Review of International Political Economy* 3 (4): 662–97.

Marshall, Monty G., and Keith Jaggers. 2000. Polity IV project: Political regime characteristics and transitions, 1800–2000. http://www.cidcm.umd.edu/inscr/polity/. Accessed March 2003.

Mauro, Paolo. 1995. Corruption and growth. *Quarterly Journal of Economics* 110 (3): 681–712.

———. 1997. The effects of corruption on growth, investment, and government expenditure: A cross-country analysis. In *Corruption and the global economy*, ed. K. A. Elliott, 83–107. Washington, DC: Institute for International Economics.

———. 2002. The effects of corruption on growth and public expenditures. In *Political corruption: Concepts and contexts*, ed. Heidenheimer and Johnston, 339–52.

Mazzuca, Sebastian. 2000. Evolving conceptions of democracy: Access to power versus exercise of power. Department of Political Science, University of California at Berkeley.

McCann, James A., and Jorge I. Dominguez. 1998. Mexicans react to political corruption and electoral fraud: An assessment of public opinion and voting behavior. *Electoral Studies* 17 (4): 483–504.

McFarlane, Anthony. 1996. Political corruption and reform in bourbon Spanish America. In *Political corruption in Europe and Latin America*, eds. Little and Posada-Carbó, 41–64.

Medina, Luis, and S. Stokes. 2002. Clientelism as political monopoly. Unpublished manuscript. University of Chicago.

Meier, Kenneth J., and Thomas M. Holbrook. 1992. I seen my opportunities and I took 'em. *Journal of Politics* 54:135–55.

Mendez, Juan, Guillermo O'Donnell, and Paulo Sergio Pinheiro, eds. 1999. *The (un) rule of law and the underprivileged in Latin America*. Notre Dame: University of Notre Dame Press.

Miller, William L. 2006. Corruption and corruptibility. *World Development* 34 (2): 371–80.

Mishler, William, and Richard Rose. 2001. What are the origins of political trust? Testing institutional and cultural theories in post-communist societies. *Comparative Political Studies* 34 (1): 30–62.

Mishra, Ajit. 2006. Persistence of corruption: Some theoretical perspectives. *World Development* 34 (2): 349–58.

Mitchell, Paul. 2000. Voters and their representatives: Electoral institutions and delegation in parliamentary democracies. *European Journal of Political Research* 38 (3): 335–51.

Mizrahi, Yemile. 2003. *From martyrdom to power: The Partido Acción Nacional in Mexico*. Notre Dame: University of Notre Dame Press.

Mocan, Naci. 2004. What determines corruption? International evidence from micro data. National Bureau of Economic Research Working Paper 10460, Washington, DC.

Montinola, Gabriella R. 1996. The efficient secret revisited: The emergence of clean government in Chile. Ph.D. diss., Stanford University, Palo Alto, CA.

Montinola, Gabriella R., and Robert W. Jackman. 2002. Sources of corruption: A cross-country study. *British Journal of Political Science* 32 (1): 147–70.

Moreno, Alejandro. 2002. Corruption and democracy: A cultural assessment. *Comparative Sociology* 1 (3–4): 495–507.

———. 2003. Corruption and democracy: A cultural assessment. In *Human values and social change: Findings from the values surveys*, ed. Ronald Inglehart, 265–77. Boston: Brill.

Morris, Stephen. 1991. *Corruption and politics in contemporary Mexico*. Tuscaloosa: University of Alabama Press.

———. 1999. Corruption and the Mexican political system: Continuity and change. *Third World Quarterly* 20 (3): 623–43.

———. 2003. Corruption and Mexican political culture. *Journal of the Southwest* 45 (4): 671–708.

———. 2005. Corruption in Latin America: An empirical overview. *SECOLAS Annals* 36:74–92.

———. 2008. Disaggregating corruption: A comparison of participation and perceptions in Latin America with a focus on Mexico. *Bulletin of Latin American Research* 27 (4): 388–409.

Nef, Jorge. 2001. Government corruption in Latin America. In *Where corruption lives*, ed. Gerald E. Caiden, O. P. Dwidedi, and Joseph Jabbra, 159–73. Bloomfield, CT: Kumarian Press.

Nielsen, Richard P. 2003. Corruption networks and implications for ethical corruption reform. *Journal of Business Ethics* 42:125–49.

Nieto, Francisco. 2004. Demitificando la corrupción en América Latina. *Nueva Sociedad* 194:54–68.

Nóbrega, Maílson da. 2005. *O futuro chegou: Instituições e desenvolvimento no Brasil*. São Paulo: Editora Globo.

Norton, Edward C., Hua Wang, and Chunrong Ai. 2004. Computing interaction effects and standard errors in logit and probit models. *Stata Journal* 4 (2):103–16.

NotiSur. 2002. Latin American Countries Rated Badly in Corruption Index. September 6.

Nye, Joseph S. 1967. Corruption and political development: A cost-benefit analysis. *American Political Science Review* 61 (2): 417–27.

———. 2002 [1967]. Corruption and political development: A cost-benefit analysis. In *Political corruption: Concepts and contexts*, ed. Heidenheimer and Johnston, 281–302.

O'Donnell, Guillermo. 1994. Delegative democracy. *Journal of Democracy* 5 (1): 55–69.

————. 1998. Horizontal accountability in new democracies. *Journal of Democracy* 9 (3): 112–27.

————. 2001. Democracy, law, and comparative politics. *Studies in Comparative International Development* 36 (1): 7–36.

————. 2003. Horizontal accountability: The legal institutionalization of mistrust. In *Democratic accountability in Latin America*, ed. Mainwaring and Welna, 34–54.

————. 2004a. Human development, human rights, and democracy. In *The quality of democracy: Theory and applications*, ed. O'Donnell, Vargas Cullell, and Iazzetta, 9–92.

————. 2004b. Why the rule of law matters. *Journal of Democracy* 15 (4): 34–54.

O'Donnell, Guillermo, Jorge Vargas Cullell, and Osvaldo Iazzetta, eds. 2004. *The quality of democracy: Theory and applications*. Notre Dame: University of Notre Dame Press.

O Estado de São Paulo. 2005. Maioria das comissoes não conclui trabalhos. Entrevista com Argelina Figueiredo. June 5.

Olken, Benjamin A. 2007. Corruption perceptions vs. corruption reality. Harvard University and NBER.

Olson, Mancur. 1982. *The rise and decline of nations*. New Haven: Yale University Press.

Oppenheimer, Andres. 2001. *Ojos vendados: Estados Unidos y el negocio de la corrupción en América Latina*. Buenos Aires: Editorial Sudamericana.

Paldam, Martin. 2002. The cross-country pattern of corruption: Economics, culture, and the seesaw dynamics. *European Journal of Political Economy* 18 (2): 215–40.

Pardinas, Juan E. 2004. Índice estatal de información presupuestal. Centro de Investigación para el Desarrollo (CIDAC).

Parker, Richard. 1994. Policy, activism, and AIDS in Brazil. In *Global AIDS policy*, ed. D. A. Feldman. Westport, CT: Bergin and Garvey.

Pedone, Luiz. 1995. Magistrates and political corruption: New roles and new attitudes in comparative perspective. Paper presented at the meeting of the Latin American Studies Association, September 28–30, in Washington, DC.

Peltzman, Sam. 1976. Toward a more general theory of regulation. *Journal of Law and Economics* 19 (August): 211–40.

Persson, Torsten, Guido Tabellini, and Francesco Trebbi. 2003. Electoral rules and corruption. *Journal of the European Economic Association* 1 (4): 958–89.

Peruzzotti, Enrique, and Catalina Smulovitz, eds. 2006. *Enforcing the rule of law: Social accountability in the new Latin American democracies*. Pittsburgh: University of Pittsburgh Press.

Peschard-Sverdrup, Armand B., and Sara R. Rioff, eds. 2005. *Mexican governance: From single-party rule to divided government*. Washington, DC: Center for Strategic and International Studies.

Peters, John G., and Susan Welch. 1980. The effects of charges of corruption on voting behavior in congressional elections. *American Political Science Review* 74 (3): 697–708.

————. 2002. Gradients of corruption in perceptions of American public life. In *Political corruption: Concepts and contexts*, ed. Heidenheimer and Johnston, 155–72.

Petras, James. 1969. *Politics and social forces in Chilean development*. Berkeley: University of California Press.

Pfeiffer, Silke. 2004. Vote buying and its implications for democracy: Evidence from Latin America. In *Global corruption report 2004*, ed. Transparency International, 76–83. London: Pluto Press.

Phelan, John. 1960. Authority and flexibility in the Spanish imperial bureaucracy. *Administrative Science Quarterly* 5:47–65.

Philip, George. 2003. *Democracy in Latin America*. Cambridge: Polity.

Philip, Mark. 1997. Defining political corruption. *Political Studies* 45:436–62.

———. 2002. Conceptualizing corruption. In *Political corruption: Concepts and context*, ed. Heidenheimer and Johnston, 41–57.

Pino, Patricio. 2003. Juez Aránguiz inhabilita por seis anos a diputados Pareto, Jiménez y Lagos. *El Mercurio*, December 16.

Pinto-Duschinsky, Michael. 2002. Financing politics: A global view. *Journal of Democracy* 13:69–86.

Polsby, Nelson. 1968. The institutionalization of the U.S. House of Representatives. *American Political Science Review* 62 (1): 144–68.

Porto, Roberto, and José Reinaldo Guimarães Carneiro. 2005. Corrupção—impunidade versus cárcere. *O Estado de São Paulo*, July 27.

Posada-Carbó, Eduardo. 2000. Electoral juggling: A comparative history of the corruption of suffrage in Latin America, 1830–1930. *Journal of Latin American Studies* 32 (3): 611–45.

Power, Timothy, and Mary Clark. 2001. Does trust matter? Interpersonal trust and democratic values in Chile, Costa Rica, and Mexico. In *Citizen views of democracy in Latin America*, ed. Roderic Camp, 51–70. Pittsburgh: University of Pittsburgh Press.

Przeworski, Adam. 1991. *Democracy and the market: Political and economic reforms in Eastern Europe and Latin America*. Cambridge: Cambridge University Press.

Pujas, Véronique, and Martin Rhodes. 2002. Party finance and political scandal: Comparing Italy, Spain and France. In *Political corruption: Concepts and contexts*, ed. Heidenheimer and Johnston, 739–60.

Punch, Maurice. 2000. Police corruption and its prevention. *European Journal on Criminal Policy and Research* 8 (3): 301–24.

Putnam, Robert D. 1993. Making democracy work: Civic traditions in modern Italy. Princeton: Princeton University Press.

———. 2000. *Bowling alone: The collapse and revival of the American community*. New York: Touchstone.

Ranis, Gustav. 1990. Contrasts in the political economy of development policy change. In *Manufacturing miracles: Paths of industrialization in Latin America and East Asia*, ed. Gary Gereffi and Donald L. Wyman. 207–30. Princeton: Princeton University Press.

Rauch, James, and Peter Evans. 2000. Bureaucratic structure and bureaucratic performance in less developed countries. *Journal of Public Economics* 75 (1): 49–72.

Rehren, Alfredo. 1996. Corruption in local politics in Chile. *Crime, Law and Social Change* 25:323–34.

———. 1999. Clientelismo político, corrupción y ética en la nueva democracia chilena. In *El modelo chileno: Democracia y desarrollo en los noventa*, eds. Paul Drake and Ivan Jaksic. Santiago: Editorial LOM.

————. 2000. Clientelismo político, corrupción y reforma del estado. Documento de trabajo 305. Santiago: Centro de Estudios Públicos.

————. 2002a. Clientelismo político, corrupción y reforma del estado en Chile. In *Reforma del Estado vol. II*, ed. Salvador Valdés, 135–40. Santiago: Centro de Estudios Públicos.

————. 2002b. Business and corruption in a re-emerging Latin American democracy: The case of Chile. Paper presented at the meeting of the International Sociological Association, July 7–13, in Brisbane, Australia.

————. 2004. Politics and corruption in Chile: The underside of Chilean democracy. *Harvard Review of Latin America* (Spring): 14–15.

Reinikka, Ritva, and Jakob Svensson. 2001. Explaining leakage of public funds. Policy Research Working Paper 2709. Development Research Group. Washington, DC: World Bank.

————. 2004. Local capture: Evidence from a central government transfer program in Uganda. *Quarterly Journal of Economics* 119 (2): 679–705.

————. 2006. Using micro-surveys to measure and explain corruption. *World Development* 34 (2): 359–70.

Reno, William. 1995. *Corruption and state politics in Sierra Leone*. Cambridge: Cambridge University Press.

————. 2000. Clandestine economies, violence and states in Africa. *Journal of International Affairs* 53 (2): 433–59.

Renovación nacional recoge denuncias de corrupción de funcionarios. 2005. *El Mercurio*, January 10.

Reyes, Leonarda. 2004. Mexico: If you don't cheat, you don't advance. In *The corruption notebooks*, 176–87. Washington, DC: Center for Public Integrity.

Rhodes, Martin. 1997. Financing party politics in Italy: A case of systemic corruption. *West European Politics* 20:54–80.

Riley, Stephen P. 1998. The political economy of anti-corruption strategies in Africa. In *Corruption and development*, ed. Mark Robinson, 129–59. London: Frank Cass.

Roberts, Kenneth M. 1995. Neoliberalism and the transformation of populism in Latin America: The Peruvian case. *World Politics* 48:82–116.

Robinson, Mark. 1998. Democracy, participation, and public policy. In *The democratic developmental state: Politics and institutional design*, ed. Mark Robinson and Gordon White, 150–86. Oxford: Oxford University Press.

Rodden, Jonathan, Gunnar S. Eskeland, and Jennie I. Litvack. 2003. *Fiscal decentralization and the challenge of hard budget constraints*. Cambridge: MIT Press.

Rodrigues, Fernando. 2004. Brazil: A protected elite. In *The corruption notebooks*, 37–42. Washington, DC: Center for Public Integrity.

Roniger, Luis, and Ayse Gunes-Ayata. 1994. *Democracy, clientelism, and civil society*. Boulder: Lynne Rienner.

Rose-Ackerman, Susan. 1978. *Corruption: A study in political economy*. New York: Academic Press.

————. 1996. ¿Una administración más reducida significa una administración más limpia? *Nueva Sociedad* 145 (September–October): 66–79.

————. 1999. *Corruption and government: Causes, consequences, and reform*. Cambridge: Cambridge University Press.

Rose, Richard, William Mishler, and Christian Haerpfer. 1998. *Democracy and its alternatives: Understanding post-communist societies.* Baltimore: Johns Hopkins University Press.

Rosenn, Keith S. 1971. The Jeito: Brazil's institutional bypass of the formal legal system and its developmental implications. *American Journal of Comparative Law* 13 (3): 514–49.

Rosenn, Keith S., and Richard Downes. 1998. *Corruption and political reform in Brazil: The impact of Collor's impeachment.* Boulder: Lynne Rienner.

Rothstein, Bo. 2005. *Social traps and the problem of trust.* Cambridge: Cambridge University Press.

Saba, Roberto, and Luigi Manzetti. 1997. Privatizations in Argentina: The implications for corruption. *Crime, Law and Social Change* 25:353–69.

Sachs, Jeffrey D., and Andrew M. Warner. 1995. Economic reform and the process of global integration. Brookings Papers on Economic Activity, 1–118.

Sadek, Maria Teresa. 2000. *Justiça e cidadania no Brasil.* São Paulo: Editora Sumaré.

Samuels, David. 1999. Incentives to cultivate a party vote in candidate-centric electoral systems: Evidence from Brazil. *Comparative Political Studies* 32(4): 487–518.

Sandholtz, Wayne, and Mark Gray. 2003. International integration and national corruption. *International Organization* 57 (4): 761–800.

Sandholtz, Wayne, and William Koetzle. 2000. Accounting for corruption: Economic structure, democracy, and trade. *International Studies Quarterly* 44:31–50.

Santoro, Daniel. 2004. Argentina: The tango of corruption. In *The corruption notebooks,* 6–13. Washington, DC: Center for Public Integrity.

Sartori, Giovanni. 1994. *Ingeniería política comparada.* Mexico: Fondo Cultural Económica.

Schedler, Andreas, Larry Diamond, and Marc Plattner, eds. 1999. *The self-restraining state: Power and accountability in new democracies.* Boulder: Lynne Rienner.

Schlesinger, Thomas, and Kenneth J. Meier. 2002. Variations in corruption among the American states. In *Political corruption: Concepts and contexts,* ed. Heidenheimer and Johnston, 627–43.

Schmidt, Steffen W., Laura Guasti, Carl Land, and James C. Scott, eds. 1977. *Friends, followers and factions: A reader in political clientelism.* Berkeley: University of California Press.

Schor, Miguel. n.d. The rule of law and democratic consolidation in Latin America. http://www.darkwing.uoregon.edu.

Schulte Nordholt, Nico G. 2000. Corruption and legitimacy in Indonesia: An exploration. In *Corruption and legitimacy,* eds. Heleen E. Bakker and Nico G. Schulte, 65–95. Amsterdam: SISWO Publications.

Scott, James C. 1969. Corruption, machine politics, and political change. *American Political Science Review* 43:1142–58.

———. 1972a. *Comparative political corruption.* Englewood Cliffs, NJ: Prentice-Hall.

———. 1972b. Patron-client politics and political change in Southeast Asia. *American Political Science Review* 66 (1): 91–113.

Seligson, Mitchell A. 1997. Los Nicaraguenses hablan sobre la corrupción: Un estudio de opinión pública. Arlington, VA: Casals and Associates, Latin American Public Opinion Project.

———. 1999. Nicaraguans talk about corruption: A follow-up study of public opinion. Arlington, VA: Casals and Associates, Latin American Public Opinion Project.

———. 2001a. Transparency and anti-corruption activities in Colombia: A survey of citizen experience. Arlington, VA: Casals and Associates, Latin American Public Opinion Project.

———. 2001b. Corruption and democratization: What is to be done? *Public Integrity* 3 (3): 221–41.

———. 2002. The impact of corruption on regime legitimacy: A comparative study of four Latin American countries. *Journal of Politics* 64 (2): 408–33.

———. 2004. Victimization scale. In *Global corruption report 2004*, 307–10. Transparency International. London: Pluto Press.

———. 2005. Democracy on ice: The multiple challenges of Guatemala's peace process. In *The third wave of democratization in Latin America: Advances and setbacks*, ed. Frances Hagopian and Scott Mainwaring, 202–31. Cambridge: Cambridge University Press.

———. 2006. The measurement and impact of corruption victimization: Survey evidence from Latin America. *World Development* 34 (2): 381–404.

Serra, Danila. 2006. Empirical determinants of corruption: A sensitivity analysis. *Public Choice* 126: 225–56.

Shefter, Martin. 1977. Party and patronage: Germany, England, and Italy. *Politics and Society* 7 (4): 403–52.

Shelly, Louise. 2001. Corruption and organized crime in Mexico in the post-PRI transition. *Journal of Contemporary Criminal Justice* 17 (3): 213–31.

Shleifer, Andrei, and Robert Vishny. 1993. Corruption. *Quarterly Journal of Economics* 108:599–617.

———, eds. 1998. *The grabbing hand: Government pathologies and their cures.* Cambridge: Harvard University Press.

Siavelis, Peter. 2000. Disconnected fire alarms and ineffective police patrols: Legislative oversight in postauthoritarian Chile. *Journal of Interamerican Studies and World Affairs* 42 (1): 71–99.

Sives, Amanda. 1993. Elite behavior and corruption in the consolidation of democracy in Brazil. *Parliamentary Affairs* 46 (4): 549–63.

Skidmore, Thomas. 1999. Collor's downfall in historical perspective. In *Corruption and political reform in Brazil: The impact of Collor's impeachment*, eds. Rosenn and Downes, 1–20.

Smallman, Shawn C. 1997. Shady business: Corruption in the Brazilian army before 1954. *Latin American Research Review* 32 (3): 39–62.

Smith, Adam. 1939 [1776]. *An inquiry into the nature and causes of the wealth of nations.* New York: Modern Library.

Smith, Peter H. 2005. *Democracy in Latin America: Political change in comparative perspective.* New York: Oxford University Press.

Smulovitz, Catalina, and Enrique Peruzzotti. 2000. Social accountability in Latin America. *Journal of Democracy* 11 (4): 147–58.

Snyder, Richard. 1999. Politics after neoliberalism: Regulation in Mexico. *World Politics* 51:173–204.

Soares, Rodrigo. 2004. Development, crime, and punishment: Accounting for the international differences in crime rates. *Journal of Development Economics* 73 (1):155–84.

Souza, Ammaury de. 2004. Political reform in Brazil: Promises and pitfalls. Center for Strategic and International Studies, April.

Souza Martins, José de. 1996. Clientelism and corruption in contemporary Brazil. In *Political corruption in Europe and Latin America*, ed. Little and Posada-Carbó, 195–218.

Speck, Bruno Wilhelm. 2002. *Caminhos da transparência*. São Paulo: Editora da Universidade Estadual de Campinas.

———. 2004. Campaign finance reform: Is Latin America on the road to transparency? In *Global Corruption Report 2004*, 32–35. Transparency International. London: Pluto Press.

Spector, Bertram I., ed. 2005. *Fighting corruption in developing countries: Strategies and analysis*. Bloomfield, CT: Kumarian Press.

Spector, Bertram, Michael Johnston, and Phyllis Dininio. 2005. Learning across cases: Trends in anticorruption strategies. In *Fighting corruption in developing countries*, ed. Spector, 212–32.

Stigler, George J. 1971. The theory of economic regulation. *Bell Journal of Economics and Management Science* 2 (1): 3–21.

Stokes, Susan. 2005. Perverse accountability: A formal model of machine politics with evidence from Argentina. *American Political Science Review* 99 (3): 315–26.

Sturzenegger, Federico. 2003. *La economía de los argentinos: Reglas de juego para una sociedad próspera y justa*. Buenos Aires: Ediciones Planeta.

Subero, Carlos. 2004. Venezuela: With me, or against me. In *The Corruption Notebooks*, ed. Center for Public Integrity, 365–72. Washington, DC: Center for Public Integrity.

Swamy, Anand, and Stephen Knack. 2001. Gender and corruption. *Journal of Development Economics* 64 (1): 25–55.

Tanzi, Vito, and Hamid Davoodi. 1997. Corruption, public investment and growth. IMF Working Paper. Washington, DC: International Monetary Fund.

———. 1998. Corruption around the world: Causes, consequences, scope, and cures. IMF Staff Paper 45 (December): 4.

Taylor, Lewis. 2000. Patterns of electoral corruption in Peru: The April 2000 general election. *Crime, Law and Social Change* 34:391–415.

Taylor, Matthew M. 2008. *Judging policy: Courts and policy reform in democratic Brazil*. Palo Alto, CA: Stanford University Press.

Taylor, Matthew M., and Vinicius C. Buranelli. 2007. Ending up in pizza: Accountability as a problem of institutional arrangement in Brazil. *Latin American Politics and Society* 49 (1): 59–87.

Thacker, Strom C. 2000a. *Big business, the state, and free trade: Constructing coalitions in Mexico*. New York: Cambridge University Press.

———. 2000b. Private sector trade politics in Mexico. *Business and Politics* 2 (2): 161–87.

Theobald, Robin. 1982. Patrimonialism. *World Politics* 34:549–58.

Thompson, Dennis F. 1993. Mediated corruption: The case of the Keating five. *American Political Science Review* 87 (2): 369–81.

Tirole, Jean. 1996. A theory of collective reputations with applications to the persistence of corruption and to firm quality. *Review of Economic Studies* 63:1–22.

Tomz, Michael, Jason Wittenberg, and Gary King. 2003. *CLARIFY: Software for interpreting and presenting statistical results.* Version 2.1. Stanford University, University of Wisconsin, and Harvard University. January 5. http://gking.harvard.edu/.

Transparencia Mexicana. 2001. *Encuesta de Corrupción y Buen Gobierno (ECBG).* Mexico City: Transparencia Mexicana.

Transparency International. 2001. *Global corruption report.* London: Pluto Press.

———. 2003a. *Corruption fighters' tool-kit: Civil society experiences and emerging strategies, 2002–03.* Berlin: Transparency International.

———. 2003b. *Global corruption report.* London: Pluto Press.

———. 2004. *Global corruption report.* London: Pluto Press.

———. 2005a. *Global corruption barometer 2005.* Berlin: Transparency International.

———. 2005b. *Global corruption report.* London: Pluto Press.

Treisman, Daniel. 2000. The causes of corruption: A cross-national study. *Journal of Public Economics* 76:399–457.

———. 2007. What have we learned about the causes of corruption from ten years of cross-national empirical research? *Annual Review of Political Science* 10:211–44.

Tulchin, Joseph S., and Ralph H. Espach, eds. 2000. *Combating corruption in Latin America.* Washington, DC: Woodrow Wilson Center Press.

Ungar, Mark. 2002. *Elusive reform: Democracy and the rule of law in Latin America.* Boulder: Lynne Rienner.

United Nations, Economic and Social Council. 2002. Civil and political rights, including questions of independence of the judiciary, administration of justice, impunity. Report of the Mission to Mexico. Commission on Human Rights E/CN.4/2002.

USAID. 2005a. USAID anticorruption strategy (PD-ACA-557). Washington, DC: USAID.

———. 2005b. Anti-corruption and transparency coalitions: Lessons from Peru, Paraguay, El Salvador and Bolivia. Washington, DC: USAID.

Valdés-Prieto, Salvador. 2002. Las "Coimas": Las medidas del gobierno y las propuestas del CEP. Puntos de Referencia No. 264. Santiago: Centro de Estudios Públicos.

Valenzuela, Arturo. 1977. *Political brokers in Chile: Local government in a centralized polity.* Durham, NC: Duke University Press.

———. 2004. Latin American presidencies interrupted. *Journal of Democracy* 15 (4): 5–19.

Valor Econômico. 2005. Prisão encerra desencontros no cerco a Maluf. *Valor Econômico*, September 26.

Van de Walle, Nicolas. 2001. *The politics of permanent crisis: Managing African economies, 1979–1999.* Cambridge: Cambridge University Press.

Vanhanen, Tatu. 1990. *The process of democratization: A comparative study of 147 states, 1980–88.* New York: Crane Russak.

Van Klaveren, Jacob. 1978. The concept of corruption. In *Political corruption: A handbook*, ed. Heidenheimer, Johnston, and LeVine, 149–63.

Van Rijckeghem, Caroline, and Beatrice Weder. 2001. Bureaucratic corruption and the rate of temptation: Do wages in the civil service affect corruption? *Journal of Development Economics* 65 (2): 307–32.

Varese, Federico. 1997. The transition to the market and corruption in post-socialist Russia. *Political Studies* 45 (3): 579–96.

Vargas Cullel, Jorge. 2004. Democracy and the quality of democracy: Empirical findings and methodological and theoretical issues drawn from the citizen audit of the quality of democracy in Costa Rica. In *The quality of democracy: Theory and applications*, ed. Guillermo O'Donnell, 93–162. Notre Dame: University of Notre Dame Press.

Velloso, Carlos Mário da Silva. 2005. Poder judiciário: Reforma. A emenda constitucional No. 45, De 08.12. *Revista Forense* 101, no. 378 (March–April 2005): 11–26.

Wantchekon, Leonard. 2003. Clientelism and voting behavior: A field experiment in Benin. *World Politics* 55:399–422.

Warren, Mark E. 2002. Corrupting democracy. Paper presented at the meeting of the American Political Science Association, August 29–September 1, Boston.

———. 2004. What does corruption mean in a democracy? *American Journal of Political Science* 48 (2): 328–43.

Waterbury, John. 1976. Corruption, political stability, and development: Comparative evidence from Egypt and Morocco. *Government and Opposition* 11 (4): 426–45.

Webb, Douglass. 2004. Legitimate actors? The future roles for NGOs against HIV/AIDS in Sub-Saharan Africa. In *The political economy of AIDS in Africa*, ed. Nana K. Poku and Alan Whiteside, 19–32. Aldershot, Hants, England: Burlington Ashgate.

Weber, Max. 1968. *Economy and society*. New York: Bedminster Press.

Weber Abramo, Claudio. 2007. How much do perceptions of corruption really tell us? Economics Discussion Papers 2007–19.

Wertheim, W. F. 1970. Sociological aspects of corruption in Southeast Asia. In *Political corruption: Readings in comparative analysis*, ed. Arnold Heidenheimer, 195–211. New Brunswick, NJ: Transaction Books.

Weyland, Kurt. 1998. Politics of corruption in Latin America. *Journal of Democracy* 9 (2): 108–21.

———. 2004. Neoliberalism and democracy in Latin America: A mixed record. *Latin American Politics and Society* 46 (1): 135–57.

———. 2006. Reform and corruption in Latin America. *Current History* 105 (668): 84–89.

White, Gordon. 1996. Corruption and market reform in China. *IDS Bulletin* 27 (2): 6–12.

Whitehead, Laurence. 1989. On presidential graft: The Latin American evidence. In *Political corruption: A handbook*, ed. Heidenheimer, Johnston, and LeVine, 781–800.

———. 2000a. Institutional design and accountability in Latin America. Paper presented at the meeting of the Latin American Studies Association, March 16–18, in Miami.

———. 2000b. High level political corruption in Latin America: A "transitional" phenomenon? In *Combating corruption in Latin America*, ed. Joseph S. Tulchin and Ralph H. Espach, 107–29. Washington, DC: Woodrow Wilson Center Press.

———. 2002. High level political corruption in Latin America: A "transitional" phenomenon? In *Political corruption: Concepts and contexts*, eds. Heidenheimer and Johnston, 801–18.

Wigley, Simon. 2003. Parliamentary immunity: Protecting democracy or protecting corruption? *Journal of Political Philosophy* 11 (1): 23–40.

Williams, Robert. 1987. *Political corruption in Africa*. Aldershot: Gower.

———. 2001. *The politics of corruption*. Cheltenham: Edward Elgar Publishers.

World Bank. 2002. Public expenditure tracking survey: Peru. Washington, DC: World Bank.

———. 2003. World development indicators CD-ROM. Washington, DC: World Bank.

Xin, Xiaohui, and Thomas K. Rudel. 2004. The context for political corruption: A cross-national analysis. *Social Science Quarterly* 85 (2): 294–309.

Yarrington, Doug. 2003. Cattle, corruption, and Venezuelan state formation during the regime of Juan Vicente Gomez, 1908–35. *Latin American Research Review* 38 (2): 3–28.

Zaller, John. 1992. *The nature and origins of mass opinion*. Cambridge: Cambridge University Press.

Zagaris, Bruce, and Shelia Lakhani. 1999. The emergence of an international enforcement regime on transnational corruption in the Americas. *Law and Policy in International Business* (Midsummer): 53–93.

Zepeda Lecuona, Guillermo. 2004. *Crimen sin castigo: Procuración de justicia penal y ministerio público en México*. Mexico City: CIDAC and CFE.

Zovatto G., Daniel. 2000. Political finance in Latin America: Comparative study of the legal and practical characteristics of the funding of political parties and electoral campaigns. Paper presented at the meeting of the International Political Science Association, August 1–5, Quebec, Canada.

LORENA ALCÁZAR is senior researcher at GRADE (Group for the Analysis of Development). She has a Ph.D. in economics from Washington University in St. Louis and an advanced studies degree in public policy research from the Kiel Institute of World Economics in Germany. She has served in various research capacities with OSITRAN (National Regulatory Institution of Public Transportation Infrastructure), the Instituto Apoyo, the World Bank's Policy Research Department, and the Brookings Institution, and as an international consultant. Dr. Alcázar has done extensive research and published widely on social and education programs, budget monitoring, decentralization, regulatory policies, and institutional reform.

CHARLES H. BLAKE is professor of political science at James Madison University. His research on the political economy of public policy and of corruption has been published in *Comparative Political Studies; Democratization; Journal of Inter-American Studies and World Affairs; The Review of International Political Economy;* and *Studies in Comparative International Development.* His most recent book, *Politics in Latin America* (Houghton Mifflin, 2008) serves as a college textbook on Latin American politics. With Jessica Adolino, he has coauthored a book on comparative public policy in the G-7 countries, *Comparing Public Policies,* for CQ Press.

JOHN BAILEY is professor of government and foreign service at Georgetown University. His most recent book (coedited with Lucía Dammert, FLACSO-Chile), *Public Security and Police Reform in the Americas* (University of Pittsburgh Press, 2006), compares the experiences of six countries. His current research project analyzes the problem of security traps and their effects on democratic governability in Latin America.

ADAM BRINEGAR holds a Ph.D. in political science from Duke University and has taught at Duke, Georgetown, and Humboldt. His dissertation focuses on the nexus of partisanship and corruption reform in Latin America. He has been published in numerous books and journals, including *Party Politics* and *European Union Politics*. He is currently a consultant in Washington, D.C., where he leads large multinational, quantitative survey projects investigating various problems related to the development and management of human capital.

JOSÉ R. LÓPEZ-CÁLIX, a native of El Salvador, is lead economist in the Economic Policy Group for the World Bank's Middle East and North Africa Region, with an emphasis on Morocco, Libya, and Algeria. Before joining the World Bank in 1994, he worked with the U.S. Agency for International Development, the Canadian International Development Agency, the U.S. Congress, the Inter-American Development Bank, and El Salvador's Ministry of Planning's Economic and Social Advisory Group. López-Cálix has published numerous books and articles on varied subjects, including parallel exchange markets, growth theory and practice, international coordination in economic policy, public finance, public expenditure monitoring surveys, trade policy, and family remittances.

LUIGI MANZETTI is associate professor of political science at Southern Methodist University. His work has focused on issues that include economic integration, governance, corruption, and market reforms. He is the author of *The IMF and Economic Stabilization* (Praeger, 1991), *Political Forces in Argentina* (with Peter G. Snow; Praeger, 1993), *Institutions, Parties and Coalitions in Argentine Politics* (Pittsburgh University Press, 1993), *Privatization South American Style* (Oxford University Press, 1999), and *Accountability and Market Reform Failures* (Penn State University Press, 2009). His journal articles have appeared in *Comparative Political Studies*, *Comparative Politics*, and *World Politics*.

STEPHEN D. MORRIS is director of the International Studies Program and professor of political science at the University of South Alabama. He is the author of *Corruption and Politics in Contemporary Mexico* (University of Alabama Press, 1991), *Political Reformism in Mexico* (Lynne Rienner, 1995), *Gringolandia: Mexican Identity and Perceptions of the United States* (Rowman and Littlefield, 2005) and guest editor for a special issue on corruption of *The Latin Americanist* (2006). He has taught at the Universidad de las Americas in Puebla and as a visiting Fulbright lecturer at the Universidad de Guadalajara. He is in the process of completing a second coedited volume on corruption in Latin America with Charles Blake and a book manuscript on corruption and political change in Mexico.

ALFREDO REHREN is a professor at the Instituto de Ciencia Política at the Universidad Católica de Chile. He has been a visiting professor or researcher at several universities, including the David Rockefeller Center for Latin American Studies at Harvard University. His research on political processes and national and subnational governance has been published in varied international journals, including *Crime, Law, and Social Change* and *Revista de Ciencia Política*.

MITCHELL A. SELIGSON is the Centennial Professor of Political Science at Vanderbilt University and Fellow of the Center for the Americas and the Vanderbilt Center for Nashville Studies. He is also founder and director of the Latin American Public Opinion Project (LAPOP). Seligson has published over eighty articles and more than two dozen books and monographs, including recently *The Legitimacy Puzzle: Democracy and Support in Latin America* (with John Booth; Cambridge University Press, forthcoming) and *Development and Underdevelopment: The Political Economy of Global Inequality* (with John Passé-Smith; 4th ed., Lynne Rienner Press, forthcoming).

MATTHEW M. TAYLOR is assistant professor of political science at the University of São Paulo. His research on courts, judicial politics, political economy, and corruption has been published in such journals as *Comparative Politics, Economics of Governance, Journal of Latin American Studies, Latin American Politics and Society,* and *Latin American Research Review.* Taylor is also the author of *Judging Policy: Courts and Policy Reform in Democratic Brazil* (Stanford University Press, 2008).

STROM C. THACKER is associate professor of International Relations and director of Latin American Studies at Boston University. His current research focuses on the long-term relationship between democracy and development and on the politics of human development. He is a faculty affiliate of the David Rockefeller Center for Latin American Studies at Harvard University and a fellow at the Frederick S. Pardee Center for the Study of the Longer-Range Future at Boston University. He has been a visiting associate professor of government at Harvard University, a Susan Louise Dyer Peace Fellow at Stanford University's Hoover Institution, and a Fulbright Scholar.

CAROLE J. WILSON is assistant professor of political science at the University of Texas at Dallas. Her research interests include elections in Latin America and Western Europe, citizen and party responses to the European Union, and the effects of corruption on public opinion and voting. Her research appears in such journals as *American Journal of Political Science*, *British Journal of Political Science*, *Comparative Political Studies*, and *Political Behavior*.

INDEX

accountability, 33, 85, 96, 128, 132, 147; and the accountability process, 155–57, 163, 200; in Brazil, 21, 151, 154–55, 158, 161–65; and clientelism, 78, 83; and decentralization, 21, 127; deficit of, 167–68; and democracy, 3, 6, 9, 16, 61, 167, 170, 194–95; and elections, electoral system, and voting, 81, 171–72, 185, 187, 198; horizontal, 12, 95, 135, 169, 195, 202; impact on corruption, 152, 195; impact of the perception of corruption on, 132; and the judicial system, 71, 159–60; and Klitgaard's equation, 150–51, 154, 168; in Mexico, 169–70; and presidential power, 55–56; vertical 12–13, 15, 53, 165, 169, 171, 195–96, 202

Africa, 10, 30, 35, 113, 209n12

age, impact on tolerance of corruption, 100–101

Alemán, Arnoldo, 70

alternation in power: impact on corruption, 173–74, 180, 182, 196

anticorruption, 9–10, 14–20, 33, 55, 58–59, 149, 197; in Brazil, 161–65, 200, 202; in Chile, 55, 131, 136–37, 139, 198–99; failure of, 193–94, 196; government programs, 94–95; historically, 106–7; at the international level, 78, 95; in Mexico, 169; needed reforms, 199–202; and transparency, 18, 185

Argentina, 41, 90, 105; clientelism in, 69,

82; corruption in, 12, 46–47, 52–54, 65–66, 94–96, 131; perceptions of corruption in, 2, 18, 48, 85, 103

authoritarianism, 27, 38, 61

Bolivia, 47–48, 54, 68, 70, 79, 94, 95

Brazil, 2, 41, 54, 85, 103, 105; anticorruption in, 164–68, 200, 203; corruption in, 10–11, 14–15, 19–21, 46, 65–66, 84, 94–95, 151–71; perceptions of corruption in, 2, 151

bribery, 13, 17, 62–66, 69, 72–73, 131, 140, 142, 144–46, 166, 210n23. *See also* Caso Coimas; corruption: types of

budgeting. *See* fiscal policy

bureaucracy, 10, 51–52, 58, 69, 85–86; in Brazil, 162, 165; in Chile, 133, 135; in Mexico, 169, 190

Cardoso, Fernando Henrique, 164

Caso Coimas, 136

Chávez, Hugo, 14, 46

Chile, 2, 20, 21, 41, 43–44, 47, 55, 57–58, 72, 85, 94–95, 96, 100, 103, 105, 131–48, 194, 198

citizens, citizenship, 69, 92, 96; link to government, 3, 12, 74; role in corruption, 80, 100, 128; role in fighting corruption, 14–15, 56, 72,106, 132, 139–40, 145, 147; and support for corrupt leaders, 77, 84–85, 90–91

civil society, 52, 167; and anticorruption,

federalism, 11, 205. *See also* decentralization

fiscal policies: impact on corruption, 31–32, 38, 154

Foreign Corrupt Practices Act, 5

Fox, Vicente, 16, 185

Fujimori, Alberto, 19, 46, 52–53, 91, 94, 208n5

functionalism/functionalist theory, 5, 9, 67, 78

Global Corruption Barometer. *See* Transparency International

governability, 20, 21, 60, 61, 64, 71, 75

government effectiveness, 86, 88

government spending, 8, 9, 112, 153. *See also* fiscal policies

Guatemala, 47–48, 70, 94–95, 112

Haiti, 47, 94

Hong Kong's Independent Commission against Corruption (ICAC), 166

impunity, 12, 53, 71, 75, 96, 152, 193–94, 202

incentive structures, 163–64

Indice de Corrupción y Buen Gobierno (ICBG), 175–76

inequality, 9, 11, 59, 60, 65, 105, 197, 198, 203

inflation, 32, 34, 38–39, 76, 87, 153

information: impact on attitudes toward corruption, 132

Institutional Revolutionary Party (PRI) (Mexico), 16, 29, 46, 52, 169–70, 17374, 179-80, 182-83, 187, 191

International Monetary Fund (IMF), 5–7, 78, 91

investments, 6, 9, 27, 31, 33, 94, 205

Italy, 51, 77, 80, 101, 112, 165, 171

Japan, 77, 80, 171

judicial reform, 15, 158–60, 163

judiciary: confidence in, 159–60, 212n5; corruption in, 57, 59,73–75, 97; role in anticorruption, 9, 56, 58, 85; weakness

of, and corruption, 12, 46, 53, 56, 159, 185, 196

kleptocracy, 80, 211n5

Klitgaard's equation, 150, 152, 168

Lagos, Ricardo, 2, 47, 55, 94, 101, 135–37, 199

Lalau scandal, 156–57, 160

Latin American Public Opinion Project (LAPOP), 187

Latin American Research Review, 10

Latinobarómetro, 2, 18, 47

law enforcement, 1, 62, 70, 75, 97, 98, 163, 196, 197. *See also* police

leakages, 113, 121–22, 124, 214n7; measuring, 118, 129–30

legitimacy, 9, 14, 29, 46, 49, 56, 58–59, 63, 79, 83, 97, 173, 175

liberalization. *See* neoliberal economic reforms

life satisfaction, link to tolerance of corruption. *See* satisfaction

local government, 112, 119–20, 123. *See also* decentralization

Lula da Silva, Luis Inácio, 19, 94, 151, 153, 159–60, 162

Maluf, Paulo, 161–62, 217n12

Mani Puliti (Clean Hands) (Italy), 165–66

market-oriented economic policies. *See* neoliberal economic reforms

media. *See* press

Menem, Carlos, 11, 46, 52–53, 91

mensalão scandal, 151, 153

Mexico, 2, 14, 16, 18, 20–22, 29, 41, 46, 48, 52-54, 57, 65, 72, 85, 95, 100, 104-05

Ministério Público (Brazil), 154–57, 161–66

monetary policy: impact on corruption, 31–32

money laundering, 11, 161, 164

municipalities. *See* local government

National Action Party (PAN) (Mexico), 180, 182-83, 191

neoliberal and anti-statist bias, 17
neoliberal economic reforms, 3–8, 11, 26, 30–31, 44, 46–47, 62, 69, 111, 134–35. *See also* privatization
neopopulism, 11–12, 52–53, 195
NGOs, 28–29, 52, 114, 127, 147, 199. *See also* civil society

openness. *See* neoliberal economic reforms
Organization for Economic Cooperation and Development (OECD), 6, 19
Organization of American States (OAS), 6, 12, 15–16, 19

Paraguay, 2, 41, 47–48, 79, 94
partisanship, 21, 86, 131–32, 136, 139, 142–48, 198; impact on attitudes toward corruption, 132, 139
party: and electoral systems, 11, 153; switching, 153, 158. *See also* elections; electoral campaigns; proportional representation
Party of the Democratic Revolution (PRD) (Mexico), 180, 182–83
patronage, 51–52, 62, 81, 83–84, 88–91, 135, 137, 158, 171
Pérez, Carlos Andrés, 10–11, 46, 94
personnel policy, 122, 153
Peru, 2, 14, 20–21, 46, 52–53, 57, 68, 77, 91, 94–95, 104–5, 112–24, 161, 205
Pinochet, Augusto, 133–35
police: and corruption, 2, 57, 67, 70–71, 73–75, 96–97, 99, 162, 190. *See also* confidence: in the police; law enforcement; and Federal Police (Brazil)
political participation, 9, 14, 55, 65, 72, 101, 173
political parties, 2, 21, 29, 51–53, 56–57, 69, 73–74, 97, 100, 133, 135, 142, 153, 158, 180
political will, 15, 53, 163, 165
Portillo, Alfonso, 70
poverty, 5, 59, 115, 118, 120, 122, 132, 197–98; and clientelism, 69, 82, 90, 100, 197; impact of corruption on, 9,

18; impact on corruption, 65, 137, 199, 203
presidential power, 53, 205n3; in Brazil, 152; in Mexico, 16, 29, 66, 133, 135, 137, 142, 156, 169, 170
press: and corruption, 8, 58, 65–66, 73, 75, 77, 148, 168, 169, 210n14; impact of democracy on, 3, 9–10, 28, 147, 170–71
price stability, 32–34. *See also* inflation
privatization, 1, 47, 51, 52, 78, 205n10. *See also* neoliberal economic reforms
proportional representation, 65, 81, 153, 158, 211n2
Protestantism: and corruption, 8, 35–36, 39
public financing, of parties and campaigns, 20, 53–55
public opinion, 11–15, 18–19, 21–22, 49, 58, 62, 63, 96

regime (as distinct from state), 60–64, 66, 72, 74, 76
regulatory burden, controls, and oversight, 8, 11, 67, 95, 153, 164, 205n11
rule of law, 16, 106; and anticorruption, 10, 15; and corruption, 3, 8, 12, 173, 185, 196; and democracy, 29, 71, 83, 85, 171; and the police, 96–97

Salinas de Gortari, Carlos, 52
sanguessuga (leech) scandal, 151, 166
satisfaction: with democratic governments, 14, 44, 75, 85, 88, 89,152, 167, 173; with economic situation, 87; with life, 100, 103–6, 197
scandal, 1, 10, 19, 58, 70; in Brazil, 151–52, 156, 159, 165; in Chile, 55, 131, 133, 135–39, 141, 146–49, 198–99; impact of, 79–80, 94, 132, 146, 194, 198, 200, 202. *See also* Lalau scandal; *mensalão* scandal; *sanguessuga* (leech) scandal
service delivery, 67, 69, 114, 127
skepticism, culture of, 16, 22, 172
sobresueldos scandal, 131, 135, 137
social capital, 101, 171

tolerance of corruption, 8, 10, 12, 15, 20, 89–90, 92, 96, 98-106, 167, 197–98, 202, 212n5

trade, 6, 9, 31–35, 38–39, 44, 78, 195. *See also* neoliberal economic reforms

Transparencia Mexicana, 73, 175

transparency: and anticorruption, 148, 185; and democracy, 6, 54, 83, 85, 153, 195; lack of, 12, 18, 32, 56, 59, 96, 124, 128; laws mandating, 54, 137

Transparency International, 6–7, 9, 18, 47, 200; and Corruption Perception Index, 2, 18, 47, 131, 172, 174–75, 206nn13–14; and Global Corruption Barometer, 2, 18, 57, 73

treaties on corruption, 6–7, 10, 12, 15–16, 19, 48, 95

Tribunal de Contas da União (TCU) (Brazil), 155–57, 162, 164

trust: and democracy, 3, 75, 150, 170, 172–73, 175; in government, 9, 14, 55, 79, 99, 145, 159, 167, 172, 210n23; inter-

personal, 8–9, 13, 58, 75, 79, 101, 103–4, 167

United Nations, 6, 48, 95, 165

United States, 5–7, 14, 27, 72–73, 78, 85, 133, 147–48, 154, 165, 171, 174

Uruguay, 2, 41, 44, 47, 58, 95, 104–5

Venezuela, 2, 10, 14, 41, 46–47, 85–86, 94, 104–5, 205

vertical accountability. *See* accountability

vote-buying, 65, 67, 210n15

vote choice or voting, 21, 132, 139, 141–42, 146–49, 198; impact of corruption on, 14, 63, 65, 140–41, 170, 173, 179, 186–87, 190; models of, 140, 142, 146-47

whistleblowing, 166

World Bank, 5–7, 33–35, 39, 41, 47–48, 78–79, 91, 113, 150, 165, 200, 206n12

World Values Survey, 2, 72, 85, 96, 98–99, 101–2, 132